Studies in the Social and
Cultural Foundations of Language No. 6

Culture and language development

As children are learning to become competent members of their society, so also are they learning to become competent speakers of their language. In other words, socialization and language acquisition take place at the same time in a child's experience. In this book, Elinor Ochs explores the complex interaction of these two processes.

Focussing in particular on the experiences of children in Samoa, Ochs examines both the cognitive and socio-cultural dimensions of children's language development. She shows that language competence includes not only knowledge of grammatical principles and sentence construction, but also knowledge of the norms that link language to social and cognitive context; and that local social and cultural systems, as well as children's individual psychological and biological capacities, organize their understanding and production of particular language constructions. She also illustrates how children are socialized through language and socialized to use language, examining in particular the way in which the verbal strategies used by caregivers socialize children into theories of local knowledge; how literacy instruction socializes children into notions of task accomplishment as they are learning to read; and the way in which children come to understand the socio-cultural organization of emotion through learning the norms and expectations surrounding its linguistic expression.

This innovative study will appeal widely to anthropologists, developmental psychologists, psycholinguists, sociolinguists, communication specialists, and educationists interested in child development and caregiver–child communication.

Studies in the Social and
Cultural Foundations of Language

The aim of this series is to develop theoretical perspectives on the essential
social and cultural character of language by methodological and empirical
emphasis on the occurrence of language in its communicative and interactional
settings, on the socioculturally grounded 'meanings' and 'functions' of linguistic
forms, and on the social scientific study of language use across cultures. It will
thus explicate the essentially ethnographic nature of linguistic data, whether
spontaneously occurring or experimentally induced, whether normative or
variational, whether synchronic or diachronic. Works appearing in the series
will make substantive and theoretical contributions to the debate over the
sociocultural–functional and structural–formal nature of language, and will
represent the concerns of scholars in the sociology and anthropology of
language, anthropological linguistics, sociolinguistics, and socioculturally
informed psycholinguistics.

Editorial Board

Keith H. Basso
John J. Gumperz
Shirley Brice Heath
Dell H. Hymes
Judith T. Irvine
Wolfgang Klein
Stephen C. Levinson
Elinor Ochs
Bruce Rigsby
Michael Silverstein

1. Charles L. Briggs: *Learning how to ask: a sociolinguistic appraisal of the role
   of the interview in social science research*

2. Tamar Katriel: *Talking straight:* Dugri *speech in Israeli Sabra culture*

3. Bambi B. Schieffelin and Elinor Ochs (eds.): *Language socialization across
   cultures*

4. Susan U. Philips, Susan Steele, and Christine Tanz (eds.): *Language, gender,
   and sex in comparative perspective*

5. Jeff Siegel: *Language contact in a plantation environment: a sociolinguistic
   history of Fiji*

6. Elinor Ochs: *Culture and language development: language acquisition and
   language socialization in a Samoan village*

Culture and language development

Language acquisition
and language socialization
in a Samoan village

Elinor Ochs

University of Southern California

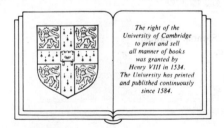

The right of the
University of Cambridge
to print and sell
all manner of books
was granted by
Henry VIII in 1534.
The University has printed
and published continuously
since 1584.

Cambridge University Press
Cambridge
New York   New Rochelle   Melbourne   Sydney

Published by the Press Syndicate of the University of Cambridge
The Pitt Building, Trumpington Street, Cambridge, CB2 1RP
32 East 57th Street, New York, NY 10022, USA
10 Stamford Road, Oakleigh, Melbourne 3166, Australia

First published 1988

Printed in Great Britain at the Bath Press, Avon

British Library cataloguing in publication data
Ochs, Elinor
Culture and language developments:
language acquisition and language socialization in a Samoan village.
– (Studies in the social and cultural foundations of language; no. 6).
1. Children – Samoan Islands – Language
I. Title II. Series
401'.9 LB1139.L3

Library of Congress cataloguing in publication data
Ochs, Elinor.
Culture and language development.
(Studies in the social and cultural foundations of language; no. 6)
Bibliography: p.
Includes index.
1. Language acquisition. 2. Sociolinguistics – Samoan Islands.
3. Socialization. 4. Samoan language – Usage.
I. Title II. Series
P118.O24 1988 401'.9'099613 87-23822

ISBN 0 521 34454 9 hard covers
ISBN 0 521 34894 3 paperback

SE

Contents

		page	
List of photographs			vi
Foreword by Shirley Brice Heath			vii
Acknowledgments			xv
1	To know a language		1
2	Methodology		40
3	Introduction to Samoan language usage: grammar and register		53
4	The social contexts of childhood: village and household organization		71
5	Ergative case marking: variation and acquisition		86
6	Word-order strategies: the two-constituent bias		105
7	Clarification		128
8	Affect, social control, and the Samoan child		145
9	The linguistic expression of affect		168
10	Literacy instruction in a Samoan village		189
11	Language as symbol and tool		210
Appendix I	Transcription conventions		228
Appendix II	Canonical transitive verb types in children's speech		232
	References		238
	Index		253

Photographs

Between pp. 144 and 145

1 Mother with children and *matai* of the family

2 Infant under mosquito net

3 Older children taking care of younger children

4 Girls returning from plantations with coconuts

5 Preparing breadfruit

6 Houses on family compound

7 Learning to read and interpret the Bible

8 First literacy experience

Foreword

This case study will be of considerable interest to linguists, anthropologists, and psychologists who study child language. The Samoan language and culture present rich examples for those who have puzzled over links between the evidence for universal innate linguistic capacities and accounts of widely differing conditions of socialization. Social stratification, together with the emphasis the society places on learning by observing, determines the ways children have access to, can participate in, or are rewarded for responding to or producing specific language forms.

Those who study and theorize about child language acquisition, as well as those who have attempted to document the widely varying contexts of socialization for children around the world, will find much here to challenge their theories and inspire further fieldwork. For example, those who have focused on theories of 'learnability' to account for the innate capacities that underlie language growth will find relevant and rich language data, described in the contexts of what adults do with language and the extent to which young children have access to these language forms. Those who concern themselves with possible ways in which children reorganize their knowledge of language rules as they grow older will find numerous examples of system building in which children broaden and narrow certain categories to which rules apply as they grow older and receive more consistent exposure to forms of both 'good' and 'bad' speech. Those who wonder about ways children pick up registral variation and tie this variation to factors such as audience, topic, and relations between speaker and listener will find good evidence on which to make judgments about the extent to which principles of conventionality become salient at certain points in children's maturational development as well as in coordination with their growing social awareness of themselves as members of a culture. In short, this book demonstrates how interdisciplinary approaches to child language can help us consider in new ways both the potential of the 'human bioprogram' for language and its interdependence with sociocultural factors.

Fundamental to the assumption that language is innate are particular approaches to uses of theory and types of data collected, as well as the very methods of collection and analysis. Until the past few years, psychologists and linguists heavily influenced by methods and theories of psychology predominated in the study of language acquisition. Much of the work of these researchers focuses on the individual development of what might be termed mainstream children of nuclear families – strongly oriented to formal education and committed to the view that adults hold primary responsibility for nurturing and educating the young in the skills and knowledge of their elders. Mainstream adults, whether acting as parents or researchers, generally embrace some version of a developmental model of learning that assumes a linear and relatively orderly progression of learning in which earlier stages will not normally be repeated, and behaviors characteristic of later stages will not precede or appear in the place of behaviors judged as simpler or more fundamental than others. Mainstream families facilitate research with children in both laboratory and home settings. They exercise a high degree of control over unpredictable interruptions; they honor time commitments and keep appointments for data collection scheduled at intervals; and their geographic and economic stability offers considerable assurance of long-term studies. Often adults in the household can be enlisted to provide data in audio or written form to supplement the data collection of researchers.

Those who study nonmainstream sociocultural groups often have no such predictable supports for their data collection. They cannot assume biological parents as agents who control the spatial and temporal commitments of young children; neither can they assume that the researcher's focus on an individual's development will evoke cooperation from either adults or children. Adults of the society may not accept the notion of research on human behavior as a worthwhile – or even reasonable – activity, and the study of something so 'natural' as children learning to talk, listen, and respond may seem a particularly irrational pursuit. That Ochs chose to work in a society that acknowledged almost none of the givens of research into mainstream language acquisition is a credit to her ingenuity and persistence. In the Samoan village she studied, the child is community member, not individual; that which is to be learned need not be verbally displayed; demonstration and apprenticeship with numerous young sibling caregivers provide the major means for learning.

For most researchers in child language, the absence of expected contexts for research poses insurmountable difficulties; thus the patterns of language acquisition of many speech communities do not receive consideration. Moreover, a priori approaches worked out before field investigation rarely turn out to be either feasible or appropriate in nonmainstream settings. Ochs makes clear the details of her research methods and demonstrates how the ongoing analysis of her data in the field led her to alter methods, consider new hypotheses, and test theories as she collected more data. We can be grateful that Ochs chose to lay her methodology out carefully for the benefit of others who want to study language acquisition among societies of widely differing socialization contexts.

At least three guidelines from Ochs's collection and reporting of data can serve others who choose to work in nonmainstream societies: (1) acquire intimate knowledge of daily lifeways of the contemporary group as well as oral histories of individuals and recurring situations; (2) take a comparative perspective on interactions among group members as well as with outsiders; and (3) place oral language within the range of symbolic systems and communicative forms of the society. Of primary importance was Ochs's extended fieldwork within the village as well as her familiarity with prior research carried out in the region. She and her co-workers operated as unobtrusive adult members of Samoan village life to the extent possible, and they were also helped by the happy coincidence of having their own young children present during the fieldwork. Any long-term participant–observer study of child language acquisition gains by comparing adult–child interactions with those that take place only among children.

Besides descriptions of daily life and talk of Samoans among themselves, Ochs also gives us data on their relations with Western-based institutions and individuals. For example, her examination of the school's literacy expectations, task orientations, and patterns of reward and punishment highlights differences between within-group communication patterns and those that include outsiders. She clearly documents the interplay of affect, sensory perceptions and responses, and oral or written language uses that distinguish indigenous institutional habits from practices in the school.

Finally, Ochs's study of language socialization among the Samoans lets us know the importance of recognizing that oral language performance stands within an array of other communication forms. Gesture, written language, song, and numerous other symbol systems hold different levels and types of influence in different societies. Ochs's account of role assignments and the nature of their distribution – fluid or rigid – tells us much about the extent to which Samoan children of different social standings have access to language models beyond the intimate caregivers of kin and friendship ties. The wider the net of these associations, the greater the possibility of familiarity with a range of communication forms and language reinforcements and restrictions that include those of such Western-based institutions as the school.

Data for those who take up Ochs's guidelines will consist primarily of the scenes which surround children as they perceive, store, and make patterns of the communication systems that surround them. Details of these situations provide fundamental data of cues that repeatedly attract and sustain the attention of language learners. In addition, features of their environments will be seen to co-vary with different types of learning that children display without prior modeling or with only single occurrences. Close recording and analysis of such data can suggest the most salient paths of access to meaning that different sociocultural systems provide their young.

Beyond these methodological guidelines, what does Ochs's work suggest about the uses of such detailed case studies of small-scale nonmainstream societies? We cannot read this book without being struck by the need for more comparative work that will allow us to look at specific linguistic features, patterns of development, and approaches to parenting across societies. This current study certainly benefited greatly from earlier work in Samoa, as well as from the studies of Kaluli speakers of Papua New Guinea carried out by Ochs's colleague Bambi Schieffelin. As the research community provides more such case studies, we shall have the particulars with which to search for possible universal patterns of co-occurrence of language and social interactional habits. However, if such universals are to be at anything more than the most general level, fieldworkers must continue to work toward improved ways of observing, recording, and analyzing their data and demonstrating the interdependence of language structures and uses and social and cultural patterns.

Reaching such a goal begins by acknowledging the need for more researchers to set aside some time-honored premises of child language research and to take up new starting principles: cross-cultural studies cannot regard the basic socializing agent as the mother, a single dialect (or language) as the norm, the referential function of language as consistently primary, or spoken forms as uniquely favored for abstraction (and hence presumed maximum transfer potential). Ochs's study makes it clear that the concept of childhood and its relation to adulthood vary across cultures and shift across time. Samoan adults do not see infants of their community as conversational partners; they do not believe they have to teach directly or model speech for their children to learn to talk. In past first-language research, assumptions about a mythical universal notion of childhood have led us to accept the view that infants are exposed primarily to caregiver speech and acquire their early speech within certain structural routines and predictable contexts. Within such interactions, we have expected children to learn to take turns and negotiate the social meaning of utterances. Underlying such assumptions are implicit notions about the speaker as individual who pits his or her speech against that of others in a one-at-a-time exchange. Instead, among the Samoans, multiparty talk that is not directed to young children or talk 'through' children to a high-status individual occurs frequently. Thus, the assumptions of those who would focus only on mother–child dyadic and direct discourse seem highly simplistic. In situations such as those described by Ochs, the search for something like negative evidence becomes impossible even with the most sophisticated equipment, since overlapping and layering of utterances with nonverbal communications as support or parallel structuring are the norm. Moreover, young children are not expected to be verbal among adults. Adult models, conversational exchanges, and purposeful mediation of the environment through adult language, as these are generally conceived in the literature on mainstream child language, occur rarely or in highly marked circumstances. In this society, the biological mother serves primarily the feeding needs of her young and adopts an early monitoring role through which she evaluates the caregiving responsibilities of those older siblings who gradually take more and more charge of the infant.

Though anthropologists such as Ochs agree that the potential for grammar and development of cognitive schemata rests in the human neurological and biochemical systems, they also strive to describe how the shaping and, to some extent, the ordering of the realization of grammar and cognitive organization depend in large part on practices of language socialization. For two central points related to key mechanisms and processes of language growth – the role of affect and the interdependence of social perception and language learning – Ochs provides considerable evidence. Moreover, she demonstrates that the acquisition of certain grammatical forms believed to be universally acquired before other forms depends in large part on the amount and kind of exposure children have to these forms. In particular, the sorting out of the kin system and the hierarchy of social stratification rests with the ability of children to perceive subtle behavioral differences and to link these with variations in language forms and uses.

Ochs's work bears close links with current neurological and biochemical research with both humans and lower-order animals that underscores the fundamental role of both the perceptual and affective environment of the young. In this research, learning is a form of selection in response to environmental presentations. Patterns of neural connections are selected and made more or less active in recombinations at synaptic junctions in response to environmental contexts. Cross-correlations or patterns of presentations with varying degrees of affectual support stimulate highly variable and individual patterns of such neural connections.

Ochs's work should serve as a model of the rigor with which those who study child language in nonmainstream societies must document the kinds and degrees of displays and cuing systems that these environments present to children. With more and more such studies, we can hope that we shall eventually be able to establish fundamental social communicative operating principles that enable children to come to their sense of individual and group identity and to function as communicating members of their particular primary group. Moreover, we can hope that studies such as that presented here will draw increased scholarly attention not only to the role of affect – a little-understood phenomenon in language development – but also to ways that visual perception of the social relations of others gets mapped onto grammatical forms as the social role of the child changes during maturation. This kind of understanding takes us farther than we have yet come in accounting for ways in which children sort out semantic or role relations of agent/patient, etc. These issues relate directly to our need to understand how infants develop selective attention to certain cues that become especially salient in leading them to hypothesize and to automate the numerous decisions that direct and monitor grammatical competence and role relations in language learning.

There is much else in this case study that speaks to the future of child language research, as well as related topics, such as language varieties, the role of nonverbal symbols, and literacy acquisition and retention. Ochs reminds us of the need to recognize that many children of the world grow up learning two or more language varieties, either as dialectal or registral varieties or as different languages. Samoan children learn two registers at the same time, but sometimes from different speakers and in different settings, and often with dissimilar role relations to speakers of these varieties. Yet another reminder from Ochs's study is the fact that the spoken form of communication is not uniquely favored for young children across cultures. Indeed, some cultures downplay spoken language in daily activities and stress nonverbal signals of environmental and emotional states. The Samoan society illustrates how the spoken language of children stands relative to numerous other symbolic forms – gesture, spatial distancing, and affectual displays. Moreover, language in this society cannot be considered apart from its coordinated supports – demonstration of activities, apprenticing of roles, or ceremonial keying. These and other variations in the ways that societies approach symbolic systems can tell us much about why and how certain societies take to literacy more readily than others and how and why certain children learn to recognize and respond to conditions and elements dominant in the environment but rarely labeled. The Samoan case of literacy learning in school and in conjunction with church uses stands in sharp contrast to the 'natural' patterns of learning oral language the children followed before their entry into classrooms and 'lessoned' language.

The American poet Wallace Stevens has said, "There is nothing in the world greater than reality. In this predicament we have to accept reality itself as the only genius." The clearly and carefully detailed realities of a small-scale society in a place far distant from most of the readers of this book leave little doubt of what we may call the human genius that lies within the variety of patterns of language acquisition and language socialization around the world. I hope that this book will not only challenge our current theories of language acquisition but also stimulate other child language researchers across disciplines to take up similar studies that will enable us to accept reality as genius.

Shirley Brice Heath
Linguistics Dept.
Stanford University

Acknowledgments

Throughout the preparation and writing of this book, I have received support from colleagues, family, and the adults and children of Falefaa. The study undertaken in this book attempts to articulate relations between language acquisition and culture. Such an enterprise could not be attempted without the availability of detailed linguistic and anthropological accounts of Samoan language, society, and culture. Luckily, Samoan has recently been the object of several rich grammatical descriptions, a circumstance I have taken advantage of throughout this study. I have also benefited from the previous research of Keith Kernan and Claudia Mitchell-Kernan on Samoan language acquisition. The Kernans generously provided me with their transcriptions of children's speech prior to my own field research. In terms of encouragement, facilitation, and ethnographic wisdom, Bradd Shore has been invaluable. My decision to carry out this project in Western Samoa was very much due to Bradd's support and the breadth and insight of his accounts of Samoan social life. Bradd not only provided an ethnographic context for our acquisition study, he also facilitated our entry into the village of Falefaa, where we remained throughout the course of our field research.

Three people – Sandro Duranti, Martha Platt, and myself – composed the research team who went to Falefaa in 1978. Martha's linguistic fluency and integration into the social life of the village were always a marvel to me. The solidness of the study rests on her systematic efforts to gather, transcribe, and understand the utterances of children and others. Sandro played many roles in the course of our stay in Falefaa. I can't imagine the study's success without his efforts as sociolinguist, cameraman, *matai* 'titled person', and family man. My son David contributed valuable insights into the cultural construction of childhood as he established friendships and immersed himself in the life of his school-aged peers. In 1981, when we returned to Falefaa for a second round of fieldwork, my eight-month-old son Marco was, unbeknownst to him, a contributor to our research. As Samoans have a simplified foreigner talk register but not a simplified baby talk register, we wondered how they would talk to an infant foreigner. Babyhood won over!

xvi   *Acknowledgments*

Our stay and work in Falefaa were possible primarily because of the hospitality and support of Pastor Fa'atau'oloa Mauala and his wife Sau'iluma, who introduced us to the families of Falefaa and helped us to build a house on the Congregational Christian Church land. Fa'atau'oloa and Sau'iluma helped us to locate families for our study and allowed us to tape and film the pastor's school. Most valuable of all, they gave us their friendship, which we have sustained throughout these years. During both periods of fieldwork John and Dotsy Kneubuhl and Tate Simi and Noumea Pesetaa opened their homes to us and offered us good counsel and good company. I am particularly grateful to Dotsy Kneubuhl for her insights into the expression of emotion in childhood.

The study itself involved entering the lives of six children – Pesio, Niulala, Kalavini, Matu'u, Iakopo, and Naomi – and their families. These children, their peers, and their caregivers tolerated the presence of the intruding researchers with their recording equipment and their insistence on remaining for entire mornings or afternoons or sometimes both. I owe a tremendous debt to these households.

In the course of our stay, several thousand pages of transcription were completed. Such a massive data base depended on the efforts of several field assistants, who transcribed five or six days a week, working hours on end each day. At times, our house looked like a transcription factory as we listened, consulted over difficult passages, wrote, and checked the data. I am grateful to all those who assisted in this task.

Since leaving Falefaa, I have been working very closely with my colleague Bambi Schieffelin, who carried out similar research in Papua New Guinea. We have woven our insights into a comparative perspective, and it is this perspective that pervades the present study. I have also benefited from numerous talks with my departmental colleagues and from long lunchtime discussions with Manny Schegloff about clarification and with Patricia Greenfield, Pat Zukow, and Judy Reilly about language-acquisition theory. All of these scholars have read earlier versions of chapters and offered valuable suggestions. My initiation into the theoretical intricacies of Soviet psychological research has been greatly facilitated by conversations with Mike and Sheila Cole, Peg Griffin, and Jim Wertsch. The interface between language socialization and the social construction of development is the point of departure for our continuing dialogues.

In preparing the final manuscript, I have worked closely with Lori Powell. I am indebted to her for preparation of the list of references and close readings of various drafts. I am also grateful to other members of the departmental staff, particularly David Srebnik, for their help in getting the manuscript completed.

Throughout data collection and analysis of the Samoan speech data I have been fortunate enough to receive financial support from several institutions. The National Science Foundation supported my initial field research and analysis from 1978 to 1980 and has awarded further support for a three-year (1986–9) study of the acquisition and use of genitive noun phrases in Samoan. From 1980 to 1981 the Research School of Pacific Studies, Australian National University, supported a second field trip to Western Samoa and the writing up of the Samoan data. A grant from the Howard Foundation in 1982–3, a stipend and office space from the Istituto di Psicologia (Consiglio Nazionale di Ricerche) in Rome, 1983–4, and a Guggenheim Fellowship, 1984–5, supported my research on cross-cultural patterns of language socialization. I wish to thank all of these research institutions for funding this study.

This book is dedicated to my husband and intellectual partner, Sandro Duranti.

1. To know a language

I.   GUIDING PRINCIPLES

When I first began recording Samoan children and their caregivers in the summer of 1978, I encountered a serious methodological problem. Instead of engaging in the usual range of everyday household activities and interactions, the children would sit very properly on mats near my own mat and either wait for me to tell them what to do or perform at the command of an older sibling, parent, or other relative. Worse for the poor researcher, instead of conversing in the register typical of most social interactions in the village (the register Samoans call 'bad speech'), caregivers and children appeared to use only the register Samoans call 'good speech', characteristic of written Samoan and of Samoan spoken in school, church, and certain business settings and to foreigners who know Samoan. 'Please', I would say over and over to members of the household, 'just go on doing what you usually do and do not pay attention to me.' I hoped somehow that this formula would magically create the context for the 'spontaneous' talk of children and caregivers that is characteristic of longitudinal studies of child language in other societies. How else would I be able to bring back 'comparable' data? The failure of my magic and the prospect of loss of face in the world of developmental research led me to a full-scale analysis of the basis of this problem.

In transcribing the first tapes I discovered that while most of the talk was 'good speech', some of it was not. Initially it seemed that caregivers switched to 'bad speech' when they spoke to persons some distance from the area around the tape recorder and microphone. My first hypothesis was that caregivers would switch when they thought the microphone was not picking up what they were saying. That is, they had on-stage and off-stage (Goffman 1959, 1963) registers. I pursued this hypothesis, checking the locations of different addresses through my notes on context taken during recording sessions. I found that talk to anyone seated on mats in the central area of the room was in 'good speech', whereas talk to those hanging around the periphery of the house, either standing or seated on pebbles or the bare

1

floor, was in 'bad speech'. A closer look showed that the central area was actually toward the front of the house, with my mat always the closest to the front. Those in the peripheral areas stayed toward the sides and back of the house. My methodological dilemma was partially resolved when I realized that the ethnographer Bradd Shore's analysis of spatial contrasts in Samoan society had a linguistic counterpart. In Shore's account (1977, 1982), the orientations of front versus back and center versus periphery are associated with more-controlled versus less-controlled demeanor and activities. Front versus back is also associated with the place of higher-ranking persons (see also Duranti 1981a). It became obvious to me that, whereas I saw myself as a researcher coming to record speech, the rest of those in the house saw me as a guest and a foreigner. The placing of my mat in the front of the house and my sitting on it defined me as a relatively high-ranking person and defined the social event as formal. As was appropriate to this identity, the disposition of others was to serve my needs. Knowing that I was a teacher, the children waited to be instructed, and when this expectation was not met the caregivers initiated a series of performances that displayed for me the skills and knowledge of the children. Given that I was a foreigner and that the situation was partially defined as 'doing school', all of the talk oriented toward the goal of satisfying my needs was in 'good speech'.

You might wonder why I introduce my study of Samoan language development with such an episode. My primary intention is not to convey the hazards of cross-cultural research and ways to overcome them. It is, rather, to communicate to my readers, who I presume are primarily researchers in child language, the theoretical import of this methodological crisis. I temporarily resolved my methodological dilemma by becoming more familiar with the household and by sitting in the back of the house, often off a mat. I also learned to exploit my knowledge of space and language to elicit a wide range of speech styles from children and caregivers. But this is not all I learned. These methodological problems moved me to analyze the language of children over developmental time and the language of caregivers in the context of the Samoan social order and cultural ideology. My odyssey at the start of data collection turned into a piece of data in itself, for I realized that in a very general sense an odyssey of this sort is also experienced by every child acquiring language. In making sense out of what people are saying and in speaking in a sensible fashion themselves, children relate linguistic forms to social situations. Part of their acquired knowledge of a linguistic form is the set of relations that obtain between that form and social situations, just as part of their acquired knowledge of a social situation includes the linguistic forms that define or characterize it. My incompetence lay precisely in this area: I could not figure out the overall goals of household members that linked one speech act to another, and I could not figure out why my request that they ignore me was not heeded.

My request was absurd or at least difficult to carry out, given that I defined the event as a formal visit through my seating pattern. Meaning is embedded in cultural conceptions of context, and in this respect the process of acquiring language is embedded in the process of socialization of knowledge.

Like other language-acquisition studies, this book is dedicated to understanding the process of becoming a competent speaker–hearer, attending to both universal and particular aspects of this process. The present study should not, however, be read as a 'standard' psycholinguistic consideration of language acquisition. It is important for the reader to note that the author is an anthropologist by training and that the processes under consideration in this book are relevant to the sociocultural as well as the intra-individual cognitive domain. Certain chapters dwell almost exclusively on one of these domains, while others evaluate both dimensions of a particular linguistic structure. For example, Chapter 6 focuses primarily on how word-order preferences in Samoan adult and child language use relate to saliency and ordering of particular concepts. Chapter 7 focuses on the social and cultural information indexed in the clarification sequence, a discourse structure pervasive in children's conversations with others. On the other hand, Chapters 5 and 9 consider both cognitive and sociocultural parameters of children's acquisition of case (Chapter 5) and affect (Chapter 9) morphology.

There are many who wish that research would display once and for all a clear division between areas of language that are insulated from social processes and areas that are vulnerable. The story of language turns out not to lend itself to slick generalizations of this sort, however. My own view is that the relative importance of intra-personal cognitive processes and society depends less on a particular area of language structure and more on the question posed concerning language. Social processes will be highly relevant to questions concerning patterns of language production and comprehension. Social processes figure largely in discussions relating linguistic forms to meaning. On the other hand, social processes are not of immediate explanatory relevance (even though a sociolinguist will likely take this as a challenge to prove otherwise) when one is investigating whether or not particular lexical items are constituents of the same type.

Acquisition research is still a long way from an account of how children perceive and conceptualize events, states, and objects (including persons) in the world and how they map this information onto lexical, grammatical, and discourse structures. An idea supported by several researchers, including Nelson (1981), Peters (1983), and Slobin (1986), is that children organize information in terms of conceptual scenes or frames (Bateson 1972). In Slobin's account, any one event or situation is a complex outcome of different kinds of knowledge, e.g. sensori-motor, perceptual–cognitive, social interactional. Language encodes these different facets of scenes. Thus far, acquisition research has generated numerous studies and hypotheses concerning children's strategies for mapping sensori-motor and perceptual–cognitive concepts onto linguistic structures. Much less is understood about children's concepts of affect, social acts, social activities, social events, social relationships, and other areas of sociocultural knowledge and how these concepts relate to children's understanding of scenes on the one hand and language on the other. The acquisition of language entails coming to tacitly know the multiple kinds of information or meanings that linguistic structures index. The task of the researcher is to characterize this process as accurately as possible. Such a task involves resources from several disciplines. The present study offers primarily an anthropological linguistic orientation to this theoretical concern.

This volume explores ways in which Samoan children and adults represent events, activities, and object (including person) relations through language and ways they use language as a social tool (Vygotsky 1978). It asks what kinds of meanings are expressed and what kinds of structures express these meanings in the course of children's verbal interactions with others and in the course of children's language development. A major guiding principle of this book is that interpretation and meaning are necessarily embedded in cultural systems of understanding. If language is a meaning-making system and speaking and listening are meaning-making activities, then accounts of these phenomena must at some point draw on accounts of society and culture.

A number of scholars have contributed to the view I am advocating, namely that language participates in a network of semiotic systems (Sapir 1921) and that speaking and listening are social practices (Bourdieu 1977; Garfinkel 1967; Giddens 1979, 1984; Hymes 1974; Leontyev 1981) with social histories and consequences (Bakhtin 1981) and social expectations and preferences (Gumperz 1982; Schegloff, Jefferson & Sacks 1977). The relations obtaining between particular linguistic structures and linguistic practices become part of a language acquirer's linguistic knowledge, part of his or her understanding of those structures. As language acquirers develop – indeed throughout individuals' lifespans – they use linguistic structures to engage in different practices and in so doing continually modify their conceptions of these linguistic structures.

II.   A SOCIOCULTURAL FRAMEWORK FOR LANGUAGE ACQUISITION

Specifying precisely what constitutes a sociocultural perspective of language acquisition is no simple matter. We need an understanding of how sociocultural knowledge, linguistic knowledge, and the processes of social-ization and language acquisition impact each other. Let us begin with a brief overview of society, culture, and the process of socialization. After this discussion, we shall consider the relation of these phenonema to language and its acquisition.

A.   Society, culture, and socialization

One of the distinctive characteristics of the human species is that it transmits both social skills and cultural knowledge to its young. The transmission of cultural knowledge has been referred to as *enculturation* (Mead 1963), but a term that covers transmission of both procedures ('knowing how') and premises ('knowing that') is *socialization* (Cicourel 1973). For purposes of the discussion here, socialization will be considered as a more general term referring to the process by which one becomes a competent member of society (Ochs & Schieffelin 1984; Schieffelin & Ochs 1983, 1986a). An important point put forward in this book is that children's speech behavior over developmental time will be socially and culturally organized. To understand the form and content of children's language, it is necessary to incorporate a sociocultural level of interpretation.

A theory of socialization will draw on theories and definitions of cultural and social systems. As numerous reviews have pointed out (Geertz 1973; Keesing 1974; Leach 1982; Sapir 1924; Tyler 1969), the definition and significance of culture vary from school to school within the field of anthropology. Most approaches, however, treat culture as a system of implicit and explicit ideas (Keesing 1974) that underlies and gives meaning to behaviors in society. Culture has been defined as a world view of members of a society (Sapir 1921; Whorf 1941), as premises that order thought and feeling (Tindall 1976), as a cognitive map (Goodenough 1957; Wallace 1970), as a system of symbols and meanings (Geertz 1973; Lévi-Strauss 1968, Schneider 1968). These orientations are related (in various ways, to varying extents, according to 'school' and paradigm) to social behavior, including political, economic, religious, and kinship relations, events, interactions, and institutions; to values; to conceptions of the world; to theories of knowledge and procedures for understanding and interpreting.

One of the major points of disagreement in anthropology concerns the locus of culture – the extent to which it is in the heads of all members (Conklin 1962; Frake 1964; Goodenough 1957); the extent to which it is created, negotiated, and redefined continually between persons (Geertz 1973) participating in some context or situation (Malinowski 1978).

Within the first theoretical approach, socialization might be viewed as the transmission of cultural knowledge (and its corresponding behavioral expression) that is shared by adult members of the society to which a child belongs. Socialization consists, in this framework, of transferring principles for making sense out of the world and procedures for engaging in it from one generation to the next. Socialization is complete when a child has acquired this knowledge.

In the extreme of this view, culture is a closed system of ideas. As such, this approach assigns a relatively static role to culture. But we know that cultures evolve and change and that not all of these changes can be accounted for as responses to changes in the physical environment or contact with another society and its cultural system.

A more comprehensive approach is to view culture as a loose set of guidelines and premises, shared to varying extents by members of a society. To adopt the view taken by Keesing (1974), certain basic orientations will be shared and lie in the heads of all competent members of a society, whereas others will vary among members within the society. Among other routes, members of a society may alter their 'theories' of the world through exposure and reaction to other's orientations. That is not to say that the orientation of one member becomes the orientation of another. Rather, the messages and actions of one member are interpreted in terms of and integrated within the existing orientations or 'frames' of the other (Goffman 1974). The extent to which we as adults transform our theories about the social and physical world will be limited, as will children's, by our egocentric tendencies and our willingness to empathize with others (Langness & Frank 1981).

Socialization, in this view, is not a process limited to early childhood; instead, socialization is a lifespan experience (see Cicourel 1973; Ochs & Schieffelin 1984; Schieffelin & Ochs 1986b for extended discussions of this point). Throughout our lives, we are socializing and being socialized by those we encounter (including by our own children).

The effects of social experience on culture and culture on social experience are complex and have been the subject of philosophy of social science for some time (Bleicher 1982; Heidegger 1962; Husserl 1970; Ricoeur 1971) as well as a major point of dispute dividing social and cultural anthropology (see discussion by Leach 1982). Simply put, for social anthropologists, cultural beliefs and values are byproducts of social institutions, and function to sustain those institutions. That is, social organization creates culture. Cultural anthropologists, for the most part, have viewed culture as broader in function and significance – a complex system, (partially) shared and created among members of a society, that organizes meanings of events at different levels. This system may facilitate the perpetuation of social institutions and the survival of the group, but these goals cannot account for the breadth and complexity of the system of ideas generated among members of society.

The relation of social behavior to culture is not simple in any current view. First of all, for any social behavior, there may be different *realms* of understanding that experience. This is Geertz's point about culture being an 'assemblage of texts' (1973; Keesing 1974). Second, members of the same society may not have identical conceptualizations (implicit and explicit) of social behaviors. Indeed, having partially different understandings of a social activity does not seem to preclude participating in that activity (if we can still refer to it as the same activity). Students attending a university may have somewhat different notions concerning what students are doing, what professors are doing, etc., but they interact with one another rather smoothly nonetheless most of the time (though not, for example, in the 1968 student revolt in Paris). Third, culture and social interaction have a cybernetic relation (Bateson 1972, 1979), each affecting the other. Culture emerges through social interaction, and at the same time it organizes social interaction. Giddens (1979, 1984) refers to a similar relation between social systems and social activity as the 'duality of structure': 'By the duality of structure, I mean the essential recursiveness of social life, as constituted in social practices. Structure enters simultaneously into the constitution of the agent and social practices, and "exists" in the generating moments of this constitution' (1979:5).

In our concept of socialization, we want to provide for these complex relations between cultural systems and social behavior. On the other hand, we need to recognize that the attainment of an adequate account of these relations is beyond current reach. Though structural analytic methods have been used for isolating different levels and structural relations characteristic of cultural systems (Goodenough 1957; Lévi-Strauss 1968), there is still no acceptable means of validating these accounts. Further, there is no clear means of determining variation and sharedness of assumptions within a social group. And this leads to problems in defining and demarcating the boundaries of a culture (Sapir 1924; Wallace 1970). Is one a member of a culture because one identifies oneself as such? because one acts in appropriate ways? because one shares a way of interpreting social behavior? How much or what has to be shared? Certainly these are very real problems, particularly for those carrying out research in complex, multiethnic societies (see Gumperz 1982 for a discussion of this point). Finally, the process or socialization element in culture seems particularly difficult to document. While the broad outlines of the negotiation of meaning, drawn from the phenomenological, ethnomethodological, and hermeneutic literature, have been presented (see Wentworth 1980), the details of this very important process have not been provided. Close analysis of the sociolinguistic organization of the speech activities in which children (novices) engage is a means of getting at just these details linking communication to culture.

B.   Language and language acquisition

Just as the concept of socialization implies notions of society and culture, so one's understanding of language acquisition depends on how one conceptualizes language. We take for granted that language is organized in terms of a set of principles (Slobin 1986) or rules (Chomsky 1986) constraining form–form and form–meaning relations. From the perspective of generative grammar, these principles or rules are seen as generating grammatical sentences in a language. (We shall take up this point later in discussing alternatives to this view of the *langue–parole* relation.)

While recognizing the extraordinary complexity and systematicity of grammar, we consider language to have forms of organization beyond the sentence. 'Discourse' typically refers to multiclausal, multisentential, or multiutterance structures; the term is also widely used to refer simply to relations between clauses, sentences, or utterances and context. Rather than referring to structures directly, I believe that 'discourse' should refer to a set of norms, preferences, and expectations relating linguistic structures to context, which speaker–hearers draw on and modify in producing and interpreting language in context. Discourse in this sense is comparable to the notion of grammar, although grammatical principles are formulated as rules and constraints that generate all allowable sentences in a language.

Structures covered by discourse principles include speech acts, conversational sequences, episodes, rounds, speech activities, speech events, genres, and registers, among others. Part of every native speaker–hearer's competence is a tacit understanding of these constructions. This understanding involves tacit knowledge of norms, preferences, and expectations surrounding linguistic form–form, form–meaning, and form–function relations. Knowledge underlying form–form relations includes knowledge of co-occurrence (e.g. to form registers) and sequential-order (e.g. to form conversational sequences and speech events) relations. Knowledge of form–meaning and form–function relations includes knowing how forms index contextual information, such as speaker and/or situation goals, social identities and relationships, affective and epistemic stances.

The use of linguistic forms to signal that a particular context is in play has been a major concern of those interested in pragmatic properties of language. Let us consider here some facets of this context-generating capacity of language and its acquisition by young children.

1.   Metacommunicative and paradigmatic relations

'*Metacommunicative*' is a term borrowed from Bateson (1972, 1979), who in turn draws on the notion of *indexicality*, introduced by Peirce (1931–58).

Indexicality refers to the property of a sign as an indicator of some aspect of the situational context in which the sign is used. The notion has been developed in a series of articles by Silverstein (1976a, 1981a, b), who has distinguished 'referential indexes' and 'nonreferential indexes', the latter being 'features of speech which, independent of any referential speech events that may be occurring, signal some particular value of one or more contextual variables' (1976a:29). Nonreferential indexes, for example, may signal something about the social organization of a speech event, such as the social rank of participants, or they may refer to affective or epistemic stances vis-à-vis some expressed proposition.

Bateson's writings concern indexes that signal the type of action or speech event taking place. *Metacommunicative markers* provide listeners with information concerning what actors/speakers are doing. They indicate the contextual 'frame' in which verbal and non-verbal behavior is to be interpreted. These markers are similar to what Hymes has called 'keys' (1974), Goffman calls 'keyings' (1974), and Gumperz (1977, 1982) and Gumperz & Cook-Gumperz (1982) have referred to as 'contextualization cues' or 'contextualization conventions'. Most of Bateson's discussion focuses on metacommunicative markers that signal that an act is not serious, that it is to be taken as 'play'. Bateson contends species other than humans have metacommunicative markers that signal this information and have the capacity to recognize them in their interactions; hence, dogs distinguish the 'playful nip' from the 'bite' (1972).

The kind of knowledge that we are discussing here could be subsumed under knowledge of paradigmatic relations among contexts. Metacommunicative knowledge helps members of society to relate an action (including an utterance) to one or more contexts out of a set of alternative contexts. Part of what it means to participate in a society is to have what Schutz would call 'stock knowledge' (1967) of the conventions for marking metacommunicative information. Members of a community partially share postures, movements, and verbal means for indicating the nature (in Bateson's terms, the 'logical type') of the activity occurring (e.g. 'This is play', 'This is a serious threat').

This does not mean that participants always provide the same contextual frame for a verbal or nonverbal action. Certain behaviors may be ambiguous with respect to their interpretive frames. The ambiguity may be consciously exploited, as in the case of threats. It may not always be clear whether a threat is a 'mock threat' or 'serious threat'. Speakers/actors may 'play' on this ambiguity, letting the listener entertain the more serious interpretation (see Kochman 1981 for an extended discussion of this strategy in black culture). Indeed, disagreements often arise concerning just this type of information ('I was only kidding.' 'No, you weren't').

Although children's capacity to play has been a traditional concern in child-development research (see for example Bruner 1972, 1975; Garvey

1977; Piaget 1926, 1929, 1951), it is only recently that children's understanding of others' messages as playful or nonliteral has been considered. A series of studies of *teasing* (Briggs 1986; Demuth 1986; Eisenberg 1982; Heath 1983; Miller 1986; Mitchell-Kernan & Kernan 1975; Ochs 1986b; Schieffelin 1986b; Watson-Gegeo & Gegeo 1986) indicate that there is cross-cultural variation in when and how teasing is directed to small children and in the developmental point at which children are expected to recognize and produce markers of this activity. In many white middle-class American families, mothers do not frequently tease infants and small children, although fathers may do so, particularly their young sons (Gleason & Greif 1983; Gleason & Weintraub 1976). On the other hand, teasing by both parents and others of infants and toddlers of both sexes is frequent in many other societies, including working-class American (Heath 1983; Miller 1982, 1986), Mexicano (Briggs 1986; Eisenberg 1982, 1986), Kaluli of Papua New Guinea (Schieffelin 1986b), Basotho of South Africa (Demuth 1986), Kwara'ae of the Solomon Islands (Watson-Gegeo & Gegeo 1986), and Samoan (Mitchell-Kernan & Kernan 1975; Ochs 1982a). In these societies, caregivers will alter their voice quality and their facial expressions as they engage their young charges in teasing. Briggs reports that Mexicano family members speaking to a girl of one year and nine months 'alter the pitch, quantity, rhythm, and patterns, and the speed of utterance of their speech. In some cases, these are used in marking an utterance as motherese or baby talk. But they are also used by [the caregiver] in framing the relative ludic vs. admonitory character of her statements' (1984:8). Both Briggs and Eisenberg report that Mexicano children just over the age of two can produce and recognize certain metacommunicative markers of this distinction.

To be competent communicative partners, children must acquire knowledge of both contextual frames for interpreting actions and metacommunicative markers indicating which frames should be supplied. Bateson's major point in two volumes of collected writings is that communication is related to species survival. We can see here that communication and survival rest on one's capacity to distinguish the metacommunicative markers of 'play' from those associated with other activities. The film *War Games* dwells on this theme. The major plot revolves around the inability of humans and machines to communicate with each other. While able to understand the computer's printout statements concerning enemy offensive movements, Defense Department officials are unable to understand that the computer is playing a war *game* and not war itself. We are saved from World War III by a last-minute appearance of the original creator of the program, who interprets the true goals of the computer for the top brass with their fingers on the button. This film resembles the scenarios drawn by Bateson of cross-species miscommunication. The theme has parallels as well for interethnic misunderstandings, as when white federal officials in the 1960s (mis)interpreted the rhetoric of black English performance speech at civil-rights marches in their own literal contextual frames (see Kochman 1981).

2.   Syntagmatic relations

Syntagmatic relations indicate those linguistic structures that may co-occur, given one or more specified dimensions of context, such as a particular type of social relation (doctor–patient, parent–child, etc.), speech act (e.g. request, wish, disagreement), or setting (e.g. home, restaurant, church, courtroom, on the road, in the bush). Co-occurring linguistic structures may also display a sequential organization (Sacks, Schegloff & Jefferson 1974). The syntagmatic relations between linguistic structures and contextual dimensions may be quite complex. Usually communicative competence involves relating a number of linguistic forms to a number of contextual dimensions. A speaker–hearer must know what structures to use, given goals, roles, statuses, settings, and so on (Hymes 1974).

Tacit knowledge of syntagmatic relations includes tacit knowledge of *registers* (Andersen 1977; Ellis & Ure 1969; Ferguson 1977) within a language. Registers are varieties associated with situations of use (Andersen 1977); examples of registers in different societies are baby talk, foreigner talk, religious speech, formal registers, newscasters' talk, mother-in-law speech (Dixon 1972), and doctor–patient speech. Andersen (1977), Sachs & Devin (1976), and Shatz & Gelman (1973) among others have demonstrated that American middle-class children can speak appropriately (but with varying degrees of sophistication) in a variety of registers in English in their preschool years. Samoan children also display a certain amount of competence in register switching early in their development, with most displaying two phonological registers in their speech before the age of two and a half years.

Acquirers often indicate that they do not yet know local norms that relate linguistic forms to particular contexts, producing utterances that are grammatical but not quite appropriate. For example, after one American middle-class mother would ask her two-and-a-half-year-old child, 'Shall we go to bed now?' the child would repeatedly respond, 'No, thank you.' Young Samoan children, to cite another example, use primarily one of three phonological markers of 'good Samoan' register, in situations that require that register. (The phoneme /t/ is favored over /n/ or /r/. See Chapters 3 and 10 for a discussion of these registers.)

Acquirers may receive explicit instruction in the use of linguistic features and constructions appropriate to particular situations. Research in several societies, including Kaluli of Papua New Guinea (Schieffelin 1979, 1986a, b), Western Samoan (Ochs 1982a), Kwara'ae of the Solomon Islands (Peters & Boggs 1986; Watson-Gegeo & Gegeo 1986), Hawaiian (Boggs 1985; Watson-Gegeo & Boggs 1977), Mexican American (Eisenberg 1982), American middle-class (Greif & Gleason 1980), and American working-class (Heath 1983), indicates that caregivers will tell children what to say and how to say it, utterance by utterance, turn by turn. These instruction sequences are themselves linguistically marked (e.g. prosodically). They may be relatively brief, as reported of middle-class socialization, or go on for dozens of turns, as reported of socialization in several Oceanic societies.

Interest in children's knowledge of syntagmatic relations between linguistic forms and situations has increased in the past decade in the social sciences. The concern is manifest in sociolinguistic research in the notion of *speech event* (Hymes 1962, 1972, 1974) and *speech activity* (Levinson 1979). In psychology, two major lines of research focus on the relation of language to situational knowledge. The first line of research stems from Soviet psychology, particularly Leontyev (1981), Luria (1976, 1981), and Vygotsky (1962, 1978), and is currently represented in such works as Cole (1985), Griffin & Cole (1984), Hickman (1985), LCHC (1983), Lee (1985), Scribner & Cole (1981), and Wertsch (1980, 1985a, b), among others. The research focuses on the link between communication, social activity, and cognitive development, promoting the hypothesis that how language is used in culturally organized activity settings impacts the development of higher mental functions. This idea is rooted primarily in Vygotsky's claim that 'the internalization of socially rooted and historically developed activities is the distinguishing feature of human psychology, the basis of the qualitative leap from animal to human psychology. As yet, the barest outline of this process is known' (1978:57).

A second line of research, in the area of cognitive science, has been considering mental representations underlying *scripts* (Schank & Abelson 1977). A major focus has been children's schemata for recurrent activities and relations between linguistic structures and these schemata. Nelson's (1981) research relating lexical knowledge to situational knowledge among young children illustrates this interest. This research stresses the role of situational knowledge in the acquisition of word meanings. Other research (E. Clark 1974; Peters 1983) suggests that some children produce whole predicates and complex constructions in appropriate social situations but do not 'know' these constructions in an analytic sense, i.e. do not systematically vary components of these constructions in other situations.

3. Preference relations

When children acquire knowledge of relations between linguistic features and contexts of use, they acquire knowledge of *expectations* associated with these relations. For example, members of society have attitudes or, rather, preferences concerning the various linguistic structures that could be put to use, given a particular situation. There are preferences about which linguistic forms are most suited to carrying out particular speech acts, activities, and events; which forms best index degrees and kinds of speaker–hearers' knowledge and affective dispositions and so on. Children acquire a range of expectations: what is required, what is preferred, what is possible but unusual, what is awkward, and what is altogether out of bounds of the appropriate (Ervin-Tripp 1972, 1979; Hymes 1974; Philips 1970). This knowledge provides young children with a basis for understanding the *social meaning* (referring to social context of use) of utterances they hear. They learn to interpret certain constructions in context as unusual or marked and can assign special significance to them, e.g. a change in social distance or affect between speaker and addressee.

The literature on language development indicates that children early on are socialized to use the most preferred linguistic forms vis-à-vis particular situations of use. Greif & Gleason (1980) report that in American families children are often explicitly told to supply the preferred form for a situation (in this case, the preferred is also the polite alternative).

Prompting occurred in virtually all of the families. . . . Parents were most insistent that their children say *thank you*, prompting them 51% of the time if they did not produce the routine when receiving the gift. The children were also remarkably compliant: they said *thank you* 86% of the time when they were told to. On the rare occasion when a child actually refused to say *thank you*, the parent insisted relentlessly. (Greif & Gleason 1980:162)

Similar forms of preferred-form prompting for a wide range of situations (including insults, challenges, and teasing) are found in a number of other societies, including Kaluli, Basotho, Kwara'ae, Mexican American, and Samoan (see Schieffelin & Ochs 1986a, b for a review of these practices).

To summarize, within the perspective proposed here, acquisition is seen as increasing competence in both the formal and functional potential of language. By functional, I mean the multiplicity of relations between language and context, including that in which language creates context. Over developmental time, children acquire repertoires of constructions and lexical items associated with such contextual dimensions as role relationships (e.g. doctor and patient, teacher and student), social acts (e.g. refusing), and events (e.g telling a story, playing a game). Children's understanding of the meaning of the propositions associated with these constructions and words is in part based on their knowledge of such contextual associations as well as on their understanding of preference or markedness relations between these forms and contexts.

C.   Toward a sociocultural model of language acquisition

1.   The interdependence of linguistic and sociocultural knowledge

From the previous discussion, it is evident that acquisition of linguistic knowledge and acquisition of sociocultural knowledge are interdependent. A basic task of the language acquirer is to acquire tacit knowledge of principles relating linguistic forms not only to each other but also to referential and nonreferential meanings and functions (see Slobin 1986). Given that meanings and functions are to a large extent socioculturally organized, linguistic knowledge is embedded in sociocultural knowledge. On the other hand, understandings of the social organization of everyday life, cultural ideologies, moral values, beliefs, and structures of knowledge and interpretation are to a large extent acquired through the medium of language. Schieffelin & Ochs call this process *language socialization* (see 1986a, b), i.e. socialization through language and socialization to use language. Children develop concepts of a socioculturally structured universe through their participation in language activities. In this sense, we support a version of the Sapir–Whorf hypothesis (Mandelbaum 1949) and claim that not only are language practices organized by world views, they also create world views for the language users carrying out these practices.

One way of representing the interdependency of linguistic and sociocultural knowledge would be a simple model of the sort shown in Figure 1.1.

2.   The role of activity

However, such a model does not articulate the role of human activity in the development of knowledge. Activity is both a behavioral unit, in the sense of a sequence of actions associated with particular motivations and goals (Leontyev 1981), and a process, in the sense of praxis (Marx 1959; Vygotsky

Linguistic knowledge $\langle - - - - - - - \rangle$ Sociocultural knowledge

Figure 1.1.

1962). A model which relates activity to mental representations of language, society, and culture is offered in Figure 1.2. This model, which indicates that activity mediates linguistic and sociocultural knowledge and that knowledge and activity impact one another, draws on several approaches to the acquisition of knowledge, including the psychological approaches of Piaget (1952) and Vygotsky (1962, 1978) and the sociological approaches of Bourdieu (1977) and Giddens (1979, 1984). What is common to all of these approaches is the view that knowledge and praxis create each other.

Piaget's fundamental point is that children bring into their experiences biological predispositions and capacities for cognizing and developing; however, at the same time, in a very important sense children construct their own development through their actions in the world they experience. Here we can see that knowledge structures activity and activity structures knowledge. This relationship is expressed in Piaget's notions of assimilation and accommodation. Until recently, Piagetian research has not concentrated on children's interactions with other persons nor the social cultural construction of children's activities. Hence, whereas Piagetian research examines children's social cognition, much of what is considered classic Piagetian theory does not emphasize the role of society and culture in intellectual development (see Cole & Cole in press; Vygotsky 1962; Wertsch 1985a, b).

Sociohistorical approaches to development, in contrast, promote the idea that higher intellectual skills of individuals develop in part through participation in socially and culturally organized activities. Novices are able to acquire cognitive skills through participation in joint activities (which require these skills) with more knowledgeable persons. That is, more knowledgeable persons provide an environment which promotes cognitive development. Critical to the development of certain cognitive skills is, then, the activity. Sociohistorical approaches claim that different social and cultural structuring of activities (demanding different cognitive skills) across social groups at particular historical moments will differentially impact the development of certain higher mental functions (e.g. abstract thinking). Quite important here is the impact of socially and culturally organized language practices in activity settings. Among other variables, the channel of communication (e.g. written, spoken), the instrument of communication (e.g. computer, television), the goals or problems addressed by these language practices, and the organization of participation in these language practices (e.g. type and extent of joint activity) influence the direction of cognitive development. This point underlies Vygotsky's notion of 'semiotic mediation' of thought (1962, 1978; Wertsch 1985a, b) and

Linguistic knowledge ⟨ − − ⟩ Activity ⟨ − − ⟩ Sociocultural knowledge

Figure 1.2.

Scribner & Cole's (1981) research on literacy practices and cognitive development.

The overall relevance of the sociohistorical approach to the model represented in Figure 1.2 is that sociocultural and linguistic knowledge structures activity, and activity creates (in the case of the novice/acquirer) and recreates (in the case of the member/competent language user) knowledge in both of these domains. With respect to the notion of recreating knowledge, one of the important results of recent research is that cognitive skills once acquired may be lost if the activities for which these skills are necessary are not habitual (see Scribner & Cole 1981).

These psychological approaches resonate with recent sociological approaches proposed by Bourdieu (1977) and Giddens (1979, 1984). Bourdieu's 'practice theory' proposes that the *habitus* of a social group, its socially constituted system of dispositions (cognitive and motivating structures), gives rise to practices, which in turn tend to reproduce *habitus*:

Dispositions durably inculcated by objective conditions engender aspirations and practices objectively compatible with those objective requirements.(1977:72)

The system of dispositions (*habitus*) – a past which survives in the present and tends to perpetuate itself into the future by making itself present in practices structured according to its principles . . .   (1977:82)

This same orientation is maintained in Giddens's theory of structuration, in which structures are seen as sources and products of social behavior. As noted earlier in this chapter, this idea is captured in Giddens's notion of 'duality of structure'. Both Bourdieu and Giddens critique structuralist theories for their failure to link structure with practice, except in a unidirectional manner, where structure generates practice. They criticize de Saussure, Lévi-Strauss, and Chomsky for their views that *langue* (structure) creates *parole* (practice/performance) but that *langue* is unaffected by *parole*. Both practice theory and structuration theory along with the constructivist theory of Piaget and sociohistorical theory make the claim that structure and practice enjoy a complex, cybernetic relationship. From the point of view of these theories, *parole* generates *langue* as well as the converse. From this point of view, linguistic knowledge is at least partially generated from language practices. This idea is captured in sociolinguistic research on language change, such as that of Labov (1966), Sankoff (1980), and Trudgill (1974).

With respect to the point that use affects structure, we would, then, predict that contextual conditions inherent in communicative practices would impact the linguistic competence of language users universally. That is, certain aspects of the activity of communicating always present will influence not only linguistic practices but the organization of linguistic knowledge as well. This point is stressed in psycholinguistic research relating typological and universal preferences for particular linguistic structures (e.g. preference hierarchies for relative-clause formation, word-order preferences, etc.) to processing constraints associated with actual language use (see Antinucci, Duranti & Gebert 1979; Hawkins in press; Slobin 1986). Here the argument is that linguistic structures difficult to process in actual communicative activities are less common and less preferred across the world's languages than alternative structures that are easier to process.

The same idea is held here in the theory of language acquisition I am proposing. Children's language practices are partially engendered by grammatical, discourse, sociocultural, and general cognitive structures. However, these structures of knowledge are created in part through children's participation in temporarily and spatially situated practices/activities.

The notion of practice or activity is central to an integrated theory of language acquisition in other ways as well. I noted earlier that activities play a *mediating role* vis-à-vis linguistic and sociocultural knowledge. By this I mean several things. First, language activities are at the same time linguistic and sociocultural phenomena. They are structured by linguistic and sociocultural principles. Second, the sociocultural contexts that language activities engender or reflect become part of the pragmatic or social meaning of particular linguistic structures carrying out these tasks. This idea is rooted in the work of Vygotsky (1962, 1978), Leontyev (1981), and Wittgenstein (1958). Drawing on Marx, Leontyev used the notion of 'objectivization', that objects (and hence words) take their meanings from the variety of activities in which they participate. Wittgenstein emphasized that language is a form of life, that speaking is part of an activity (language game), and that meanings of words consist of their uses in these activity contexts. The net effect is that children are acquiring linguistic and sociocultural knowledge hand-in-hand as they assume various communicative and social roles in language activities.

3.   Discourse theory and developmental theory

One of the more striking generalizations to emerge from this perspective is that theories of development imply theories of communication and hence theories of discourse. The converse is also the case: theories of communication/discourse have implications for cognitive developmental research. What is common to both cognitive development and communication/discourse is that both involve the acquisition of knowledge ('information'). In discourse, the acquisition of knowledge spans a relatively short period of time, and various paradigms consider the *microgenesis* of knowledge during this period. Developmental research not only considers microgenetic change in behavior and knowledge (e.g. over the course of an experimental task), it also considers the genesis of knowledge and skills over a longer period of time. The point I wish to make here is that conceptualizations of macrogenesis of knowledge have microgenetic counterparts.

3.1.   *Behaviorism and speech-act theory*

Consider, for example, behavioristic formulations of how meaning or knowledge emerges in development. This paradigm emphasizes that children's understanding of words and objects is shaped by reinforcing particular responses emitted under the control of particular stimuli (Skinner 1957). In this paradigm, the child is a passive recipient of knowledge, a mimic conditioned by controlling stimuli. This is how children come to associate forms with meanings.

This concept of development corresponds to theories of communication in which recipients of information (hearers) are relatively passive receivers and meaning is controlled by those who emit linguistic signals (speakers). This image of communication is expressed in the so-called conduit metaphor of communication (G. Lakoff & Johnson 1980). In this metaphor, communication is seen as 'sending' messages or information by a transmitter to a receiver. Many information-processing approaches adopt this perspective. Among discourse models, speech-act theory displays a number of parallels to the behavioral model of development (Searle 1969, 1979, 1983). In their views of activity and the acquisition of understanding, both approaches prioritize the knowledge structure of the performer of an action (speaker of a speech act) over the knowledge structure of the audience for that action (hearer/addressee). In both stimulus–response and speech-act approaches, the orientation toward communication is decidedly from the perspective of the sender rather than from the receiver or from a social-interactional perspective (Duranti 1984b; Rosaldo 1982). Searle, for example, tends to examine perlocutionary dimensions of speech acts in terms of perlocutionary *effects*, and goes on to discuss these effects in terms of whether or not they are intended by the speaker (1983). Communication as well is visualized from the point of view of the speaker: 'Communicating is a matter of producing certain effects on one's hearers' (1983:165). While speech-act theory incorporates the hearer's knowledge structure or disposition in terms of the notion of perlocutionary act, this dimension of meaning is subordinate to speaker's knowledge/disposition (the illocutionary act) in establishing meaning. In speech-act theory, it is the illocutionary act which constitutes the core of meaning and the goal of communication. Understanding here is a matter of hearers recognizing the intended acts of speakers. This idea is similar to the behavioristic idea of meaning being a set of responses to controlling stimuli. A consequence of this approach to meaning and its acquisition is that, in both theories, the definition of the activity in play is primarily in terms of a knowing party whose job it is to transmit his or her definition of the activity to an unknowing party. This approach contrasts with approaches that allow situations to be defined by hearers or allow hearers to play an active role in the co-construction of situational definitions (Duranti & Brenneis 1986).

3.2.   *Innatism and deconstructionist theory*

Various developmental models have been proposed criticizing behavioristic assumptions about the acquisition of knowledge. The best-known of these is the innatist theory proposed by Chomsky in various forms (1965, 1971, 1975, 1986). Whereas behavioristic models prioritize the stimulus (the set of existing conditions and meanings), innatist theory prioritizes the knowledge structure of the acquirer. In this paradigm the acquirer of knowledge is actively creating his or her own knowledge structures in the course of engaging in communicative activities. The acquirer draws on innate resources (Universal Grammar) and formulates hypotheses about the linguistic forms used in the course of these activities, and in so doing constructs a grammar. Like the behaviorist approach, the innatist approach is interactional only in a limited sense. Once grammatical principles are acquired, they are not affected by communicative interactions with other native speakers. The model presupposes that all native speakers share the same grammatical rules; hence, negotiation of rule construction is a moot point.

In many but certainly not all respects, innatist approaches to the acquisition of knowledge are similar to deconstructionist approaches to the meaning of texts. As put forward by Derrida (1977), text meaning lies primarily in the hands of the listener/reader. Thus, like innatist models, deconstructionist theory prioritizes the acquirer. The acquirer/audience is an active constructor of knowledge/meaning and will draw on her or his own resources in the meaning-making process. The two theories differ in that Chomsky's locates these resources in biology, whereas Derrida locates them in experience. Another similarity is that both approaches do not see meaning making as a process of negotiation between producers of texts and acquirers. The interaction is between the text/corpus and the interpreter/ acquirer. That there may be differences between producers' and acquirers' mental representations of texts is irrelevant to both innatist and deconstructionist paradigms.

3.3.   *Sociohistorical theory and dialogic models*

More explicit comparisons have been made between the sociohistorical approach to development and certain models of discourse and communication. For example, both Holquist (1983) and Wertsch (1985a, b) have drawn parallels between Vygotsky's ideas and those of Mikhail Bakhtin. Further, Duranti (in press) has compared Vygotskian notions of development with interpretive and conversation-analysis approaches. As noted earlier, sociohistorical theory emphasizes that development of higher mental functions (e.g. those associated with language, computational reasoning, memory) is achieved through socially mediated activities. These higher mental functions are not learned responses to activity stimuli, but rather are discovered by the child through socially mediated experiences. In the sociohistorical framework, activities, especially ways in which language is used, create contexts for the child to create new kinds of thinking. Particularly important in this approach is the idea that individual development is both a social and an individual process. One facet of this idea is that mental activity can be carried out jointly or socially, as when children and adults jointly solve a problem. Individual skills develop in part as a consequence of such mental partnership (see Rogoff 1984; Wertsch 1985a, b); in this sense, ways of thinking are both social and individual. From a developmental point of view, society permeates the individual. While physiologically individuals may be distinguished from society, mentally they cannot be.

The notion that higher intellectual functions are both social and individual and have a social history parallels Bakhtin's notion of discourse and meaning as primordially social (Bakhtin 1981). No discourse is an individual product in Bakhtin's framework. Words have histories, and propositions address previous and anticipated audiences. Speakers use the 'voices' of others explicitly, as in reported speech, or implicitly. Speakers and writers use other voices strategically to make their points; in Bakhtin's terms, speakers/writers ventriloquate through others' voices what they wish to communicate. Accounts of whose message and whose intention are being communicated become highly textured, incorporating not only the speaker/writer but a range of social identities and relations.

The idea that acquisition of knowledge is socially mediated and negotiated is compatible as well with the broad outlines of hermeneutic and conversation-analysis approaches to discourse (see Duranti 1984a, in press). Like the sociohistorical notion that development emerges from social interaction, *hermeneutic philosophy* (Bleicher 1980, 1982; Gadamer 1976) stresses that meaning is acquired through complex interactions between speaker/writer and interpreter, including conditions of production and interpretation. Thus, like sociohistorical theory, hermeneutic theory considers understanding to be social and individual at the same time.

Similarly conversation-analysis research demonstrates in rich detail ways in which talk and meaning making are co-constructed or joint activities. For example, Schegloff, Jefferson & Sacks's research on repair (1977) indicates how clarification and remembering are interactionally achieved.

Goodwin's studies (1981, 1986) of multiparty interactions indicate the role of others' eye gaze or other signs of involvement in structuring an individual's speech act (e.g. reminder) or activity (e.g. telling a story). In these studies, the construction of the talk activity and hence the construction of meaning is socially accomplished and is negotiated within and across turns. This idea parallels the sociohistorical-based notion that worlds of meaning (within the individual) are created through social activity.

In both sociohistorical and dialogic approaches, the acquirer of knowledge is active; and, further, production and meaning of a text or activity lie neither in the hands of a speaker/knowledgeable participant or a hearer/acquirer alone, but rather are a complex engagement of both participants. This is not to suggest that all texts or activities involve balanced or equal social and psychological participation among those engaged. Where one participant enjoys more power or more knowledge than the others, the asymmetry may affect how meaning is constructed. For example, in traditional Samoan interactions, meaning is influenced heavily by higher-ranking persons, whether they be speakers or hearers (see Chapter 7). In the case of titled persons communicating with untitled persons, meaning tends to be controlled by the titled party. In the case of caregivers communicating with young children, meaning tends not to be negotiated but rather lies primarily in interpretive frames imposed by the caregiver.

4.   Summary

The perspective promoted in this chapter emphasizes that children develop in a linguistically and socioculturally structured environment and that these two domains interface as the child acquires linguistic and sociocultural competence. Such a perspective distinguishes between these domains and makes no attempt to reduce one form of competence to the other. Each domain, rather, relies on the other as an intellectual resource; it is in this sense that we say that the two domains interface with each other. Linguistic knowledge draws on sociocultural knowledge in several ways. For example, knowledge of discourse, i.e. principles relating linguistic structures to contexts, draws on sociocultural knowledge for definitions of context. Examples of relations between structures and context (metapragmatic, paradigmatic, syntagmatic, preference) are provided in section B above. In the sociocultural approach, discourse knowledge involves not only knowing how language represents or indexes contexts but how language structures are also tools for creating contexts.

In addition to the notion of interface, the notion of social activity is of central importance to the sociocultural perspective. Social activities involving language are structured by linguistic and sociocultural knowledge; at the same time it is through participation in these structured activities that children and other novices acquire knowledge in these two domains. It is through participating in conversational interactions that young children acquire tacit knowledge of how to index and create contexts.

In this framework, the acquirer is mentally active in furthering his or her intellectual competence. This approach to language acquisition advocates Vygotsky's notion that activity settings 'arrange' for development to take place (Cole & Cole in press; Vygotsky 1962, 1978; Wertsch 1985a, b). Part of the activity setting is the presence and role of knowledgeable (vis-à-vis a task) participants. In this sense, children's linguistic and sociocultural development is socially facilitated. It should be kept in mind, however, that societies differ in the ways activities are organized, both in terms of the tasks undertaken and in terms of the roles expected of more- and less-competent participants. As noted in Ochs (1982a), Ochs & Schieffelin (1984), and Schieffelin & Ochs (1986a, b), in some societies caregivers are expected to be highly accommodating to children's relative incompetence, whereas in other societies caregivers are much less accommodating. In some societies we find a wide variety of facilitating behaviors in play (e.g. repetition, structural simplification, labeling, pre-announcements and other attention-getting devices), whereas other societies rely on a limited set of such behaviors (e.g. repetition of performance). Societies also differ in the nature and scope of activities in which facilitation is expected (e.g. to accomplish goals initiated by a child, to accomplish goals initiated by an older member, to accomplish work-related tasks, to engage in play-related activities.)

Finally, the sociocultural approach to language acquisition favors dialogic approaches to production and comprehension of texts. In dialogic approaches, form and meaning of texts are partly engendered by structural expectations (have a social history) but as well are interactionally negotiated. Further, just as acquisition is both a social and an individual accomplishment, so are the processes of meaning making and text production.

III.   SOCIOCULTURAL PROCESSES IN LANGUAGE ACQUISITION

My reader might wonder why I belabor the point that children and caregivers are members of a community, with speech behaviors systematically organized and interpreted through partially shared beliefs and values and epistemologies. After all, social scientists have heard of Sapir and Whorf, though they may not concur with their views. And, as noted earlier, there are spokespersons in the field of psychology itself (Cole 1985; LCHC 1983; Scribner & Cole 1981; Vygotsky 1978; Wertsch 1985a) for the relation between language acquisition and thought and culture.

Despite these figures and their messages, there is a profound ignoring and ignorance of social and cultural systems among those carrying out research in language acquisition. As discussed in Ochs (1982a), Ochs & Schieffelin (1984), Schieffelin (1979), Schieffelin & Ochs (1986a, b), the background of society and culture has led many psychologists to assume that the patterns of speaking of middle-class children and their caregivers are ubiquitous and are guided by biologically patterned social and cognitive strategies. While all researchers will readily admit that exotic peoples have a culture, very few see themselves as having a culture and even fewer see their middle-class research subjects as having a culture (but see Lock 1981; Shotter 1978). As noted in Ochs & Schieffelin (1984), middle-class language acquirers and caregivers have an *invisible culture* (see Philips 1983). Their culture is not usually perceived because the researcher usually speaks the same language and participates in the same cultural system as the children and caregivers and/or because the researcher does not have a heightened awareness of his or her own orientations and behaviors, and does not look for these underpinnings in interpreting the behavior of others. Indeed, there is no pressing need to foreground cultural belief and values and social norms in analysis, given that most of the time researcher, subject, and academic audience share this background and unconsciously supply it in making sense out of strips of talk.

While researchers can see quite a lot by removing considerations of society and culture from their analyses of language acquisition, there is much that we do not see.

A.   Simplification

We do not see, for example, that the speech of caregivers to and in the presence of young children is organized by cultural expectations regarding the status and role of children and caregivers and regarding relative incompetence (see Ochs & Schieffelin 1984). In certain societies more than others, caregivers are expected to make rather dramatic accommodation to young children's cognitive immaturity (Sachs 1977; Snow & Ferguson 1977). One manifestation of this expectation is in caregiver speech. In societies where this expectation prevails, such as American white middle-class society, caregivers simplify their speech in addressing small children. In societies where this expectation does not prevail, such as traditional Western Samoan society and Kaluli (Papua New Guinea) society, caregivers do not simplify their speech to the extent characteristic of the American middle class. Simplified caregiver speech is one kind of caregiver speech that exists in the world's societies. It is a social register. It is not universal and not a necessary environmental condition for language acquisition to take place. Discussion of these claims is found in Chapter 7 of this volume.

Here we can see how an understanding of cultural orientations can affect theories of language acquisition specifically and more generally theories of social and intellectual development. Certainly for studies of language acquisition, our understanding of what constitutes 'input' needs some reassessment, for in many societies input is not the set of accommodations described for simplified registers.

B.   Egocentrism

The impression one gets in comparing transcripts of caregivers and children in American middle-class society and Western Samoan society is that American caregivers indulge the egocentric tendencies of children, whereas traditional Samoan caregivers resist these egocentric tendencies. American white middle-class caregivers compensate for the inability of infants and small children to meet the informational and social needs of others by carrying out a lot of this work for them. When children express themselves, caregivers will often fill in missing information or paraphrase (expand) what the caregiver interprets to be the child's intended message. In getting the caregiver's message across to the child, the caregiver will often adapt the form of the message to secure the child's attention, and so on. These caregivers may, indeed, allow the egocentric tendencies of children to flourish for quite an extended period of time through their heightened sociocentric demeanor (taking point of view of other; in this case, the child) toward infants and young children.

Samoan caregivers have another way. As will be discussed in Chapter 7, the traditional Samoan way is to sensitize infants and young children early in life to the language and actions of others around them. Infants are fed and held outward, facing toward others in the setting. They are directed to notice movements, remember names, and repeat phrases of caregivers. When small children display egocentric speech – speech that displays an inability to meet the informational/social needs of another – caregivers characteristically do not try to formulate what the child might be trying to communicate. The child is, rather, given the greater responsibility in producing a communicatively competent utterance (see the following section and the discussion in Chapter 7). These responses of caregivers and others toward egocentric speech by the child are linked to different cultural concepts and values, but of particular relevance here is that attitude that egocentric speech is appropriate only for high-status persons in certain contexts, such as orators delivering a formal speech. Children are instead socialized at a very early age into a sociocentric demeanor – to notice and take the perspective of others. This demeanor is tied to two basic forms of competence expected of young children by around the age of four or five:

the show of *respect* to higher-ranking persons and the *care of younger siblings*. By this age, Samoan children are capable of carrying out several activities at the same time – always with an eye or an ear ready to respond to a request by an elder or to notice the movements of a younger sibling.

This discussion should not be taken to mean that egocentrism is not universal or that egocentrism is not an interesting analytic concept in the study of Samoan children's behavior. On the contrary, egocentrism is a tendency in young Samoan children's actions and speech just as it has been observed of French, Italian, Swiss, British, American, etc. children. The difference is in cultural orientations toward egocentric behavior of children, as evidenced in the social behavior of others with whom the child interacts. There are cross-cultural differences in attitudes toward children's egocentric speech and actions and in responses to such behavior at different developmental points. Societies vary in the extent to which they indulge or accommodate the egocentric behavior of young children. They also vary in expectations concerning the age at which children should display sociocentric skills and the social contexts in which they should display them (e.g. caregiving, reporting news or delivering messages to higher-ranking persons, talk in the presence of guests or strangers). These expectations are linked in complex ways to social organization, concepts of person, and competence.

Before turning to another topic, I want to note here that societies differ in the extent to which they engage infants and young children as active participants in communicative exchanges that in themselves require sociocentric skills. One way of interpreting the numerous observations of middle-class mothers engaging their infants in greetings and other forms of conversation is to say that these mothers place their children in an activity (conversation) in which the children cannot competently participate (in the adult sense of competence). A child who is only twenty-four hours old (Stern 1977) can hardly be said to have the competence to greet. In other words, it looks as if middle-class mothers set up an activity (like greeting) for themselves and their children where only one participant (the mother) is competent. If the mother has the goal of carrying out the activity, then this goal can be carried out only by the mother taking on all or most of the infant's communicative roles (varying with maturity of child). These others will interpret their own messages for the infant and provide responses (Trevarthen 1979) on behalf of the infant as well, and in this manner engage in 'proto-conversations' (Bates, Camaioni & Volterra 1979). Placing very small children in communicative activities is not restricted to Western middle-class societies. Schieffelin has reported extensively (1979, in press) how Kaluli mothers in Papua New Guinea hold up tiny infants toward others and speak in a high voice for the infant, engaging some third party in conversation. (But note that Kaluli mothers do not use a simplified register or baby talk in speaking for their infants, and do not verbally paraphrase infants' actions or otherwise guess at infants' intentions.)

The traditional Samoan pattern is different from that just described. As will be described in Chapter 7, Samoan caregivers tend not to give infants an active role in communicative activities. Particularly in the first months of life, these infants are not usually treated as conversational participants in either the middle-class sense or the Kaluli sense. They are showered with affection, cuddled, and sung to, but are not usually placed in conversational exchanges as active speaker–hearers. The Samoan tendency is, rather, to hold off engaging in conversational exchanges with very young children until the children mature a bit more. In some sense, Samoan caregivers do not create situations that demand a series of accommodating, sociocentric behaviors on their part.

To summarize, many middle-class children engage in communicative exchanges practically from birth on, but their caregivers (mothers primarily) take over most of the work involved in sustaining this activity. Samoan children usually participate actively in such exchanges somewhat later in their development, but when they do, they are expected to carry out their own communicative work to a greater extent than middle-class American children of the same age.

C.   Folk epistemology

Every society has at least one theory of knowledge. These theories specify among other functions the *limits of knowledge* (what can be known) and the *path to knowledge* (procedures for arriving at knowledge). An interest in epistemologies is shared by scholars in all fields. It is, of course, a crucial component of the study of children's intellectual development; the work of Piaget has pursued this concern by examining children's concepts of reality and procedures for acquiring knowledge over developmental time. For those interested in relations between thought and language development of young children, this concern is also of considerable importance. In what ways are language skills (including formal languages like mathematics) related to the scope of children's knowledge and the intellectual operations they engage in to arrive at knowledge?

One of the major motivations for looking at young children's knowledge is the search for capacities and processes that are common to all humans, which in turn might lend credence to some particular philosophical position. Fairly recently certain psychologists have indicated that cognitive skills are not uniform across societies or within societies (Greenfield & Bruner 1966; Scribner & Cole 1981). A perspective advocated by a number of cognitive scientists (Cole 1985; Greenfield 1972; LCHC 1983) is that cognitive skills emerge through participation in particular types of social situations and that (1) the typical testing situations (including objects used in testing tasks) utilized by psychologists may not be familiar to members of a particular society and (2) other situations integral to the society may reveal the cognitive skills not displayed in testing tasks. In this approach, cultures may differ in the situations in which cognitive skills are displayed, the extent to which members participate in these situations (how many, how often, etc.), and the values or meanings associated with these situations.

In the research on cross-cultural cognition, the situations under study are usually of a special sort. Situations are defined as highly circumscribed activities. Much in the tradition of psychological testing, the situations examined in naturalistic surroundings are associated with well-articulated goals, often manifest in a material product, e.g. weaving cloth (Childs & Greenfield 1980), making a garment (Lave 1977).

A semiotic perspective would indicate that in the stream of behavior observed there are many situations/activities and associated goals. One activity that runs parallel to and participates in innumerable other activities, from the most formal and defined to the least, is that of *holding a conversation*. If we want to observe, for purposes of cross-cultural comparison, an activity that pervades experience and is common across cultures, then conversation is an appropriate locus of study.

Like many activities, conversation is a complex social endeavor, with embedded and superimposed activities requiring a variety of intellectual skills. For purposes of this discussion, I consider conversation as an activity that poses a number of problems for participants – e.g. turn-taking problems (Sacks, Schegloff & Jefferson 1974), face-saving problems (P. Brown & Levinson 1978; Goffman 1963, 1967, 1981), information-processing problems (H. Clark & Haviland 1977; H. Clark & Lucy 1975; Grice 1975) – and focus on one very common problem or task for what it can reveal about folk epistemology. The following discussion is an abbreviated version of the discussion in Chapter 7 of this volume.

Very often in conversation a participant produces an utterance that is not comprehensible to another participant. That is, very often a co-conversationalist will take some utterance to be troublesome, or, to use the terminology of conversation analysis, to be a trouble source (Schegloff, Jefferson & Sacks 1977). Of the many cases to which this applies, I am interested in those in which the speaker has not articulated clearly or has incompletely expressed some proposition as well as those in which the hearer has not been attentive to the speech act. That is, a potential recipient of an utterance has not been able to make sense out of that utterance because it was garbled, because it was telegraphic, or because it was not heard. This is emblematic of more subtle occurrences of communicative distress of the sort that are of interest in hermeneutic philosophy (the science of interpretation and understanding as outlined in Bleicher 1980, 1982; Gadamer 1976; Ricoeur 1971, 1981; and others).

These occurrences establish a series of related problems for speaker and/ or recipient of an utterance if communication is a goal. The superordinate problem is to make intelligible to the recipient the proposition(s) and the social act(s) intended by the speaker of the unintelligible utterance. Several alternatives are potentially available to conversational participants faced with this problem. Of particular interest here are the alternatives observed for recipients. Recipients may assume several different roles with respect to the process of 'making sense' out of an utterance. For example, recipients may request that the speaker alone make the utterance intelligible, or recipients may orally conjecture what the utterance/proposition might be, leaving the original speaker to validate or reject the hypothesis. I propose here that members of different social groups vary in their preferences for responding to unintelligibility and that these preferences reflect folk expectations concerning certain and uncertain knowledge and the pursuit of certain knowledge.

I noted in the previous section that Samoan caregivers expect small children to assume most of the burden of making an unintelligible utterance intelligible, and indicated that this practice is tied to expectations concerning social rank, i.e. that a sociocentric demeanor is expected of lower- to higher-ranking persons. However, it is also the case that another preference, or rather dispreference, is manifest in this response; namely, a dispreference for guessing what another person could be thinking. We find this dispreference in social interactions involving different social relations (e.g. among peers, low to high rank, high to low rank), but the dispreference is strongest in cases where the recipient of the unintelligible utterance is of higher rank and weakest where the recipient is of lower rank (see Chapter 7).

What we find in looking at transcripts of Samoan discourse is that rather than making a stab at what an unclear utterance might be, recipients tend to request a speaker to reproduce all or part of an utterance that is unclear. This is carried out orally through either a wh question ('What?' 'He went where?' etc.) or by stating that the utterance is not clear or understood.

This dispreference contrasts with what has been observed of other societies, such as white middle-class American (Schegloff, Jefferson & Sacks 1977), where recipients may respond to unintelligible utterances by guessing what that utterance might be, particularly where the speaker seems unable to provide a clearer rendition. This behavior, widespread in certain societies, reflects folk expectations that one can know what another is thinking.

The different responses to the problem of unintelligibility, then, display different epistemological principles. Principles associated with different philosophical positions, such as rationalist, positivist, realist, hermeneutic, manifest themselves differentially across cultures in these particular discourse situations. The variable we have been considering here is the extent to which individuals orally conjecture about (not simply discuss or infer) psychological states of others.

Regardless of the various philosophical positions current in Western philosophy, it is apparent that among those middle-class persons recorded and observed, there is a consistent philosophical orientation manifest in their discourse: psychological states of others are suitable objects of conjecture. We propose, test, and dispute theories concerning others' intentions, motivations, attitudes, and the like. This philosophical principle runs rampant in our everyday speech. Among other routes, it is transmitted to small children through repeated responses to unintelligible and partially intelligible utterances.

In the same way, Samoan discourse evidences an orientation toward psychological states, namely that psychological states are suitable objects of conjecture only under certain conditions. Generally, compared with the behavior of middle-class speakers observed, there is in Western Samoan communities a far greater reluctance to speculate about others' psychological states, but the reluctance varies according to rank of interactants. This reluctance is manifest not only in clarification sequences but in a range of other discourse activities, particularly those associated with judicial concerns. The orientation of discourse is toward the immediate cause of an action (agent) and its consequences rather than toward the motivations or intentions of those involved. Young Samoan children are not involved in court procedures, but they are, like children the world over, involved in communicative breakdowns that lead to culturally patterned conversational sequences. As children participate in such sequences, they acquire competence in the construction of conversational discourse, and in this process they acquire expectations concerning the limits of knowledge, the acquisition of knowledge, and the social organization of knowledge (limits and procedures as related to social status, setting, activity, etc.). In Bateson's (1972) terms, children are not only learning language; they are learning to learn. In Sapir's (1927) and Whorf's (1941) terms, children are acquiring through language a way of viewing the world.

D.   Acquisition order

Most researchers in the field of language acquisition are interested in processes that facilitate or inhibit the acquisition of linguistic structures. Children's performance, i.e. production and comprehension of language, is examined for patterns and strategies, which are then related to a variety of considerations, for example, to surface properties of grammatical systems and perceptual ease (Slobin 1973, 1982) or to conceptual distinctions encoded by lexical terms (E. Clark 1974; Nelson 1981). These generalizations provide insights into the nature of children's linguistic competence and some predictive power concerning children's linguistic performance over developmental time.

My own work (Ochs 1982a, 1986a, b), and the work of others (see, among others, Clancy 1986a, b; Eisenberg 1982; Heath 1983; Platt 1980, 1986; Schieffelin 1979, in press; Scollon & Scollon 1981; S. Scollon 1982), indicates that, among the various constraints affecting children's linguistic competence, social and cultural systems play an important role. Children's performance is organized not only by biological processes but by sociocultural processes as well. After all, children's performance is nested in social life and as such is responsive to social norms, expectations, values, and beliefs. To account for how language is acquired and to understand what is acquired, we need to look at children both as organisms and as social beings. What they do and don't do is rooted not only in physiology and intellectual maturity but in social expectations as well.

The linguistic structures most interesting for sociocultural analysis (i.e. most affected) are those that are *variable* (Labov 1966, 1972). In Samoan, these structures draw from all levels of language, including phonology (phonological registers), morpho-syntax (case marking, word order, deletion, negation), the lexicon (deictic verbs, pronouns, respect vocabulary), and discourse. The use of these structures is systematically sensitive to social organization and belief systems. Of particular interest to the Samoan study is the way in which acquisition of linguistic structures is sensitive to the *hierarchical organization* of Samoan society, to the *private–public distinction* in setting, and to the *affective demeanor* valued by members of this society.

An example of the interaction between the hierarchical organization of Samoan society and order of acquisition of linguistic structures comes from the research of Platt (1986) on acquisition of Samoan deictic verbs. In her study, Platt found the semantically less complex verb *sau* 'come' was produced later and less frequently than the more complex verb *'aumai* 'bring/give', by Samoan children aged two to four. While this pattern is the reverse of what a semantic account might predict and the reverse of the acquisition order for English-speaking children (E. Clark 1978), it is compatible with expectations concerning appropriate behavior between persons of different social rank, in this case between children and their caregivers. In particular, the expectation is that higher-ranking persons will direct lower-ranking persons to 'come' but that lower-ranking persons will not impose this directive on their higher-ranking addressees. (This expectation does not apply to the use of the verb *'aumai* 'bring/give' in imperative constructions.) Given that most of the persons surrounding young language-acquiring children are older, there are few opportunities to use the verb 'come' in directive constructions; hence the low frequency in the data collected and analyzed.

Platt's analysis indicates that the children are sensitive to the sociolinguistic constraints on the use of 'come' in imperatives. When children began to use the verb in directives, they addressed peers and lower-ranking persons predominantly. The cases in which the children used the verb towards higher-ranking persons are largely those in which a copresent caregiver has told the child to call someone on behalf of the caregiver. In the latter cases, the child is sender or addresser but not the source of the message. These contextual regularities in the use of the verb 'come' indicate that Samoan children have acquired early in their language development an understanding of both the referential and social meanings of this deictic form.

This example illustrates that social norms influence both production and comprehension of linguistic forms. On the production side, a social norm restricts the appropriate contexts for using the form. This suggests that children's production is guided not only by conceptual simplicity and perceptual ease but by social appropriateness as well. On the comprehension side, the appropriate contexts of use are acquired as components of meaning of the verb.

An example of the effects of public versus private settings on acquisition order comes from the study of the acquisition of Samoan ergative case marking discussed in Ochs (1982b) and in Chapter 5 of this volume. Young children do not use the case marker systematically until relatively late in their development, and this can be partially accounted for in terms of the register associated with the setting to which they are most exposed. As in all societies, Samoan speech varies systematically as setting moves from private to public, from intimate to socially distant. Ergative case marking is affected in that it tends to increase frequency of use as settings become more public and relationships more distant. Frequent use of the case marker is not characteristic of the speech register used in household settings. Samoan children's late acquisition of ergative case marking reflects the fact that they have acquired the linguistic features of one particular register. (We cannot say, however, on the basis of this evidence that the children at this developmental stage have tacit knowledge of the sociocultural import of these forms.)

The two examples discussed here (the verb *sau* 'to come' and the ergative case marker) indicate that nonproduction of a form does not always reflect incompetence. In both cases, children do not use the forms because they are conforming to a sociolinguistic norm. As members of Samoan society, they are acting with competence (even if, as in the example of ergative case marking, they may be doing so without an understanding of the sociolinguistic norms surrounding the use).

An example of the interactions between affect and order of acquisition comes from a study of pronoun acquisition reported in Ochs (1986b) and discussed in Chapter 9 of this volume. Like caregivers the world over, Samoan caregivers are concerned that their charges will be able to display and recognize the verbal conventions that signal feelings or dispositions. For certain tasks to be accomplished, for certain desires to be satisfied, a child must learn appropriate and effective ways to express affect. Indeed, certain tasks or speech acts have, as felicity conditions on their perform- ance, particular affects and conventional affective displays. One such speech act is *begging*. In Samoan, to count as an act of begging (*aisi*), the performance must evidence elicitation of sympathy for the speaker. Other- wise the act counts as a request or demand.

Begging is an important means for small Samoan children to obtain goods and services. They may also request or demand, but often it is necessary to shift to begging to move the addressee to satisfy the directive (see also Schieffelin 1986b for a discussion of this function among Kaluli (Papua New Guinea) children). This rhetorical effect is a strong motivation for acquiring the structures that express sympathy for self.

Among the features for expressing this affect is a set of first person pronouns that mean roughly 'poor me', 'poor my', etc., depending on grammatical role in the utterance. Samoan has in addition a complemen- tary set of first person pronouns that do not express this affect. The latter pronouns are not used in begging. I should mention here that Samoan allows deletion and ellipsis of the first person pronoun as well.

Samoan children acquire the sympathy-marked first person pronoun forms before they acquire the more neutral first person forms. That is, they either do not express the first person pronoun (deletion/ellipsis) or they express the affect-marked pronoun. The preference for the affect-marked form appears to be rooted in its rhetorical superiority. In addition to eliciting sympathy, children using this form may invoke their dependency on the addressee and the moral bonds that define their relationship with that addressee. These affects may lead to a preferred response where other dispositions fail.

In language-acquisition research, researchers have isolated a set of variables which, other things being equal, will account for the observed acquisition orders. Given two different forms, we can make strong predic- tions concerning which will be acquired earlier based on the differences in conceptual or perceptual properties of these forms. I suggest here that other things are not equal, that forms may differ in simplicity and in salience in terms of the social and cultural conditions surrounding their use.

For example, the ergative case marker in Samoan is not salient for young children because it is not frequent in the particular register to which they are exposed most often. Here we see that the social organization of speech varieties backgrounds certain grammatical structures (e.g. ergative case marking) and foregrounds others (e.g. morphological markers of affect). In the example concerning acquisition of the first person affect pronoun, we can see that salience is not always a matter of frequency in the environment. The use of appeal pronouns (elicitation of sympathy for speaker) is not a frequent strategy employed by a Samoan child's caregivers; they may apply rank as a basis for obtaining a desired response. Instead, a form (such as the affect pronoun) may be relatively salient because children are socialized to assume certain demeanors and to use forms compatible with those demeanors.

Children are acquiring language in socially and culturally organized environments. They are selectively exposed to language; they discover over developmental time different varieties, their distinguishing features and contexts, and their significance for members of the social group. In addition to the questions researchers already ask to determine the basis for simplicity and salience, we can pose questions leading to sociocultural variables, such as:

Is this form characteristic of settings to which young children are exposed?
If so, is this form associated with activities in which children participate?
If so, what role(s) (including what demeanor(s)) are children expected to carry out within these activities?
Which communicative roles is a child likely to assume relative to the use of this form in these activities – source? addresser? addressee? overhearer? etc.?

These variables interact with others, such as those based on literal meaning or perceptual dimensions, as influences on what children will say and what children will understand at particular moments in their development.

E.   The endpoint of acquisition

When researchers consider the endpoint of acquisition, they invoke the notion of competence. And when competence is brought into the discussion, the researcher has usually in mind either grammatical competence (Chomsky 1965) or communicative competence (Hymes 1972). Grammatical competence concerns the tacit knowledge underlying the grammatical structure of clauses and sentences. Communicative competence concerns the tacit knowledge underlying language use and encompasses a wider range of knowledge than that conveyed by grammatical competence. It covers knowledge of structures beyond the clause and sentence, including sequences, genres, and registers. Communicative competence involves tacit knowledge of norms relating structures to social situations. This knowledge provides, along with grammatical knowledge, the foundation for interpreting and expressing ideas and actions.

I believe that research in the area of communicative competence can provide a better understanding of the notion of grammatical competence. In particular, it can lead to more sophisticated methods for assessing grammaticality judgments and for ascertaining what is grammatically possible for a given language. The result is a more comprehensive account of the endpoint of the acquisition of language.

Trained in ethnographic and sociolinguistic methods, those carrying out research on communicative competence utilize three major sources in analysis: researcher's knowledge, language users' knowledge, and recordings of both elicited and naturally occurring language use. While sociocultural approaches to language have been most closely associated with the last method, all three methods are traditional in sociology and anthropology (Briggs 1986).

It is my understanding that it is not the sources of analysis themselves that distinguish the sociocultural perspective, but rather the methods of considering and relating these sources to each other. First of all, researchers within this perspective have a strong sense of social context, relative to, for example, formal linguists eliciting grammaticality judgments. One manifestation of this sensitivity is that formal interviews between researchers and language users are treated as one *type* of social situation, e.g. talking to outsiders. Data obtained through this source are treated as characteristic of one social context. The problem for the researcher here is to relate these data to data from other social contexts. In collecting recordings of the code in use, the researcher tries to obtain samples from other social situations in the community under study. Ideally the interview and the recorded data should together cover a representative span of situations relevant to members of a society.

Much of the discussion in anthropology and sociology concerns the extent to which members' knowledge should be admitted in defining situations of analysis. Ethnomethodological and phenomenological orientations within these disciplines as well as the strong tradition of cultural relativism in cultural anthropology advocate a strong input from members' judgments (the so-called emic orientation), but at the same time call for a dialogue with the researcher (who may have a distinct orientation) in establishing definitions of situations and evaluating meanings of verbal and nonverbal behavior. Geertz's (1973) call for 'thick descriptions' (see Ryle 1949, 1953) in anthropology, for example, advocates understanding events and structures at different levels and from several perspectives, including the theoretical constructs articulated by individuals within a social group as interpreted by the researcher, who holds his own constructs for making sense out of behaviors.

I think it is safe to say that most other approaches to language structure share neither this sensitivity to members' definitions and explanations nor the sensitivity to a social organization of settings that leads language users to different judgments and different language behavior. Other approaches, particularly formal linguistic approaches, are more oriented toward defining what 'is going on' strictly in terms of the theoretical paradigm of their training and restrict the interactions with language users to particular topics, particular genres, and particular settings. Researchers within these approaches feel comfortable with the idea that definitions and frames are controlled and explicitly value 'simplicity' in description and explanation.

These different methodological orientations have consequences for the notion of grammatical competence. Let us take for granted that grammatical competence concerns tacit knowledge associated with what is structurally possible in a language (Chomsky 1965). Those carrying out research in communicative competence generally believe that the investigation of grammatical knowledge of this sort should be pursued through ethnographic methods such as those discussed above. Language users' knowledge of what is possible in their language is gleaned through display of that knowledge in a range of situations, both elicited and naturalistic. Grammatical structures missed in formal interviews emerge in other social contexts, and the reverse is also true. Good research on communicative competence will turn up not only categorical grammatical structures but also grammatical structures that vary systematically with some property of the social context (Gumperz 1972; Gumperz & Wilson 1971; Hymes 1972; Labov 1966; Lavandera 1978; Romaine 1982; Sankoff 1980). From the point of view of research into communicative competence, the typical formal interview between linguist and native speaker reveals only a slice of that speaker's grammatical knowledge.

The endpoint of acquisition, as noted in the introduction to this discussion, is competence. And we can see here how differently the endpoint might be circumscribed, depending on the paradigms and methodologies adopted. In certain cases the structures associated with adult competence would be derived from data elicited in formal interview sessions. In other cases, the endpoint would comprise those structures derived from regularities in language behavior in and across several speech events.

Overwhelmingly it is the former that informs acquisition research. This in turn has made it difficult to compare what children know with what adult speaker–hearers know about their language. Usually children's competence is assessed on the basis of observations of language behavior outside formal interview settings which are then compared with adult competence within formal settings. What happens, then, when children are observed producing structures that are not considered part of the grammar by adult speakers in formal interviews? In certain cases we might want to say that children's grammar (hence children's tacit knowledge) differs from the adult model. Children in this case might be said to have different grammatical rules from those characteristic of adults. Very often, for example, there is a grammatical rule in the adult system which children do not apply. Looking at such cases from the adult point of view, we say that children appear to be making grammatical *errors*.

In other cases, however, such a comparison leads to false distinctions, and we find through a broader sociolinguistic analysis of the adult system that adults share with children systematic use of a structure (or systematic nonuse of a structure). My own research on morpho-syntactic structures in Samoan shows this possibility. Samoan children make use of a tense–aspect system of marking, for example, that has not been documented in formal informant sessions with adult speakers (see Chapter 3). This system incorporates locative pronouns and adverbs with certain other particles. Look ing at adult speech in formal and informal contexts outside the interview setting, we can see the same system in use. The tense–aspect system elicited in formal interviews is characteristic more of one phonological register of Samoan – 'good speech', in turn characteristic of written Samoan and Samoan used in the schools, in the mass media, and *in talk to foreigners*. The interview between linguist and native speaker can be framed (from the perspective of the speaker) as the latter type of speech event. If we took only the standard interview as the basis of adult grammatical knowledge, then we might think of the children's language behavior and knowledge as qualitatively distinct (with respect to the tense–aspect system). Instead we see the children as manifesting tacit knowledge of the grammar associated with one register of Samoan ('bad speech' register).

Other examples of child–adult comparisons are presented in this volume and include ergative case marking and word order. In both of these areas, children's strategies match those associated with a register in the adult Samoan repertoire, but one which is not captured through elicitation of grammatical patterns in formal interviews with speakers of the language.

Implicit in this discussion is the idea that intuitions about language are themselves context-sensitive. When an adult native speaker is asked to make grammaticality judgments in formal interview settings, these judgments have a sociolinguistic reality, i.e. they are judgments appropriate to the register of the interview as a speech event. The elicited paradigms of sentence types themselves are also sensitive to this context, and the researcher runs the risk of eliciting just one variant of the language and hence writing rules for only that variant.

An informal argument for this methodology has been that, despite this limitation, the variety represents the standard or high-prestige form of the language and that other varieties are 'imperfect' or less complex variations. Research in communicative competence indicates that this simply is not so for many speech communities. First of all, this idea is predicated on the assumption that communities have only one type of prestige variant, whereas many communities have a prestige variant, say, for Western-related activities (such as formal schooling, urban business, Western religions) and one or more prestige variants for traditional activities (such as formal meetings, rites of passage, and other ceremonies). As noted above, the formal informant session as characteristically constructed in linguistics captures only one of these registers.

Secondly, nonprestige variants are not always less complex than the variant captured in the informant session. As noted above, nonprestige tense–aspect structures in Samoan are comparable in complexity to prestige variants. Indeed, if the linguist uses English sentences as a basis for eliciting grammatical patterns, he may miss more complex alternatives in the target language for expressing information. For example, casual registers of Samoan are characterized by widespread use of nominalization. Thus, it is more common in these registers for a speaker to say, 'Sio's delivering of that speech was good' rather than 'Sio delivered that speech well.'

To summarize, grammatical competence is bound to context of situation, which in turn is socially and culturally organized. When a speaker judges a structure to be grammatical or not, he invokes some situation of use. My major concern here has been the scope of grammaticality, with the suggestion that what falls outside the scope of a speaker's grammar in one context may be part of that speaker's grammar in another context. When speakers reflect on what is possible in their language, they are reflecting on what is possible for them, here, now etc. To reveal the limits of grammar and speakers' grammatical competence, interview data must be put in their social context and a wider set of researcher–native speaker relationships must be initiated.

IV.   CONCLUDING REMARKS

I have pursued the point that acquisition of linguistic competence, i.e. tacit knowledge of grammar, discourse, and the lexicon, interfaces with acquisition of sociocultural competence, i.e. tacit knowledge of expectations, beliefs, goals, and values associated with social life, including definitions and structures of acts and events, conduct associated with statuses, roles, concepts of self, competence, learning, and understanding. Tacit knowledge of social organization and ideologies allows children to make sense out of words, clauses, and texts. This knowledge underlies as well their own competent production.

If this is an accurate description of what children must minimally acquire, then the job of specifying more precisely what children know about language and the mechanisms for acquiring this knowledge is an immense one. The burden of carrying out this research has rested primarily with psycholinguistics. However, the interest in structures beyond the clause and the interest in meaning beyond denotation (social meanings, implicatures, pragmatic presuppositions, etc.) have drawn other fields, particularly sociology and anthropology, into this research.

In the remaining chapters of this book, I indicate ways in which research on language development among Samoan children is informed by both cognitive/psychological and sociocultural perspectives. In cognitive paradigms, development is usually understood with reference to intra-individual psychological and biological processes. In the sociocultural approach proposed here and elsewhere (Ochs & Schieffelin 1984; Schieffelin & Ochs 1986a, b), development, including language development, is partly organized by social and cultural processes. Language is not acquired without culture.

The rest of the book is organized in the following manner. Chapter 2 discusses the methods used in collecting and analyzing the Samoan language-acquisition and socialization data. Included in this chapter is a description of the field site and the kinds of data recorded in the course of field research in Western Samoa in 1978–9 and 1981. Chapters 3 and 4 provide general information about the structure of the Samoan language and the social organization of Samoan village and domestic life. Chapters 5 and 6 focus on two major grammatical structures, ergative case marking and word order, as they characterize both adult and child speech across different social settings. Chapter 5 focuses on the impact of social expectations on acquisition strategies, and Chapter 6 discusses cognitive strategies that may account for grammatical preferences in spontaneous speech.

Chapters 7 through 11 are a series of essays concerning language socialization. These essays illustrate how language practices are structured by social expectations, or *habitus* ('dispositions') as Bourdieu (1977) would say, and how children acquire tacit knowledge of these mental orientations through engaging in such practices with caregivers, peers, and other members of their community. Chapter 7 focuses on a ubiquitous and universal conversational structure, namely the clarification sequence. It compares preferences for carrying out clarification in caregiver–child interactions in Samoan society with those in American white middle-class society. The chapter suggests that such conversational structures are powerful means of socializing children into concepts of self, knowledge, competence, and social order. Chapters 8 and 9 consider the expression of affect in Samoan speech and in Samoan social life. Chapter 8 focuses on the socialization of affect through caregiver control strategies. Chapter 9 examines the rich linguistic resources available in Samoan for expressing affect and documents the acquisition of affective constructions by young Samoan children.

Chapter 10 discusses socialization through literacy instruction in formal classroom settings in Samoan villages. It indicates ways in which both the topics of communication and the conversational organization of communication in these literacy activities differ from traditional practices and socialize Samoan children into Western values. Chapter 11 explores ways in which everyday talk encodes information on many levels – semantic, pragmatic, and sociocultural. It focuses on the capacity of situated speech to index information about context or the situation at hand and thereby to constitute a powerful medium through which socialization is achieved.

2. Methodology

I. SETTING

The research on which this study is based was carried out in the village of Falefaa on the island of Upolu, Western Samoa. Upolu is the second-largest and most populated of the four major islands that compose Western Samoa. It contains the capital, Apia, and is the major center for commercial and government affairs (see Figure 2.1). Over the past ten years, communication on the island has improved dramatically. Today there is a paved road that circles much of the island, linking villages to one another and to the capital. Bus service is available daily, along with pickup trucks and cars that taxi those waiting for a lift to the capital or the village. Newspapers printed several times a week are distributed in the capital and brought back to the village by returning travelers. In addition, news is transmitted hourly through radio broadcasting.

Falefaa lies eighteen miles east of the capital along the paved road (see Figure 2.2). It is a large village, with a total population about 1,200. Just over half the population are under the age of fifteen. Falefaa contains four internal political and residential divisions, the subvillages of Sagapolu, Saleapaga, Gaga'emalae, and Sanonu. The name Falefaa literally means 'four houses' (*fale* 'house(s)', *faa* 'four'), referring to these four political units. Each of the subvillages is associated with a chiefly title, whose holder is the highest-ranking representative of that subvillage in chiefly councils (*fono*). The four titles in turn are ranked with respect to one another. (The reader is referred to Chapter 4 for a more general description of the village social structure.)

Falefaa is historically and currently associated with three other villages (see Figure 2.2). One village, Falevao, is about two miles inland along a paved road. The other two villages, Sauano and Saletele, are somewhat farther away, along Fagaloa Bay, and can be reached by dirt road. During the rainy season, communication along this road is difficult. Representatives of the four subvillages sometimes meet along with representatives of Falevao, Sauano, and Saletele and make decisions in chiefly councils, but

40

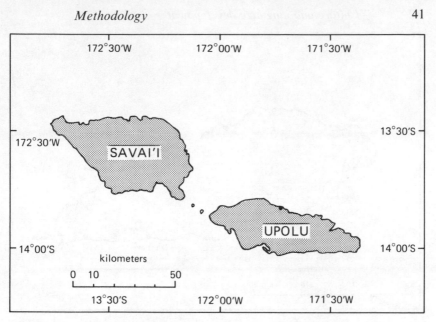

Figure 2.1.   *Western Samoa.*

typically these councils involve only the four subvillages (Duranti 1981a).

Falefaa is part of the ancient district of Atua. Historically Atua had its own paramount chief (*tui*). It is said that certain titled persons in Falefaa are descendants of one of the ancient paramount chiefs (Muagatuti'a), and other titled persons claim to be descendants of one of the three great noble families of Samoa, the Mataa'afa family. These associations are noted in various versions of the traditional ceremonial address or greeting (*fa'alupega*) delivered in the opening moments of chiefly councils and other formal events.

Falefaa is located on both sides of the main road ringing the island. The ocean is a few paces away from most households. The houses of Falefaa typically face the road and are fairly close to one another. Certainly there is a good deal of communication from one dwelling to another, and from dwellings to passersby along the main road. Farther inland lie the plantations owned by each family, where each day members of families (usually children and young untitled men and women) tend their gardens and gather taro, breadfruit, bananas, coconuts, and other foodstuffs for the family, for political or social gatherings, or for pastors and other religious leaders of a congregation to consume. Occasionally these food products will be sold in the main market in the city of Apia.

Two periods of fieldwork were carried out in Falefaa. The first focused on language acquisition and extended over thirteen months, beginning in July 1978. This research was sponsored by the National Science Foundation and

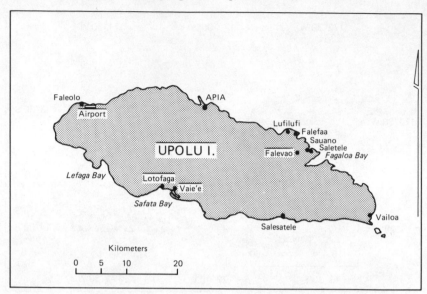

Figure 2.2. *Upolu Island.*

involved the labors of three researchers: Elinor Ochs (principal investigator), Alessandro Duranti, and Martha Platt. The second period of fieldwork was carried out in the spring of 1981 by Elinor Ochs and Alessandro Duranti. This research was sponsored by the Research School of Pacific Studies at the Australian National University and focused on the making of a Super 8 film about language use and children's activities in traditional Samoan communities.

In both periods of fieldwork, we resided in the village. In 1978, the congregation of the Congregational Christian Church agreed to let us live on church-owned land, and we built two houses next to the house of the pastor. This location was in the subvillage of Gaga'emalae, close to the main road and near the central grounds of Falefaa.

II.   RESEARCH PROJECTS AND PROCEDURES

A.   Research projects

The overall goal of this study was to document and interpret the course of language development and language socialization in traditional Samoan households. The goals of this project demanded a blend of research methods drawn from developmental psycholinguistics (e.g. longitudinal case study), sociolinguistics (e.g. sampling language use across social settings), and linguistic anthropology (e.g. observing and relating speech behavior to other social practices and cultural understandings underlying those practices). This project involved four major data-collection enterprises.

1.   The longitudinal study

The largest research project was a longitudinal study of the language development of six children. The purpose of this project was to document patterns of language use among young Samoan children and others with whom they interacted. The major grammatical features documented were ergative case marking, word order, deictic verbs and particles, and affect morphology. In addition, several conversational structures were examined. The major interest in this portion of the project was to isolate and account for grammatical and discourse preferences displayed by acquirers and competent speaker–members in this community. The children in this study tended to spend their days on the grounds of their family compounds and usually interacted with other children and adults within this setting. Interactions of children in village peer groups (*aukegi*) were not a focus of this study, as the children in this study were too young (under the age of four) to participate in these groups. This project was carried out primarily by E. Ochs and M. Platt.

1.1.   *Subjects*
The children of this study lived in two of the four subvillages of Falefaa. Two children were members of Catholic families, three of Protestant families, and one of a family of both Mormons and Protestants. The children's families differed according to social status of the child's father. Three of the fathers did not have titles, but of these one was a *faife'au* 'pastor', a very high-status figure in the village; of the three fathers who had titles, two had *tulafale* 'orator' titles, and one had an *ali'i* 'high chief' title. In this sense, the children and their families were representative of the social content of the community.

Three of the children in the study – Matu'u, Pesio, and Naomi – are female and three – Kalavini, Iakopo, and Niulala – are male. The children's ages at the onset of our observations ranged from nineteen months to thirty-five months. Table 2.1 summarizes the relevant information on age, gender, and family status for each child.

The number of children (adopted and nonadopted) dwelling in each of the households observed varied. Kalavini was the firstborn of two children. The second child was born four months after our recording of Kalavini

Table 2.1. *Age of children and family status*

Child	Age at onset (months)	Sex	Subvillage	Religion	Father's status
Kalavini	19	M	Gaga'emalae	Congregational	Pastor
Iakopo	25	M	Saleapaga	Catholic	Untitled
Matu'u	25	F	Saleapaga	Congregational	Orator
Pesio	27	F	Gaga'emalae	Catholic	Chief
Naomi	34	F	Saleapaga	Congregational	Orator
Niulala	35	M	Saleapaga	Congregational/ Mormon	Untitled

began. Iakopo was the sixth of seven children. The seventh child was born several months after the beginning of the study. Matu'u was the eighth of ten children, the tenth appearing four months into the study. Pesio was the fourth of five children; Naomi, the youngest of three. Niulala, at the onset of the study, had one older and two younger siblings. The name, sex, and age at onset of recording for each child in each of the six households is indicated in Table 2.2.

The focus of our recordings and observations was a single child in each family; the siblings were present at different times. Further, as will be discussed in subsequent chapters, each of these six families were members of extended family groups, and the children from the other member households were often present during the recordings. Our total corpus of children's speech is, then, quite extensive in terms of number and ages of children.

1.2.   *Recording schedule*
Each of the six children in this study was observed and recorded at regular intervals over a period of several months. Three of the children (Matu'u, Naomi, Niulala) were recorded over a period of nine months, two (Iakopo, Pesio) over a period of eight months, and one (Kalavini, the youngest) over a period of seven months. Kalavini was recorded every four weeks. The other five children were observed and recorded every five weeks.

Table 2.2. *Family composition*

Child	Sex	Age at onset
Kalavini's family		
Kalavini	M	1 yr 7 mo
Rossana	F	Born after study began
Iakopo's family		
Iulia	F	14 yr
Elena	F	13 yr
Lafaele	M	11 yr
Leone	M	8 yr
Iuliana	F	4 yr 3 mo
Iakopo	M	2 yr 1 mo
Malu	F	Born after study began
Matu'u's family		
Mauga	F	16 yr
Iti	M	11 yr 9 mo
Siota	M	9 yr 11 mo
Teuila	F	7 yr 2 mo
Se'emu	M	6 yr 10 mo
Feagaiga	M	5 yr 1 mo
Veni	M	4 yr
Matu'u	F	2 yr 1 mo
Losi	M	1 yr 1 mo
Mafutaga	M	Born after study began
Pesio's family		
Paula	F	13 yr 2 mo
Mika	M	11 yr 1 mo
Olagi	F	5 yr 4 mo
Pesio	F	2 yr 3 mo
Lei	M	4 mo
Naomi's family		
Maeu	M	11 yr
Aimalala	M	6 yr
Naomi	F	2 yr 10 mo
Niulala's family		
Moana	F	4 yr 2 mo
Niulala	M	2 yr 11 mo
Fineaso	M	1 yr 7 mo
Toalua (Sose)	F	4 mo

1.3.   *Recording techniques*
1.3.1.   *Taping*   For every child, both audio- and videorecordings were made. For the oldest five children in the study, three to four hours of audio- and a half-hour of videorecording were made at each five-week interval. The youngest child, in the late single-word stage, was audiotaped and videotaped for thirty minutes at each four-week session.

1.3.2.   *Observational notes*   The recordings were supplemented by handwritten notes. These notes concerned the setting, body alignments, activities, actions, and gaze of relevant persons. In taking notes, Martha Platt and I sat near the tape recorder, where we could see the tape counter. Our notes were synchronized with the audiorecorded material by the notation of a tape number along with the contextual information relevant to a particular temporal point.

In addition to taking detailed notes on ongoing behavior, we also noted information concerning events in each of the families and other information about the children that emerged between one session and another. For every family, there was contact with our research group throughout the course of our thirteen-month stay. For the youngest child, this contact was continuous, because we lived in the same family compound. We were able to observe and note developmental changes in this child's speech on a daily basis.

1.4.   *The recorded corpus*
A total of 128 hours of audio- and 20 hours of videorecording were collected in the longitudinal study. So far as I know, this is the largest longitudinal data base ever collected in a non-Western society.

1.5.   *Transcription procedures*
All of the audiotapes were transcribed in the field. The transcriptions always involved the researcher who made the recording and a Samoan intimate with the family recorded. In the first month of our study, we transcribed the tapes with the assistance of the children's mothers. However, the task was tremendously time-consuming: three hours of tape recording necessitated five weeks of transcription (roughly three to four hours a day, five days a week). The mothers simply could not spare the time to engage in this activity. Our next strategy was to engage a teenage member of the family or of a neighboring family. This strategy was successful.

Each transcriber was trained for several weeks by one of the researchers. We would listen together to tapes with two sets of earphones connected by a

Y-plug to a tape recorder. After this period, the tapes were transcribed alone by a Samoan transcriber and then relistened to by a researcher. Where differences in interpretation of the audio material emerged, we would again listen to the recording together, with the earphones, and reconcile our understandings. Where our interpretations could not be reconciled, both transcriptions were left in the notebooks. In addition, recordings were sometimes taken back to caregivers who participated in the recordings for their understandings of the utterances exchanged.

These interactions in the course of transcribing were fascinating in themselves and brought out interesting cultural differences. Most interesting was the skill with which the Samoan transcribers were able to follow simultaneous speech, in which three or four people are talking in different areas of a living space, and also speech that is quite distant from the microphone. Many times I would hear silence on the tape when my field assistant had transcribed several minutes of conversation that took place across the road or in another household. These skills seem to me to be linked to early socialization patterns, where children are expected to watch and listen to what is happening around them. Children are able early in life to monitor others' conversations as they are carrying out their own and to notice and report new information to higher-ranking persons in their families.

Other cross-cultural differences emerged in the course of making sense out of children's early utterances. Generally transcribers and members of the children's families found odd our questions about what a child's unclear utterance could be or could mean and would engage in speculating about form and meaning primarily to please or show respect for us. A characteristic first response to such questions was *Ka 'ilo?* 'How should little old me know?' Subsequently this response was culturally situated and helped me to make sense out of caregiver speech to young children and Samoan epistemology. These issues are discussed in Chapters 1 and 7 of this volume.

Transcriptions were made in large bookkeeping notebooks. Tape counter numbers were listed at the left of the page. The speech of the focus child for each family was transcribed on a separate page to the left of the speech of others. Contextual information was usually placed to the left of the focus child's speech, just after the counter number. A typical two-page format is illustrated in Figure 2.3.

The transcription conventions used were drawn from conversation analysis (Sacks, Schegloff & Jefferson 1974; Schenkein 1978) and language-acquisition literature. These conventions are listed in Appendix 1 and are discussed in Ochs (1979).

The *in loco* transcription of the audiorecordings yielded approximately 18,000 pages of transcribed material.

Transcription of the nonverbal behavior in the videotaped recordings

Page 1

Tape no. Nonverbal context

Focus Child's speech

Page 2

Tape no. Others' speech

Figure 2.3. *Transcription format.*

was made after we left the village. A certain amount of this transcription was accomplished by a Samoan research assistant (Uili Ulisese), who worked with me at the Australian National University for a short while. The bulk of the video transcription was accomplished by Martha Platt at the University of Southern California.

2.   The classroom study

In addition to collecting information on very young children's speech in the home, we also observed and recorded for a brief period children in formal classroom settings. This study was secondary to our longitudinal study. The purpose of the classroom study was to provide some documentation of the acquisition of literacy skills, both alphabetic and mathematical. Three settings were the focus of this study. The three selected represent three of the four major settings of formal education in the village.

One set of observations focused on the pastor's school. This school was located in the compound where we resided and was administered by the pastor of the Congregational Christian Church and his wife. Children begin this school quite early, most by the age of three. The school draws children from all religions and all subvillages. It is the setting in which literacy is first introduced to children. Two classes were observed and recorded. One class was the kindergarten, or youngest group of children. The second was a group of much older children, ranging from about seven to fourteen years of age.

The second setting was the village public school. This school was attended by most of the children in Falefaa. Two classes were observed and recorded, the kindergarten and first grade. One set of observations took place during the first week of school and another a month later.

The third location for this study was the village Catholic school. This school was quite large and also drew children from a variety of religious denominations within the village. A first grade and an upper grade were observed and recorded.

The classrooms were observed in both the first (1978–9) and the second (1981) periods of fieldwork. In the first period, six hours of audio- and one hour of videorecording were made of the pastor's school and the village public school. In 1981, thirty minutes of sound Super 8 film footage was made of the pastor's school and twenty minutes of sound Super 8 film footage of the village Catholic school.

3.   The contexts-of-childhood study

In both periods of fieldwork, we were very much concerned with documentation of the activities and settings in which children use language. We had in mind capturing the lifespaces of children about which Kernan (1969, 1974) and Mead (1928) spoke. We felt that documentation of the ecological dimensions of Samoan childhood would provide important information about the interface of language acquisition and Samoan society. This project was headed by Alessandro Duranti.

The contexts of children's lives were of course captured in the observational notes and videotaping made in the homes of the six families in the longitudinal study. In addition, in 1978–9 700 color slides and several hundred black-and-white photographs were taken of children of different ages in the course of their daily lives. These documented children as they carried out such tasks as food preparation, child care, cleaning, serving, carrying food from plantations, delivering messages and objects on behalf of an older person, and doing schoolwork. In addition, a range of children's play activities were captured.

In 1981, Duranti and I returned to Falefaa to shoot a sound Super 8 film that would focus on a few important social situations in the lives of Samoan children relevant to communicative competence. We shot five and a half hours of film showing children at work and at play in the family compound, at school, and on the beach. We have completed one film that contrasts task accomplishment in school and household settings. This film supplements the discussion of literacy instruction found in Chapter 10 of this volume.

4.   The adult-speech study

In addition to the documentation of children's speech and children's lives, we also observed and recorded adult speech and interviewed adult speakers. This project was the primary responsibility of Alessandro Duranti.

Our immediate goal was to document Samoan as it is used by adults across a range of statuses, social relationships, and social events. A total of fifty hours of adult-speech was recorded. Of this corpus, twenty-six and a half hours were transcribed and translated *in loco*, in cooperation with participants to the interactions recorded and/or other native speakers.

The corpus covered the speech of both untitled and titled persons of both sexes. Further, recordings were made of speech events that varied in terms of formality and in terms of private/public settings (see Chapter 3). Sample events include formal village council meetings of titled persons, chats among titled persons before and after the council meetings, ritual events such as the bestowing of a title (*saofa'i*) and the exchange of bridewealth, women's meetings, women picking weeds and gossiping by the road, women talking to masseuses of children, family discussions inside the home, host and guest discussions, teenagers telling stories to one another at night, radio broadcasts, sermons, and formal interviews with non-Samoan researchers.

B.   Summary of research procedures

This study has combined data-collection procedures from several theoretical traditions. From *developmental psycholinguistics*, it has incorporated the longitudinal case-study method for studying language development. In this tradition the study of children's linguistic competence is pursued by focusing on a few children and following their language development periodically, with detailed documentation of utterances (audiorecording) as well as the here-and-now setting and nonverbal behavior of children and others present at the time of recording (videorecording, observational notes). Transcription conventions have been drawn from this tradition as well as from the school of *conversation analysis*. Among other benefits, these procedures have provided a solid basis for evaluating the role of the immediate situation in children's communicative interactions at different developmental points in time and the choreography of turn taking and conversational sequencing in these interactions.

The *ethnographic* side of this study emerges in the pursuit of social structure and ultimately cultural ideologies that are relevant to the use and meaning of language. To this end, two traditional ethnographic procedures were used. The first was *participant observation*. Our residence in the village facilitated not only observations of the six children in the longitudinal study but routine and special events in the lives of many members of the village of all ages and social statuses. Observations of informal and formal events were recorded in the form of field notes, in photographs, on videotape, and on Super 8 film. The second ethnographic procedure used was *interviewing*. In both the adult and the child language study, members of the communities were formally and informally interviewed concerning language and other social behavior. Most of the interviews centered on recorded and/or transcribed speech. As noted earlier, we would discuss problematic recorded material with transcribers, members of the child's household, or others in the community. Starting with an immediate pragmatic need to transcribe what is being said, we were led to attitudes about communication, children, and competence. Other interviews were not centered on recorded interactions and covered a wide range of topics relevant to language and social life. In the adult speech study, A. Duranti also conducted formal *linguistic* interviews, in which grammatical structures and judgments were elicited (see Duranti 1981a: 20–1). These interviews were initially conducted in English; then, as the fieldwork proceeded, the interviews were conducted in the two phonological registers ('good speech' and 'bad speech') of Samoan. In this way, the role of the metalanguage on the judgments elicited could itself be an object of study.

III.   INTEGRATION WITH OTHER RESEARCH ON SAMOAN LANGUAGE AND SOCIETY

A study of language acquisition can be responsibly conducted only in conjunction with other resources from the language and society in which a child is expected to acquire competence. This is true for all studies but is particularly important where the language and the society are not native to or familiar to the researcher. The selection of Samoan language for the acquisition study was in large part motivated by the abundance of excellent linguistic and ethnographic analyses available. As will be discussed in the following chapter, several grammars, grammatical descriptions, and dictionaries of Samoan were available to the researchers as this study was conceived. The structures and linguistic issues that were initially a focus of study were generated from these materials. I was fortunate as well to have access to a previous study of Samoan language acquisition carried out by Keith Kernan (1969). Kernan provided me with his transcripts and field notes several months before my departure for Western Samoa.

While researchers in child language research have focused on documenting what we can call the local aspects of the speech situation (e.g. actions, changes of state, gestures, gaze), they have not as a whole gathered the kind of information that would define the situation in terms of the community of speakers. An important goal of this study was to relate speaking to other social behaviors. Children and others with whom they interact are viewed not only as children but as Samoan children, and their language is seen as guided in part by the expectations that Samoans have of children, such as their notions of childhood, development, and acquisition of knowledge. Similarly, the setting in which children are speaking in this study is viewed not only as an assemblage of here-and-now entities but also as a socially delimited and organized space. The space has an internal social organization. For example, in a Samoan house, front and back, center and periphery, even on and off a seating mat have social relevance. Further, settings are socially organized in terms of larger categories or groups of settings, such as public, private, formal, informal, sacred, secular, local and nonlocal, and so on.

We could discuss other dimensions of the speech situation (e.g. postures, actions, gaze) in these terms. The important point is that interpretation of speech rests on, indeed demands, knowledge of such sociocultural information. Samoan society and ideology are complex, the subject of a great deal of research and lively debate (Freeman 1983). To supplement our own observations and analyses, I have drawn on several valuable ethnographic sources, including, among others, Gerber (1975), F. Keesing (1934), F. Keesing & Keesing (1956), Krämer (1902/3), Mead (1928, 1930), Shore (1977, 1982), and Turner (1884). Most influential and relevant to this study of language acquisition have been Shore's Ph.D. dissertation (1977) and monograph (1982); the reader is referred to these studies for a rich account of Samoan society and the Samoan world view.

3. Introduction to Samoan language usage: grammar and register

I. INTRODUCTION

Samoan is a Polynesian language spoken primarily on the islands that compose American Samoa and Western Samoa. These islands 'lie between 13 and 15 degrees south latitude and 169 and 173 degrees [west] longitude, approximately in the center of the Pacific Ocean' (Pawley 1966:1). Samoan belongs to the Western Polynesian or Samoic-Outlier subgroup of Polynesian languages, along with languages such as East Futunan, Ellicean, Pukupukan, Tikopian, and Nukuoro (Chung 1978; Pawley 1966, 1967).

Samoan is a well-described language. There are at least three dictionaries (Milner 1966; Pratt 1911; Violette 1879), several grammars (including Churchward 1951; Marsack 1962; Neffgen 1918; Pawley 1966; Pratt 1911; Tuitele, Sapolu & Kneubuhl 1978), and dozens of grammatical descriptions (including Chapin 1970; Chung 1978; Cook 1978; Duranti 1981a; Milner 1962, 1973).

In the discussion below and throughout this volume, I shall draw on this rich body of linguistic analysis. The description of Samoan presented here will incorporate as well first-hand observations of spoken Samoan, based on fifteen months of research in Western Samoa (see Chapter 2 for discussion of research procedures). As a detailed sociolinguistic grammar of Samoan is not available, the sociolinguistic description of adult speech will necessarily be rudimentary. The description presented is intended to introduce the reader to the repertoire of registers in Samoan and the basic characteristics of Samoan grammar and lexicon. The features discussed are those that have particular relevance to subsequent chapters, in which acquisition patterns are considered. For more detailed discussions of Samoan grammar, the reader is referred to Chapters 5, 6 and 9.

II. SITUATIONAL VARIATION

As in all speech communities, language behavior in Samoan communities is situationally variable. Phonological, morpho-syntactic, and lexical constructions are associated with particular activities, affects, and social roles and relationships, and speakers often use these constructions to create or key these contexts (Gumperz 1982). Like the notion of 'appropriateness', Samoans have a notion of 'fit' (*fetaui*) between language and situation. Indeed, the notion of *fetaui* has tremendous moral weight in traditional Samoan society (Shore 1977, 1982). Actions, including speech actions, are generally not viewed as right or wrong, good or bad, in isolation (i.e. as inherently right or wrong, good or bad). Actions are, rather, evaluated in terms of the 'fit' between the actions and the situation. Disapproval is often voiced as *E lee fetaui* 'It doesn't fit'. Similarly, talk and other actions tend to be judged as good or bad with respect to some particular social circumstance. What is bad in some circumstances is not bad in others. For example, it may be bad to throw stones or insult someone publicly under many circumstances, but it is good to do these things when the honor of one's family is at stake. In Western white middle-class communities, the notion of 'fit' is also used in making moral judgments, but the notion of inherent right and wrong is often used, too. In traditional Samoan society, the notion of 'fit' figures far more prominently in moral reasoning than do inherent qualities of actions.

According to Shore (1977, 1982), the importance of the notion of *fetaui* is part of a more general preference among Samoans not to value consistency across social circumstances. Indeed, the Samoan concept of person is not associated with the enduring notion of personality or character, but rather with the notion of 'sides' (*itu*). Persons are seen as having many sides – diverse social roles and states of being – associated with particular social circumstances. These sides are seen as generated by the social situation.

The significance of context for the traditional Samoan is reflected in Samoans' awareness of settings to which behavior is sensitive. The *public–private* character of the setting is felt to have particular influence on one's conduct. As in most communities, one's mode of conduct becomes more 'proper' the more one is in the public eye: in the day more than in the nighttime; in the center of the village (especially the road) more than at the edge of the village or in the bush itself; outside one's house more than inside; within the house, in the center more than at the edge, and in the front (usually closer to the road) more than in the back of the house (ibid.)

For example, a woman may leave her shoulders uncovered if inside her house, but on the road she must wear something that covers them. Drinking and eating are to be done seated inside houses but certainly not on the public thoroughfares. Defecation should take place behind houses, as close to the bush as possible. Within one's house, the more dignified interactions take place in the central front area. Typically, interactions among lower-status family members take place in the back and periphery of a house when persons of some importance are present. In Chapter 1, I noted how phonological variation is tied to more and less public settings within dwellings. Chapters 5 and 6 discuss how case marking and word order are also sensitive to the public–private distinction.

In addition to the dimension of public versus private, the dimension of *Western versus non-western* (i.e. traditional) setting strongly constrains social behavior. Western societies have influenced the Samoan islands over generations in economic, religious, and educational domains. Institutions introduced by Western societies, such as government offices, banks, churches, pastors' schools, and public schools, are associated with a particular code of dress and verbal and nonverbal comportment (see Chapter 10). Children attending the pastor's school in the village, for example, are expected to wear shirts, and those attending the public school are expected to wear uniforms. Outside these settings, it is common to find children barebreasted. Adults and children alike wear more clothing at a Sunday church service than at other times and settings in the village. This is the setting for women to wear broad-rimmed hats and white, European-cut dresses or Samoan two-piece long suits. Men in this setting wear a European-style shirt, a plain *lavalava* with pockets, and if possible a suit jacket. In non-Western settings within the village, men and women tend to wear brightly colored floral-printed *lavalava*.

As will be discussed below and in subsequent chapters, language use is strongly influenced by the Western–non-Western distinction. Chapter 10, for example, discusses how literacy is associated with Western settings and activities associated with these settings. These settings and activities as well call for a particular phonological register and particular conversational structures not characteristic of social interactions in traditional informal and formal settings.

III.   THE SOCIOLINGUISTIC REPERTOIRE

A.   Phonology

1.   Two phonological registers

It is common knowledge to any speaker of Samoan that there are two major ways of speaking the language, namely *tautala lelei* 'good speech' and *tautala leaga* 'bad speech'. From the discussion above, the reader should realize that these descriptions must be understood as highly context-bound; they do not refer to invariably good or bad qualities of speech.

'Good speech' and 'bad speech' are distinguished on many levels of

Table 3.1. *Phonemic inventories of 'good speech' and 'bad speech'*

'Good speech'					'Bad speech'
p t		k^a	ʔ		p k ʔ
fv s			h^a		fv s
	l/r^a				l
m n		ŋ			m ŋ
			i	u	
		e		o	
			a		

^{a} Used only in lexical borrowings.

grammar and discourse. The most salient dimension, however, is phono-logical. 'Good speech' is characterized by eighteen phonemes (including /r/ and /h/ used only in English borrowings). 'Bad speech' has an inventory of fourteen phonemes. The phonemic inventory of each register is represented in Table 3.1. This table is taken from Chapter 10 by Duranti and Ochs, where phonological register is discussed in greater detail.

The two registers share a common set of vowels. Further, in both registers, vowel length is phonemic (Milner 1966; Pawley 1966). However, in 'good speech' there is a phonemic distinction between /t/ and /k/ and between /n/ and /ŋ/ (written 'g' in Samoan orthography). Thus in 'good speech', *tete* means 'shivering', but *keke* means 'cake'; *ana* means 'cave', but *aga* means 'conduct'. The bulk of the lexical items in which /k/ is used in 'good speech' are borrowings from English (e.g. *kukama* 'cucumber', *suka* 'sugar').

In 'bad speech', /t/ is not used and all lexical items that include /t/ in 'good speech' are pronounced with /k/. Thus in 'bad speech' both borrowed and nonborrowed lexical items are pronounced with /k/. In 'bad speech', *keke* can mean either 'cake' or 'shivering'. Further, the /n/ /ŋ/ distinction is not made in 'bad speech'. The lexical item *aga* can mean either 'cave' or 'conduct'.

Another phonological distinction between these varieties is that /r/ is used in 'good speech' in borrowings such as *Maria*. In 'bad speech', /l/ is used in this environment (*Malia*).

2.   Contexts of use

Currently, in most villages in Western Samoan, 'good speech' is primarily associated with Western-dominated settings and institutions (Shore 1977,

1982). It is preferred in church services, church conferences, pastors' schools, village public schools, and most situations in which Samoan is used to a European addressee. It is also the speech Samoans hear when they turn on their radios and, as will be discussed in Chapter 10, is the variety of the Bible and all literacy materials.

Samoans today link competence in 'good speech' with dignity and high status, e.g. with pastors, with high chiefs rather than orators among titled persons, and with women rather than men among untitled persons (Shore 1977, 1982). Transvestites displaying the behavior of women will exaggerate this image speaking not only with the /t/, /n/, and /r/ but moving all sounds toward the front of the mouth.

A quantitative study of phonological variation has not been carried out; however, the perception of status and 'good speech' appears to correspond only partially to language-use patterns. Within the village in which we worked, only two persons out of 1,200 inhabitants used 'good speech' in all settings. They were both women. These women were daughters of pastors. One of them had lived outside of Samoa until adulthood. The other went to a church-sponsored school in the capital, then married a student pastor and with him attended (as a spouse) a theological seminary for four years. The majority of frequent and fluent users of 'good speech' tend to be those who have completed formal education beyond the primary school, those who have an important role in church organizations (e.g. pastors, deacons), and those who have a steady job in the capital. Those villagers who are highly educated and/or work in the capital tend to be the younger adults (aged eighteen to forty) in the village.

Considerable discussion has been devoted to 'good speech', but it is 'bad speech' that prevails in village social life. 'Bad speech' is used by almost all members of the community and is understood by everyone. It is the register that prevails in formal and informal traditional (i.e. non-Western) social situations in the village – casual interactions among family members and familiars as well as highly stylized deliberations among titled persons interacting in village council meetings (Duranti 1981a, b, 1984c). 'Bad speech' cuts across several genres, ranging from personal narratives, tattling, and teasing to oratory. In these contexts, 'bad speech' is not bad but good.

From the discussion above, it is apparent that 'bad speech' and 'good speech' are associated with different social relationships. 'Good speech' tends to be used in socially more distant relationships. It is generally used where relatively impersonal relationships obtain and in speech to foreigners. It is also used where speakers who share an intimate relationship wish to take distance from their addressees. A speaker may switch to 'good speech' to a family member to signal that he or she is angry with that person.

As discussed by Duranti (1981a), the two registers have methodological implications. As 'good speech' is linked to Western settings and to talk to a

Westerner in particular, it is the medium in which a Samoan would talk to a linguist in a formal elicitation session. Most of what has been described of Samoan captures this variety of the language. As will be discussed, while many features of syntax and morphology are shared, there are important structural distinctions between 'good speech' and 'bad speech'.

B.   The lexicon

Samoan has a respect vocabulary (see Milner 1961), used in both 'good speech' and 'bad speech' when referring to or speaking to persons of high status, particularly titled persons. It is also used to persons who do not have titles when the speaker wishes to convey deference and respect (Shore 1977, 1982). For example, it may be used to an untitled person to whom a particularly important request is being directed.

When used with titled persons, this vocabulary includes many items that are appropriate only to particular statuses, e.g. only to orators, only to high chiefs. For example, there are three respect-vocabulary items for the singular verb 'come' (*sau* in unmarked vocabulary). Referring to a chief, the speaker uses the verb *afio mai*; referring to an orator, the speaker uses either *maliu mai* or *sosopo mai*. Similarly, the wife of a chief is referred to as *faletua*, whereas the wife of an orator is a *tausi* (see Milner 1966; Shore 1977, 1982). Other lexical items can refer to any person who has a title. Thus the respect-vocabulary items *finagalo* 'want' and *silafia* 'to know' are appropriate for both chiefs and orators and contrast with the unmarked terms *mana'o* and *iloa*.

The use of respect vocabulary is not characteristic of informal interaction among familiars. A shift into the use of this vocabulary brings into focus the social status or positional identity (Irvine 1979) of participants in an interaction. This is what occurs, for example, in the course of greeting exchanges when a nonfamily member arrives for a visit or is passed on the road. The greeting will include respect vocabulary that indexes (Silverstein 1976a) the positional identity of the addressee. Once the greeting is completed, the social interaction may shift to a more intimate lexical register in which ordinary vocabulary is used.

C.   Case marking

1.   Ergative and absolutive

Samoan has been described as an ergative–absolutive language (Chung 1978), that is, a language in which subjects of transitive sentences

(A) are treated differently from subjects of intransitive sentences (s) and in which subjects of intransitive sentences and direct objects (o) of transitive sentences are treated (at least in some ways) as a single category (Comrie 1978; Dixon 1979). Very commonly, this distinction is expressed through case marking, where transitive subjects (A) are in the so-called ergative case and intransitive subjects (s) and objects (o) of transitive verbs are in the 'absolutive' case.

Such a language contrasts with the more common nominative–accusative language, in which subjects of transitive and intransitive sentences are treated as one category (nominative) and are distinguished from direct objects (accusative). The different groupings in terms of case marking between the two language types are represented in the accompanying figure, taken from Dixon (1979) and Fillmore (1968).

Ergative language   *Nominative language*

Figure 3.1.

Key: s = *intransitive subject;* A = *agent/transitive subject;* o = *transitive object.*

As in most ergative languages, ergative–absolutive distinctions are expressed through nominal case marking in Samoan. The transitive subject is preceded by the particle *e* when the transitive subject follows the verb (VAO, VOA, OVA). Intransitive subjects following the verb and all direct objects receive no case marking. The difference in marking is presented below:

Transitive sentence

VAO:	'ua	fasi	e	le	tama	Sina.
	INCPTPERF	hit	ERG	ART	boy	Sina

VOA:	'ua	fasi	Sina	e	le	tama.
	INCPTPERF	hit	Sina	ERG	ART	boy

'The boy hit Sina.'

Intransitive sentence

VS:	'olo'o	moe	le	tama.
	PRES PROG	sleep	ART	boy

'The boy is sleeping.'

This case-marking system is sociolinguistically variable. Its variation is partly but not completely a function of the social distance between language users. Where social relationships are relatively impersonal and distant, there is a greater tendency for Samoans to use the ergative marker. For example, in literacy materials and in radio broadcasts, the ergative marker is always present in the grammatically feasible environments (i.e. when A follows the verb). In face-to-face social interaction, the particle is not always expressed. The social distribution of the use of this particle in spoken Samoan is discussed at length in Chapter 5 of this volume, along with its implications for language acquisition.

2.   Genitive

In Samoan, the genitive phrase follows the noun it modifies. The genitive phrase is marked with either the particle *a* or the particle *o*. The particle *a* indicates roughly alienable possession or more direct control over the 'possessed' object. The particle *o* indicates roughly inalienable possession and less-direct control over the object (Chung 1973):

Alienable possession
le   masi   a   a'u
ART   biscuit   POSS   1ST PERS
'my biscuit'

le   masi   a   Sefo
ART   biscuit   POSS   Sefo
'Sefo's biscuit'

Inalienable possession
le   lima   o   a'u
ART   arm   POSS   1ST PERS
'my arm'

le   lima   o   Sefo
ART   arm   POSS   Sefo
'Sefo's arm'

The expression of the case markers *a* and *o* varies in terms of social distance between interlocutors. The more impersonal the social relationship, the more frequently the case marker is used. In the intimate surroundings of one's family, the marker is often dropped.

Possession can also be expressed by placing an article plus possessive particle plus pronoun before the noun. In the singular form, the three items are incorporated into a singular lexical item. For example, *le* (specific determiner) + *a* (alienable possession article) + *a'u* (first person pronoun) is realized as *la'u*, as in the possessive phrase *la'u se'evae* 'my shoe'. In the plural, no article appears and the possessive particle is expressed before the pronoun in careful speech. For example, 'my shoes' in careful speech is expressed as *a a'u se'evae*.

3.   The particles *'i* and *i*

In careful 'good speech' and 'bad speech' registers of Samoan, the particles *'i* and *i* are used as case markers. The particle *'i* marks directionality (goal), causality, instrumentality, and 'aboutness' (Tuitele & Kneubuhl 1978:61).

The particle *'i* (from Tuitele & Kneubuhl 1978:57–61)

Directionality
Tu   'i   luga.
stand   DIR   up
'Stand up.'

Causality
Na   'ou   sau   'i   le   fa'alavelave.
PST   1ST PERS CLIT   come   CAUS   ART   big event
'I came because of the big event.'

Instrumentality (in sense of material from which something is made or changed)
Na   fau   le   fale   'i   laupapa   ma   simaa.
PST   construct   ART   house   INSTR   timber   CONJ   cement
'They made the house with timber and cement.'

Aboutness
Na   'ou   pese   'i   le   Atua.
PST   1ST PERS CLIT   sing   ABOUT   ART   God
'I sang about God.'

The particle *i* marks time; location (not in the sense of goal); instrumentality (in the sense of item used or item that affects one); comparison and the objects of a class of verbs (called semitransitives (Churchward 1951) or middle verbs (Chung 1978) or intransitive verbs (Tuitele & Kneubuhl 1978)) that include verbs of perception, emotion, desire, and cognition, among others.

The particle *i* (from Tuitele & Kneubuhl 1978:59–60)

Time
Na   matou   oo   i   le   lua.
PST   we (EXCL)   go   TEMP   ART   two
'We went at two.'

Location
'Ou   te   nofo   i   Masefau.
1ST PERS CLIT   NON PST   live   LOC   Masefau
'I live at Masefau.'

Object associated with semitransitive/middle/intransitive verb
'ou   te   alofa   iaa   'oe.
1ST PERS CLIT   NON PST   love   OBJ   you
'I love you.'

'ou   te   fa'alogo   iaa   'oe.
1ST PERS CLIT   NONPST   hear   OBJ   you
'I hear you.'

Instrumentality (in sense of item used or item that affects one)

Na	'ou	lavea		i	le	fao.
PST	1ST PERS CLIT	cut + TRANS SUFFIX		INSTR	ART	nail

'The nail cut/injured me' or 'I was cut by the nail.'

Comparison

'e	sili	Sina	iaa	'oe.
NON PST	beyond	Sina	COMP	you

'Sina is better than you.'

Whereas the particles *'i* and *i* are distinguished phonologically in careful Samoan, they are often not in more casual speech. Where interlocutors are familiar with one another and the interaction is relatively informal, the glottal stop in *'i* is often deleted, removing the one feature that differentiates the two particles. The dropping of the glottal stop is related not only to relatively less attention paid to speaking but to increased speed of speech characteristic of casual interactions. With the exception of certain formulaic genres (e.g. kava calling, greetings), formal speech is relatively slower than informal speech.

D.   Word order in the noun phrase

1.   Articles

There are affect-neutral and affect-marked articles in Samoan. Neutral reference to nonspecific information is expressed by *se* (singular) and *ni* (plural). *Se* and *ni* are used when the speaker is not referring to some particular entity. *Le* (singular) usually refers to specific information the speaker has in mind. There is no plural form of the specific article.

'o	le	tama
TOP	SPEC ART	boy

'the boy'

'o	tamaiti
TOP	children

'the children'

'o	se	tama
TOP	NONSPEC ART	boy

'a boy'

'o	ni	tamaiti
TOP	NONSPEC ART (PL)	children

'some/any children'

Either the singular or plural form of the specific article is obligatory when modifying NPs in the subject position, and in this grammatical context it may refer to either specific or nonspecific information.

In additional Samoan has the singular and plural affect-marked articles *si* and *nai*. These forms express sympathy toward the referent expressed by the head noun the article modifies. These forms are discussed in Chapter 9.

With one exception, the article precedes the head noun and its modifiers (e.g. the word order of genitive constructions is either ART – GEN – PRO – HEAD NOUN or ART – HEAD NOUN – GEN NP). The article may follow the head noun if it co-occurs with a demonstrative that follows the head noun (see section 3 below).

2.   Adjectives and quantifiers

Adjectives generally follow the head noun, with the exception of cardinal numerals, possessive adjectives, and the quantifier *tele*.

tagata   fiafia
people   happy
'happy people'

lua   tagata
two   people
'two people'

tele   tagata
many   people
'many people'

3.   Demonstratives

Demonstratives may appear in three word-order positions within the noun phrase: ART – HEAD NOUN – DEMONSTRATIVE, ART – DEMONSTRATIVE – HEAD NOUN, and ART – HEAD NOUN – ART – DEMONSTRATIVE. These word-order variations are illustrated below.

le   tama   nei
ART   child   this

le   nei   tama
ART   this   child

le   tama   le   nei
ART   child   ART   this
'this child'

4.   Relative clauses

The relative clause always follows the head noun. A relative pronoun (a demonstrative) may or may not appear at the beginning of the relative clause. A resumptive pronoun is needed if the relativized element acts as an oblique in the relative clause (e.g. instrument, locative, temporal, indirect object).

'Ua   popole le   tama lea   na   alu ese.
IMPERF worry ART child who PST PERF go   away
'The child who went away was worried.'

E.   The verb complex

The verb complex includes the verb and dependent structures (Seiter 1980) such as tense/aspect markers, auxiliary verbs, adverbs, deictic particles, and clitic pronouns. Only certain of these structures are covered in this chapter.

1.   Tense/aspect marking

The tense/aspect marker precedes the verb and generally is the first element in the verb complex. In 'good speech' register, Samoan uses the following tense/aspect markers:

Tense/aspect markers

Marker	*Time*
'e/te	Nonpast (*te* restricted to 1st & 2nd person clitic subjects – singular, dual, plural)
'olo'o	Present continuous
'ua	Imperfect or inceptive perfect: state/action just initiated
'o le 'aa	Future
na	Past perfect
saa	Past imperfect

Illustrations of these markers in sentences can be found below and throughout this chapter.

'e   alu   'oe?
NON PST go   2ND PERS
'Are you going?'

'ou   te   alu.
1ST PERS CLIT NON PST go
'I'm going.'

'olo'o   moe   Sina.
PRES PROG sleep Sina
'Sina is sleeping.'

'ua   alu Sina.
IMPERF go   Sina
'Sina has gone.'

'o le 'aa alu   taeao.
FUT   go   tomorrow
'(He) will go tomorrow.'

Na   fai le   mea   ananafi.
PST PREF do   SPEC ART   thing yesterday
'(He) made the thing yesterday.'

Saa   maatou   i   nei   ma   le   aaiga.
PST IMPREF   we (EXCL) in   here   with SPEC ART   family
'We were here with the family.'

The most common social context for these markers is in literate Samoan, particularly books and newspapers, where language users are socially distant. In 'bad speech' register, these forms are used much less frequently, particularly in the casual environment of one's own household. In these contexts, two additional alternatives are often employed. One alternative strategy is to completely omit the tense/aspect marker, as in the informal conversation below.

(1) P17–051*

A: Ae   va'ai,   ou   alifo   a?
    But   see   1ST PERS CLIT   go over   PRT

    Laku–   laku   o le, ((pause))
    go + DEICT   go + DEICT   there

    avaku   le   mea   i   le   oki.

    give + DEICT   ART   thing to   the   dead
    'But you see, I went over, you know?
    I went – went there, (pause)
    took the thing to the dead one.'

A second strategy is to use an alternative marker. The alternate structure may be a reduced form of one of the markers used in careful Samoan. Tuitele & Kneubuhl (1978) mention that the marker *'olo'o* may be reduced to *'o* and *'o le 'aa* may be reduced to *'a*. In our transcripts of casual conversation, *'o* is common; however, *'a* is not common. Instead, future time tends to be expressed through the particles *la'a*, *laa*, and *la*, producing such utterances as:

La'a alu.
Laa   alu.
La   alu.
FUT   go
'(I/you/he) will go.'

La'u   alu.
FUT + 1ST PERS CLIT   go
'I will go.'

La'e   alu.
FUT + 2ND PERS CLIT   go
'You will go.'

These tense/aspect particles are very frequent in the conversations transcribed in our study. The underlying form of these particles is not clear. One possibility is that they are reduced forms of *'o le 'aa*. A second possibility is that *la* is to be understood as a distinct morpheme. *La* is a deictic adverb or pronoun meaning 'there' or 'that' or 'those' (in speaker's sight, not far away). In this case, *la* may be combined with the particle *'a* to form *la'a* or *laa* (deleting glottal stop, which is also common in casual speech) or *la* (reducing vowel length, again a common process in casual speech).

Support for the second of these hypotheses comes from the use of *la* to mark other temporal dimensions. The particle *la* may precede the tense/aspect marker *e*, forming *lae*. The particle *la* is used only for third person subject and denotes present tense. The sentence *Lae moe* means roughly 'There (now) he sleeps.' *La* may also precede the marker *'ua* to become *lauaa* or *laua*. These forms express action (of a third person) that has started but is not completed. Hence the sentence *Laua moe* means roughly '(He/She) has just gone to (go to) sleep (but is not yet sleeping).'

In addition to *la*, the deictic forms *lea* (meaning 'this' or 'that' or 'now') and *loa* 'now' are used before the verb in casual speech instead of the nonpast marker *'e/te*. *Loa alu* can mean '(I) am about to go.' The semantics of these deictic forms has not been sufficiently researched to establish more precisely their scope and use as tense/aspect markers.

This brief discussion brings out two important points. First, in considering the acquisition of tense/aspect marking, one must attend to more than the system described for standard Samoan. The child's use of deictic forms for expressing time as well as omission of temporal markers is not a categorical error but rather part of the linguistic repertoire to which the child is exposed (and the register to which the child is most exposed).

The second important point to note is that casual speech is not a paler or less elaborate version of formal speech. The observations here indicate that tense/aspect may receive more complex marking (e.g. deictic forms plus particles) in the casual speech of familiars than in more formal speech and writing.

2.   Subject–verb agreement

In 'good speech' and in careful 'bad speech', some verbs agree in number with their subjects. The most common way of forming the plural consists of reduplicating the penultimate syllable of the singular form of the verb:

Singular	Plural
'ai	*'a'ai*
savali	*savavali*
moe	*momoe*

Other means of forming the plural include reduplicating two or more syllables; adding the prefix *ta-* (as in *tafasi* (sing. *fasi*)) or *fe-* (as in *feinu* (sing. *inu*)); dropping a syllable; and lengthening the vowel in the first syllable of the singular form (Pratt 1911). For certain verbs, two different lexical items are used to express the singular and plural forms of the verb. For example, the verb 'go' in the singular is *alu*; in the plural it is *oo*. The verb 'come' in the singular is *sau*; in the plural it is *oo mai*.

The use of subject–verb agreement is more restricted in language used among intimates than in the language of more socially distant interlocutors. The restriction is in terms of frequency and range of constructions used. In casual speech, one finds fewer instances of agreement and a more restricted set of verbs that are so inflected. The most common plural forms in casual speech are those of the verbs 'go', 'come', and 'eat'; outside these verbs, the use of the plural is uncommon in this context.

3.   Verbal suffix

In all social environments, a suffix may be added to verbs (intransitive, middle, and transitive). This suffix has a number of forms, including *-a*, *-ia*, *-ina*, *-lia*, *-fia*.

Verb	*Verb plus suffix*
fai 'do'	*faia*
tu'u 'put'	*tu'uina*
vala'au 'call'	*vala'aulia*
taa 'strike'	*taaia*

For transitive verbs, the suffix tends to appear in clauses whose subjects are clitic pronouns, in relative clauses whose subjects have been removed, in clauses whose subjects appear in cleft constructions, and in clauses with deleted generic agents; it is 'required' in negative imperatives and negative generic statements (Chung 1978:85–91).

Preliminary analysis by Duranti (1981a) indicates that the verbal suffix appears both more frequently and in a wider range of construction types in the 'bad speech' register used in highly formal meetings of chiefs than in more casual interaction among men. In the more formal setting, men use the suffix in the less as well as the more predictable grammatical environments (e.g. negative imperatives). In casual surroundings, the use of the suffix tends to appear only in the more predictable grammatical environments.

F.   **Word order of major constituents**

Samoan has several possible orderings of full major constituents. For all constructions, the preferred order is verb-initial, i.e. intransitives as verb–subject and transitives (with three full constituents) as either verb–subject–

object or verb–object–subject. This preference cuts across social distance and degree of formality of settings (Duranti 1981a; Duranti & Ochs 1983; Ochs 1986a). The second major preference when all constituents are expressed is subject–verb and subject–verb–object word orders. Other possible but less frequently used word orders are object–verb–subject and subject–object–verb.

Word orders in Samoan

Intransitives

VS:	'ua	sau	Pesio.
	IMPERF	come	Pesio
SV:	'o	Pesio	'ua	sau.
	TOP	Pesio	IMPERF	come

'Pesio has come.'

Canonical transitives

VAO:	Na	usu	e	Tala	le	pese.
	PST	sing	ERG	Tala	ART	song
VOA:	Na	usu	le	pese	e	Tala.
	PST	sing	ART	song	ERG	Tala
AVO:	'o	Tala	na	usu	le	pese.
	TOP	Tala	PST	sing	ART	song
OVA:	'o	le	pese	na	usu	e	Tala.
	TOP	ART	song	PST	sing	ERG	Tala

'Tala sang the song.'

Semitransitives/middle verbs

VSX:	'e	fiafia		le	pepe	i	le	letioo.
	NONPST	happy/like	ART	baby	OBJ	ART	radio
VXS:	'e	fiafia		i	le	letioo	le	pepe.
	NONPST	happy/like	OBJ	ART	radio	ART	baby
SVX:	'o	le	pepe	e		fiafia	i	le	letioo.
	TOP	ART	baby	NONPST	happy/like	OBJ	ART	radio
XVS:	'o	le	letioo	e		fiafia	iai	le	pepe.
	TOP	ART	radio	NONPST	happy/like	COPY PRO	ART	baby

'The baby is happy about/likes the radio.'

In Samoan, both intransitive and transitive subjects may be represented by a clitic pronoun as well as by a full pronoun or noun. Clitic-pronoun subjects have only one possible position, i.e. preceding the verb, usually between the tense/aspect marker and the main verb.

Clitic subject word order

SV:	Na	'ee		alu?
	PST PERF	2ND PERS CLIT	go
*VS:	na	alu	'ee?
	PST PERF	go	2ND PERS CLIT

'Did you go?'

AVO:	Na	ou		'ai	le	masi?
	PST PERF	1ST PERS CLIT	eat	ART	cracker

VAO: Na   'ai   ou   le   masi.
       PST PERF eat 1ST PERS CLIT ART cracker
       'I ate the cracker.'

* The asterisk prefix indicates ungrammaticality.

Studies of word-order strategies across social situations by Duranti (1981a) and Ochs (1982b, 1986a) indicate that word-order preferences for full pronoun and noun constituents are sensitive to gender of speaker and to degree of intimacy between interlocutors. These differences are the subject of discussion of Chapters 5 and 6 of this volume. In these chapters, a major generalization is that in relatively intimate settings, adult speakers prefer word orders in which absolutive constituents (o or s) follow the verb. For transitive utterances, the preference in these settings is for vo, voa, avo.

The relation of word order to focus is complex and the subject of considerable discussion in Chapter 6. A study by Duranti & Ochs (1983) indicates that the unmarked or usual focus position is the position immediately following the verb. Additionally, a speaker may heighten the focus (e.g. for contrast, emphasis) on a full NP constituent by placing it before the verb preceded by the topic particle *'o*, as in the avo, ova, and svx sentences above.

However, the reader should note that word order in Samoan is not the only means of differentiating what is the information focus (Chomsky 1971) in a sentence. There are intonational means; a wide range of emphatic particles that apply to verbs, adverbs, adjectives, and nominal forms; a set of verbal suffixes (discussed in section III.C.3 above); reduplication of the verb; and code switching of lexical items from 'bad speech' to 'good speech' and vice versa. Further, as will be discussed in Chapter 6, the expression of all three major constituents is itself a marked form of language use and signals a type of emphasis.

IV.   SUMMARY

We see that many structures in Samoan are variable and sensitive to social situation, particularly social distance between interlocutors, formality of setting, and gender of speaker. Among the most affected features of Samoan are the phonemes /t/, /k/, /n/, /ŋ/; the glottal stop; respect vocabulary; ergative case marking; the verbal suffix; subject–verb agreement; tense/aspect marking; ordering of subject, verb, object; and presence of all three major constituents.

Other features of Samoan do not vary across social situations. For example, the bulk of the phonological repertoire is used across situations and registers. Further, there are features that may vary in their presence or absence but that when present appear in a fixed order. For example, tense/aspect marking may or may not be used, but whenever it is used it always precedes the verb. Similarly, case markers are variably present, but when they are used they always precede the noun/pronoun they are marking.

The account of competence and error in Samoan children's language draws on this understanding of Samoan in context.

4. The social contexts of childhood: village and household organization

I. INTRODUCTION

As Samoan children mature, they participate in groups based on kinship, residence, social rank, gender, and church affiliation. Each of these groups involves networks of social relationships. Children learn what to expect from these relationships and also what they must do to maintain them. This knowledge is the core of social competence in a Samoan community. While understanding of social principles and social structures is a lifelong process, the beginnings of this understanding emerge early in the lives of Samoan children. As will be discussed in this and in subsequent chapters, the contexts of young Samoan children's development encourage sensitivity to and enactment of verbal and nonverbal behaviors associated with particular statuses and relationships and settings.

One important feature of Samoan children's socialization environment is the constant physical presence of many persons of different social status. Young children are exposed to and immersed in multiparty interactions far more often than dialogic interactions. In these interactions, each participant may display multiple social identities, depending on the social identities of others copresent. Thus, for example, a young untitled man may have higher status than a younger brother present but lower status than a titled family member also present. As persons enter and leave social settings, children and adults are constantly unconsciously calculating their social rank with respect to others. As will be noted later, associated with rank are behavioral consequences and expectations. From the point of view of children's socialization, we can see that interactions contain considerable social information. Some of this information relates to rights and duties associated with higher and lower rank. With respect to talk, children acquire a tacit understanding of who can say what to whom. Beyond this, however, Samoan children are socialized from birth into the notion of 'person' as having a number of social 'sides' (Shore 1977, 1982), which emerge and subside (from one moment to the next) in the flow of social activity at any one time and place.

71

A second feature of Samoan children's social environment is the explicit practice of caregivers of orienting the child to the persons of different social status participating in these multiparty interactions, i.e. directing children to notice and act in variable but appropriate ways to different participants. As will be discussed later, Samoan children are explicitly socialized to attend and serve. As infants they are usually held outward, often nestled on the laps of older siblings. When infants begin eating solid food, they are also often fed facing away from the feeder (usually an older sibling) and toward others present. Indeed, the core of the Samoan term for 'respect', *fa'aaloalo*, is the respect-vocabulary term *alo* 'to face (in the direction of)' (Milner 1966). When Samoan children begin to speak, they are taught not only to notice those present and those passing by, but also to call out the names of these persons. They are also socialized to attend carefully to the words of higher-status persons and are expected to repeat messages of higher status persons to others quite early in their lives. By the time children are three years old they serve higher-status family members by running messages from one family member to another and when somewhat older from one household to another.

A third, related feature of children's social environment is the expectation that children will assume child-care responsibilities for younger siblings early in life (Mead 1928). By the age of three and certainly by four, most Samoan children have a wide repertoire of demeanors appropriate to interactions with younger siblings, peers, older siblings, and a range of adult kin, guests, and strangers varying in their position in the hierarchical structure of Samoan society. In this chapter, I shall introduce certain elements of this structure. In much the same way as I presented the linguistic repertoire of Samoan in Chapter 3, I now highlight certain fundamental properties of Samoan social organization. We shall see in a series of essays how this organization enters into children's socialization and language development.

II.   VILLAGE STRUCTURES

A.   The council of *matai*

Every Samoan village is governed by a council (*fono*) of persons who hold chiefly names or titles called *matai* titles. Each village has its own set of *matai* titles, and each title has its own history, associated with a particular descent group (*'aaiga potopoto*) and its family lands. When a title holder dies, the family elects another to assume the title. Occasionally the title is split and given to two persons. Claims to titles may be made through either the male or female descent lines (*tamatane/tamefafine*), although the male line is the preferred one. Selection of a title holder is based on several considerations, including number and magnitude of services rendered to the family, kinship link to the deceased title holder(s), and economic status, education, and demeanor of the candidate (Shore 1982). From the point at which the title is bestowed, the title holder is referred to and addressed by that title in public and private settings.

There are two major categories of *matai* titles. One may have the title of *tulaafale* 'talking chief' or the title of *ali'i* 'high chief'. Usually an *ali'i* title is associated with a *tulaafale* title, although there are cases in which a particularly low-ranking chief may not in fact have his own orator, and there are other cases in which a very high-ranking chief may have several orators at his service. The *tulaafale* carries out certain services for the *ali'i*, such as distributing goods, delivering messages, and speaking on his behalf in a variety of formal events. For these services, the *ali'i* provides food and other goods to the *tulaafale*.

Within each village, the particular titles are ranked and associated with a particular position in the seating plan of council (*fono*) meetings. Verbally, the relations among titles are codified in the village *fa'alupega* 'greeting' and in the calling out of cup names in the kava ceremony that precedes or initiates formal gatherings of chiefs. Although a title holder may gain or lose political power and effectiveness through his or her personal qualities, it is the title and not the person that is of primary importance: 'Names and their rank, not individuals, are the units of construction' (Mead 1930:11). 'Personal qualities may certainly enhance political power in Samoa, but power per se is clearly separable from any particular person who may wield it. Political power lies primarily in a title and is conceived of as external to the person who might happen to bear it' (Shore 1982:69).

Although women may hold *matai* titles, overwhelmingly the title holders are men. In some villages, only one or two women may have *matai* titles.

Chiefly councils may involve the entire village, i.e. the whole group of *matai* in the village; or two or more villages; or a subvillage (*piton'u*). Additionally there are committees of *matai* that adjudicate in minor disputes and accusations and that administer particular village projects, such as the building of a public structure or carrying out an agricultural program.

The competitive nature of title assumption, the importance of rank, and the distinction between positional and personal identity (Irvine 1979) have been the subject of considerable discussion in the anthropological literature on Samoa (see especially Mead 1930; Sahlins 1958; Shore 1982). As will be discussed later, these three elements underlie not only adult but children's earliest social experiences as well. Infants and small children develop their understanding of social structure and their social skills as they participate in day-to-day interactions that are organized according to these principles. Caregivers implicitly or explicitly socialize children to assert and defend themselves and to assess the relative rank of those present and conduct themselves accordingly.

B.   Other village groups

In addition to the village *matai*, there are several other formal organizations that carry out important tasks within the village, including the *'aumaga*, or organization of untitled men, the *'aualuma*, or organization of unmarried, widowed, and divorced women and wives of untitled men (Mead 1930:31), and the *faletua ma tausi*, or organization of chiefs' wives (Shore 1982:103). The *'aumaga* serves chiefs during their gatherings and also performs the upkeep of village lands. The women's groups have a variety of concerns, including maintenance of sanitary conditions in the village, weaving of mats, and entertaining on certain occasions.

Churches, too, have their organizations, including committees to organize the pastor's and Sunday schools and committees to supply the pastor's house with mats, dishes, silverware, or other needed items, to supply the church with furniture and otherwise maintain the church building, to serve in the pastor's house meals before and after church services or on other church occasions, to maintain congregational grounds, and to administer special church projects.

Small children are not excluded from the activities of these various village organizations. Indeed, groups of small boys will hang around the *'aumaga* young men who are serving at the chiefly council meetings and will assist them in food preparation. Occasionally *matai* meeting for village or church-related affairs will bring along a toddler grandchild, who will sit just behind or pressed against the side of the *matai* grandparent in the course of the meeting. When food is served, the toddler will be given a portion. Similarly, as groups of women weed or weave, they will have their young children or grandchildren by their sides. The children will be asked to fetch items, to deliver messages, or otherwise assist in limited ways. The children may play by themselves for a while off to one side but for the most part stay close by the women to watch and listen.

III.   THE HOUSEHOLD

A.   Membership

Mead (1930:23) discusses both ideal and actual membership patterns of residential groups. The preferred residential pattern is patrilocal. The ideal household would be headed by a *matai* and consist of his untitled brothers and their families, his parents, his wife, his sons and their wives, his unmarried or widowed daughters, and so on. In fact, however, a variety of circumstances lead to frequent matrilocal residence. A family may shift residence from the family of the wife to the family of the husband or vice versa one or more times over a period of time. A common pattern is for an untitled man to live in the household of his wife initially; if he receives a title through his own family, he will move his wife and children to the land associated with that title. Additionally, one finds in a household adopted as well as natural children and various relatives who are temporarily residing there.

A household, then, is best understood as simply a group of persons related by blood and/or marriage who live and work together and affiliate themselves with one or occasionally more than one *matai* (Mead 1930; Shore 1982).

B.   The household compound

Members of a household may live in several locations within a village but usually reside together in a cleared area. The area may be on one or both sides of the coastal road that circles the island.

A household compound may contain one dwelling but more often contains several houses that are a short distance apart. One among these, usually the house in which the *matai* sleeps, is considered the main house, where important events take place. In addition to these living spaces, the household compound has at least one cooking house. Most household compounds also have outhouses and small houses for resting or relaxing.

Samoan houses are of two major types. Either they are traditional rectangular, oval, or round open-sided structures, where only poles are used to support the roof; or they are European-style structures, using walls. The traditional structures are usually round or oval, but some are rectangular. European houses are rectangular. Roofing material on traditional houses may be either pandanus or corrugated tin; European-style houses use tin. Traditional houses use blinds to shield the interior from the heat of the sun, the cool of the night, rains. European houses use glass windows and wooden doors in addition to the wooden walls. In traditional houses, there are no internal walls; European houses may contain more than one room.

By far the more common type of house is the traditional structure with no external or internal walls. The openness of this structure, the proximity of houses, and the number of family members within a family compound create a particular interactional and communicative setting. In these settings, people witness a wide range of activities and discussions. What

others are doing in different areas of the compound or even in different compounds or on the road is a source of constant comment. As noted earlier, children are socialized to notice and attend. This demeanor is expected of lower-ranking persons. Hence, rarely does an action take place unnoticed or a conversation not overheard. Further, the openness of the domestic setting encourages multiple and multiparty conversations. It is common for several persons at once to hold conversations between the house and the road or between two houses. Further, within a single house, members will move in and out of several conversations that are taking place. As noted earlier, children come to understand something of Samoan social organization and epistemology through acquiring knowledge of the organization of communication in these settings (see also Chapter 7).

C.   Kinship relations

Members of a Samoan family are typically addressed by their personal or chiefly names but referred to by a relational term. These terms are distinguished primarily on the basis of generation and gender. Those in the same generation and of the same sex as the speaker are referred to as *uso*. The sister of a male is referred to as his *tuafafine*; the brother of a female as *tuagane*. These terms can apply to a wide range of kin relations close in age to the speaker, including children of one's parents' siblings, siblings of one's parents, and so on. A younger sibling, particularly one for whom daily care is provided, is called one's *tei*. The term *tei* is loaded with positive affect and is frequently used to evoke feelings of sympathy between siblings. One often hears the term preceded by the affect determiner *si* (meaning 'the dear') and the possessive pronoun *ou* 'your', producing the noun phrase *si ou tei* (in 'good speech') or *si ou kei* (in 'bad speech').

One's father, the *matai* of the compound, and other resident male kin in the father's generation are referred to as one's *tamaa*. One's mother is referred to as *tinaa*, as are certain other older female relatives, such as the wife of the household *matai* or siblings of a father or mother (if they are much older than the speaker). A woman refers to her children as *tamatane* 'son' and *tamafafine* 'daughter'; a man refers to his children as *atali'i* 'son' and *afafine* 'daughter'. The classification of these terms does not imply that all referents for a term are treated in similar fashion or have the same rights or obligations with repect to the speaker.

The most widely discussed of these relations is that between brother and sister. Both Mead (1928, 1930) and Shore (1977, 1982) indicate that sisters command considerable respect from their brothers. From about the age of eight or nine (Mead 1928), brothers and sisters take distance from one another, avoiding intimate activities such as sharing meals or sleeping in close contact. Shore portrays the brother–sister relation as that of server to served, as that of one who moves to one who remains stationary. Ideally, the sister is the refined member of the pair. Further, while brothers are more likely to assume authority in adulthood through *matai* titles, sisters exercise considerable control over the selection of new *matai* and the everyday activities of their brothers.

The relationship of brother to sister differs from that between *uso*, which is characterized rather as both intimate (Mead 1928) and competitive (Shore 1977, 1982). We have noted, for example, that brothers will compete for family *matai* titles.

D.   Economic activities

Members of a household cooperate to maintain family lands, to feed, clothe, and shelter family members, and to supply them with fine mats and cash needed for important occasions. Every able-bodied member of the residential group contributes to these ends, but their particular activities are organized in terms of gender, age, and title.

As in most of the world's societies, women's work differs to a certain extent from that of men. For example, weaving of mats for everyday and ceremonial purposes is restricted to women and young girls. As described by Shore (1977, 1982), women are associated more with lighter and cleaner work. Men more than women carry out heavy labor in the dense plantations that surround the village, whereas women's work tends to be centered in the compound itself or in the shallow waters of the reef that borders the village shore. In food preparation, cooking taro, breadfruit, fish, and other traditional foods in traditional open ovens dug into the ground is associated with men; cooking European food in European-style ovens and using European pots is associated with women.

The division of labor based on gender is complicated by the status distinctions of title and age. First of all, one often sees young untitled women or women who are wives of untitled men engaged in the carrying of very heavy loads and messy chores in the back of the compound and in the plantations as well. Similarly, one is far more likely to find younger men without titles in the village carrying out the heavy work than men with titles, particularly high-ranking titles.

With other members of their peer group (*aukegi*), children assist in a variety of tasks in the compound area and plantation. Younger children will clean up the compound and assist older children in food preparation, laundry, and dishwashing chores. School-age children are responsible for bringing foodstuffs from the plantation, from the sea, or from other sources to the compound. Throughout the afternoon these children can be seen carrying by themselves or in pairs baskets of taro, coconuts, or breadfruit, bunches of bananas, or bundles of firewood along the road or footpaths of the village. Many are found along the reef at low tide getting sea urchins or small fish for dinner.

In addition to doing village and plantation work, certain members of the household have salaried jobs. Most of these jobs take individuals outside the village. These adults will usually take the bus to the capital, Apia, each morning and return to the village in the evening. In some cases, the jobs take individuals outside the country, to American Samoa or to New Zealand for limited periods. As will be discussed in Chapter 10, the salary is earned by one individual but is seen as the property of the family and is turned over to the head of the family to be distributed and used as he sees fit.

In general, tasks are accomplished with the assistance of more than one person. The nature of the assistance varies according to social status and rank. The strong preference is for relatively high-ranking persons to carry out those aspects of the task that require low levels of physical activity. An important form of low-activity assistance is that of *tapua'i* 'support' or 'supporter'. The *tapua'i* facilitates the accomplishment of the task through supportive remarks and encouragement directed toward one or more persons who are engaged in or who have just completed some physical activity. Both the *tapua'i* and the one(s) performing the more active aspects of the task are seen as carrying out the task. In other cases, low-activity assistance in a task is in the form of directives from (stationary) higher-ranking to (moving) lower-ranking persons. And in other cases it is simply that the higher-ranking person is carrying out some other activity that does not require a great deal of movement. Thus, one with an *ali'i* 'high chief' title may sit in his house twisting fibers into twine for a new roof for one of the compound structures. His wife similarly may sit and weave pandanus leaves into roof shingles. In the meantime, their adult son may be standing, directing younger men who are actually on top of the structure, readying it for the roofing material. In this way, the task is cooperatively and collectively accomplished and is seen as such in Samoan custom. In Chapter 10 of this volume, Duranti and I compare this concept of task with that characteristic of classroom tasks in European-oriented schools in the village. We propose that as Samoan children are instructed in literacy skills in formal schooling settings, they are being socialized into a more individualistic view of task accomplishment.

IV.   THE SOCIAL ORGANIZATION OF CAREGIVING

A.   Range of caregivers

Passing by household compounds, we can see several characteristic scenes. In one house, a young boy is tucking a mosquito net around his infant sibling, who is fast asleep. His mother sits somewhat apart, watching and directing the boy as she weaves. In another house, a group of young girls are holding infants and toddlers on their laps while their mothers are fishing or otherwise engaged. When one of the infants cries, he may be brought to his mother to be fed. He may be rocked or carried in an attempt to soothe him. Or he may be admonished. In other houses, a toddler is snuggled next to a grandparent, watching, assisting, or following in his or her footsteps. In all of these scenes, one or more persons are doing what Samoans call *tausi le pepe* 'look(ing) after the baby'.

As reported by Mead (1928) and Kernan (1969), Samoan infants and toddlers are under the care of a number of older persons in the family. In this practice, they are not unique. As reported in Barry & Paxson (1971) and discussed in Weisner & Gallimore (1977), of a controlled sample of 186 societies most have a caregiving system in which other persons as well as the mother have caregiving roles. Further, in 43.5 percent of the societies, infants are 'cared for by others in IMPORTANT caretaker roles or cared for more than half the time by others' (Weisner & Gallimore 1977:170). In the societies examined, the role of the mother as caregiver diminishes as infants become toddlers; for only 19.4 percent of the sample was the mother the principal caregiver of children beyond infancy.

When their children are infants, Samoan mothers take primary responsibility for child care. However, the mother is usually assisted by others in the family, most typically by her or her husband's younger siblings, her other children, her mother, or her mother-in-law. The infant's father may provide occasional care during the early weeks of life, but generally he is not present in the house during the day. By far the most common pattern is to use older children who are siblings of the infant.

Mead (1928) reports that at the time of her observations on the island of Manu'a in American Samoa, sib caregiving was primarily the responsibility of older sisters. She reports that older brothers tended to carry out tasks and roam outside the compound, whereas their sisters tended to remain in the compound, providing child care. Although this gender preference prevails in the village of Falefaa, it does not appear as strong as described by Mead. In the families we observed, older brothers up to twelve or thirteen years of age often provided care. Those older than that were usually recruited for tasks in the plantation or elsewhere.

Mead (1928) also reports that an older sibling developed a special one-to-one relationship with a young sibling under care. This relationship is referred to by the term *tei*, as discussed in section III.C above. From our observations, this practice is not typical of current sibling child care. In the families we observed, the older siblings took turns in child-care tasks. The difference in these observations may stem from the changing role of European formal schooling in traditional Samoan communities. Currently, Samoan children from the age of five to adolescence regularly attend school. Most attend a local village school. We found that the families had an informal rota system of sibling caregivers. The children would take turns staying at home from school to help out in caregiving and other tasks. This meant that an infant or toddler would sometimes be in the care of one sibling and sometimes another. Where both older sisters and older brothers were available, I did not observe a tendency for older sisters to be kept at home more often than their brothers.

In some families, the older siblings regularly went to school and a younger sibling of the mother or father was recruited for the school hours. Once school let out, care was shifted to the children. Thus in the course of a day infants and toddlers are handled by a number of different relatives.

As described for other societies, Samoan mothers have a central role in the care of very small infants, but as an infant begins to crawl and then walk, responsibility is gradually shifted to other caregivers. When an infant is new born, the mother stays close by constantly, nursing and cuddling her child often. When the infant is several months old, he or she is left for periods of time with one or more siblings. These older siblings may bring their charges with them to other activities in the village, for example to watch a game or to visit with friends. At four or five in the afternoon, the village is dotted with groups of children holding their younger sibs on their laps or straddled on their hips.

While children assume a large share of child-care responsibilities, they are monitored by the adults in the family. Given the openness of the Samoan house, it is easy to see what the children are doing even at some distance. Everyone in the family is concerned to see that the children handle their younger siblings with consideration and is aware that this is not always the case. In Falefaa, as in many villages, there are women who specialize in massaging infants and small children. Among the ailments these women cure is muscular soreness that results from the way in which the infants are handled by their sib caregivers. When an infant cries for a long time during the night, a mother will often say that the child is *gau* 'sore' or 'sprained' from the way an older sibling has handled him or her. Early the next morning, she will wait in line for the masseuse to soothe and heal her child.

B.   The caregiving hierarchy

1.   High- and low-ranking caregivers

As noted in the first part of this chapter, one of the most salient features of Samoan society is that of *social stratification*. Titled persons have higher rank than untitled persons, and within each of these groups there are further rank distinctions.

Of concern here is the group of untitled persons. As noted earlier, the majority of household members are untitled. Within this group, rank distinctions are made on the basis of relative age and, to a lesser extent, relative generation. I have noted that caregiving, like many traditional tasks, is carried out by more than one person. Here I want to point out that caregiving, like other household activities, is also hierarchically organized. When two or more caregivers are present, they assess their position in the caregiving hierarchy. Certain persons will be assessed as *high-ranking caregivers* and others as *low-ranking caregivers*. For example, if an infant's mother and an older sibling are present, the mother is the high-ranking caregiver and the sibling the low-ranking caregiver. If there are two sibling caregivers, the older of the two will be the high-ranking caregiver. If the mother is alone with the mother of her husband or her own mother, then either of these older-generation women will be the higher-ranking caregiver.

It is important to note that the relative rank of a caregiver is fluid from one moment to the next as participation in the household setting fluctuates. If a twelve-year-old child is alone with the mother, then he or she is the lowest-ranking caregiver. If a younger sib walks in, then this child assumes this position. The twelve-year-old is of low rank with respect to the mother but high with respect to a younger sibling. If the mother leaves the setting, then the twelve-year-old assumes her role in the caregiving hierarchy, and so on.

In summary, it became evident to us as researchers that to understand the caregiving system it is crucial to assess the relative rank of those carrying out this activity. That is, what different caregivers do hinges more on their relation to other caregivers present, such as sibling, mother, grandmother, and so on, than on their kinship relation to the infant or child under care. A sib and a mother and a grandmother may provide child care in similar or dissimilar ways; it is their position in the caregiving hierarchy at any one moment that accounts for their behavior.

2.   Caregiving roles

Persons in Samoan society who have high status and/or who command respect in some social situation are expected to conduct themselves differently from others present. *Ali'i* 'high chiefs' are expected to conduct themselves differently from *tulaafale* 'orators'; titled persons, from untitled persons; guests, from hosts; and so on. Although there are specific behaviors expected of particular statuses in the village, there are certain demeanors that are generally associated with high position. Two of these are (1) low-activity level and (2) minimal involvement in activities of lower-ranking persons in the immediate surroundings.

In his ethnography of Samoa, Shore (1982) has pointed out the correspondence between social status and activity level. In a variety of social contexts, persons who have prestigious positions are expected to restrict their movements. They are expected to move about less often and at a slower pace than others who do not have this status. Thus, as I noted earlier in this chapter, in economic activities carried out by members of a household, the *matai* and his wife, particularly those of the older generation, tend to carry out tasks that require very little gross motor activity. Young untitled persons tend to perform the more active tasks. Generally, in a household, these persons serve food and fetch other items, such as cigarettes, for the household head. If a relatively high-ranking person goes outside the household compound, ideally he or she should move slowly and unencumbered. Usually those with *matai* titles walk on the road with their hands free from objects, except for an umbrella for protection from the sun or rain or perhaps a briefcase imported from New Zealand. Younger untitled persons are usually asked to carry needed items to the destination of the higher-status person.

Additionally those who are older or titled are expected to remain somewhat apart from the activities of younger or untitled persons in their surroundings. That is, they are to assume a somewhat detached or uninterested air. Though much takes place under the eyes of high-status persons, given the openness of Samoan living spaces, these persons often do not evidence awareness or interest. This does not mean that persons of high position never involve themselves in the goings-on of lower-ranking persons. This happens, but the involvement has social consequences. Generally, a high-status person will involve himself or herself when a problem arises that cannot be resolved by others. But this involvement defines the problem as a more serious one. The greater the involvement of high-status persons, the more serious the problem becomes and the heavier the negative sanction imposed on the offender.

The caregiving activities of high- and low-ranking caregivers are also organized in terms of these two behavioral parameters – activity level and involvement. The two parameters help us to understand both the nonverbal and verbal comportment of caregivers. Overwhelmingly, the more active child-care tasks are the responsibility of lower-ranking personnel, and the less active care is provided by the higher-ranking caregiver. Just as with other prestigious positions, the high-ranking caregiver is expected to be relatively stationary. If a younger caregiver is present, then the older caregiver will try to remain seated on a mat, while the other carries out various tasks requiring movement from one location to another. Younger caregivers are primarily responsible for removing soiled clothes, washing them, bringing clean clothes and food for the young child, and cleaning up spilled food and dishes once the child has eaten. They also carry young infants to their mothers for breastfeeding and/or cuddling until the infant has learned to crawl to the mother on his or her own. When the mother is through nursing her infant or otherwise comforting him or her, she will usually hand the infant back to a younger caregiver, who will either *fa'amoe* 'put to sleep' the infant, take the infant visiting, or simply watch over the infant inside the house.

Another manifestation of the distinction in activity levels among high- and low-ranking caregivers is in food distribution. If certain food items (such as bread, sugar cane, or 'twisties') have been given to the household or brought by a member of the family, higher-ranking caregivers decide who gets what and in what order and direct lower-ranking caregivers to carry out these decisions. That is, higher-ranking caregivers remain seated while lower-ranking caregivers fetch items and deliver them to children and other family members.

In other situations, a small child may simply be hungry and need food of a more substantial sort. In these cases, the higher-ranking caregiver directs one of the younger members of the household to bring food from the cookhouse to where she or he is seated. The higher-ranking caregiver may call out directly or tell the small child to call out. In the latter case, the child calls out on behalf of the higher-ranking caregiver, acting as his or her mouthpiece. The caregiver directs the child to call out to someone and often articulates for the small child the exact directive to be relayed, as in the example below.

(1) Iakopo I:2:132

Iakopo, aged two years and one month, with mother (A) and several other members of the household compound. Iakopo is eating a banana but wants more.

Iakopo	*A*
	Vala'au Kaukala aumai le fa'i.
	'Call to Kaukala to bring the banana.'
ala/'Kaukala.'	
	Ia vala'au.
	'So call.'
ala/'Kaukala.'	
ala/'Kaukala.'	
	Fogo aumai sau fa'i.
	'Call out to bring your banana.'
ala/'Kaukala.'	

If a younger caregiver is present, older caregivers also prefer not to involve themselves directly in the activities of small children in the imme- diate surroundings. If, for example, an argument takes place among a group of three-year-olds, the caregivers leaves it initially to these peers to resolve. If it is unresolvable at this level, the preference is for one of the lower- ranking caregivers to handle it and for the higher-ranking caregiver to become involved and take action only if this fails. Similarly, there is a preference for lower-ranking caregivers to attend to the spontaneous actions of small children (i.e. actions not motivated by some directive from the higher-ranking caregiver). Ideally, if lower-ranking caregivers are present, they will be responsible for ensuring that an infant or small child does not injure himself or herself or damage the property of another.

This preference for higher-ranking caregivers to be somewhat detached is sensitive to certain contextual variables. I have already noted that caregiving responsibilities vary as an infant matures. When the infant is very young, the mother is the primary caregiver. During the early months of her infant's life, the mother remains in close proximity to the infant and closely monitors the infant's well-being. In the first few weeks this monitoring is most intense, and the mother usually does not leave her house except for brief periods.

The extent to which a high-ranking caregiver can be detached also depends on the ages of the other caregivers available. If the younger caregivers are above the age of ten, then the higher-ranking caregiver is usually able to carry out some independent activity and not attend closely to the smaller children. If, on the other hand, the other caregivers are themselves quite young, for example, five or six years old, then the higher-ranking caregiver remains somewhat apart but monitors the younger caregivers, who in turn are monitoring smaller children. For example, a mother or grandmother with a six-year-old and a two-year-old will periodically direct the six-year-old to perform various child-care tasks for the two-year-old. If the two-year-old has a younger sibling, the six-year-old may direct the two-year-old to do something on his or her behalf. If a mother is alone with the two-year-old and the younger infant, then she may direct the two-year-old. One such interaction is illustrated below. In this example, a mother (Ak) is alone with her son Niulala (N), who is three years and three months old, and her infant daughter Sose (S), who is eight months old. Ak directs N to stop S, who is ripping up a picture.

(2) Niulala IV:312

N	Ak
	'Aua!' Fai 'Aua.'
	'"Don't!" Say "Don't."'
aua!/	
'Don't!'	Mai
	'Give (it).'
	Fai 'Aua.'
	'Say "Don't."'
aua/	
'Don't.'	

Of course, even if competent teenage caregivers are available, they are not always eager to carry out their caregiving duties or may be unwilling to share food, and an older person may have to prod them into action. These directives are different in tone and affect from those to very young caregivers; usually the higher-ranking caregiver is irritated and sharply orders the mature caregiver to carry out the expected acts.

During this period, the younger caregiver learns child-care skills and procedures. On a more general level, both the child under care and the child as caregiver are learning demeanors associated with social rank. There are those who move more and those who move less; those who move quickly and those who move slowly; those who attend and those who are detached; those who are directed and those who direct (i.e. control, have authority over) others.

To summarize, Samoan children are immersed in a highly stratified social environment. Hierarchical relations are manifest not only in the distinction between titled and untitled persons, but among untitled persons as well. Persons in the immediate environment of the child as well as the child himself or herself assume a particular social status vis-à-vis those copresent and vis-à-vis the social activity at hand. As Samoan interactions in public and private settings typically involve a number of participants, any one person may assume a number of social identities vis-à-vis others present. These social identities may involve a range of expected roles and demeanors. As bystanders and as direct participants, Samoan infants and young children early in their lives develop an understanding of these expectations. As noted in Chapter 1, small children are encouraged in a variety of ways to be sociocentric, to notice others and take their point of view (see also Chapter 5). This disposition is the core of respect, the expected demeanor of a lower-ranking party to a social interaction.

Young Samoan children evidence their understanding of social rank in the course of their language development. Indeed, as noted in Chapter 1, we can say that their understanding of social rank impacts their language development. For example, Samoan children's production of deictic verbs (e.g. *sau* 'come', *alu* 'go', *aumai* 'give, bring', and *ave* 'take') is deeply affected by their understanding of just who can use these lexical items to whom and in what type of speech-act context (see Platt 1982, 1986). Children under the age of three avoid using deictic verbs (such as *sau* 'come') inappropriate to their speaker–addressee relationship and prefer more appropriate alternatives (even though the alternatives are semantically more complex than the inappropriate forms). Samoan children also acquire an understanding of social order through the organization of directives and responses in domestic settings. Responses to such speech acts display for the child the verbal and nonverbal demeanors expected of different parties copresent, including the child, siblings, and other members of the household. The interface of social order and language development is pursued in Chapters 7 through 10.

5.   Ergative case marking: variation and acquisition

I.   INTRODUCTION

This chapter, along with Chapter 6, considers the interaction of grammar, conceptual relations, and social context. With respect to social context, the discussion will focus primarily on the social distribution of case marking and word-order patterns across a range of speakers and social settings. The discussion will relate these patterns of language usage to children's acquisition of case marking and word order and more generally consider the interface of social and cognitive processes in language development. The reader should note that this chapter and the next will not analyze patterns of language usage specifically for their cultural import, linking patterns of speaking to local ideologies and values.

The present chapter will examine how the notions of agent and patient are encoded morphologically in Samoan grammar and the extent to which this morphology actually characterizes spontaneous speech of adults and children recorded in the course of our field research. Chapter 6 will attend to alternative ways available in Samoan for encoding these transitive relations and their impact on language acquisition. Both chapters are centrally relevant to current acquisition research, in that linguistic transitivity is reported to be one of the earliest grammatical relations encoded by young children acquiring their first language (for example, Bever 1970; Bloom 1970, 1973; Bowerman 1973; R. Brown 1973; Greenfield & Smith 1976; Radulovic 1975; Schieffelin 1986). On such evidence, Slobin proposes that one of the earliest or prototypical scenes children map onto grammatical structure is the Manipulative Activity Scene (1986). The Manipulative Activity Scene is a conceptual gestalt composed of several concepts including 'the concepts representing the physical objects themselves, along with sensorimotor concepts of physical agency involving the hand and perceptual–cognitive concepts of change of state and change of location, along with some overarching notions of efficacy and causality, embedded in interactional formats of requesting, giving, and taking' (1986:1175).

Interest in transitive relations has focused on the underlying explanations for these patterns of acquisition, including language-specific and more general cognitive and perceptual considerations that may impact children's language-making capacity. Certain discussions of transitivity in acquisition research have been centrally concerned with locating the source of children's expression of these relations in linguistic or nonlinguistic cognitive capacities (see Bloom 1970; Chomsky 1975; McNeill 1970; Piatelli–Palmarini 1980), and other discussions have adopted a more eclectic approach in which children's grammars have multiple possible origins (Karmiloff-Smith 1979; Slobin 1986).

One of the major topics addressed in discussions of children's expression of transitivity has been the conceptual and grammatical status of referring expressions associated with transitive verbs. Specifically a major issue has been the relation between the notion of agent and grammatical subject on the one hand and the notion of patient and direct object on the other. Is the child marking the notion of agent or the grammatical notion of subject? Is she or he marking patient or direct object? Are subjects and direct objects (and hence perhaps other fundamental grammatical relations) rooted initially in the transitive relations of agent and patient? Regardless of the perspective taken on each of these questions, the vast majority of these discussions (1) have focused on nominative–accusative languages, and (2) have assumed a particular relation between semantic roles and grammatical relations. What is represented by the grammatical notion of subject in adult grammar, for example, is taken for granted; only the developmental point at which children evidence knowledge of this grammatical notion is disputed. The acquisition study presented here challenges these assumptions in that it documents the acquisition of an ergative language, where mapping of transitive relation onto grammatical relations such as subject and object is both different from what happens in nominative–accusative languages and quite complex.

Ergative–absolutive languages have received considerable attention within linguistics, because they appear to violate (to varying degrees) the notion that 'subject' is a universal, basic grammatical relation (Comrie 1978, 1979; Dixon 1979; Plank 1979). In contrast to nominative–accusative languages, these languages distinguish morphologically intransitive subject and transitive subject on the one hand, and on the other treat intransitive subject and transitive object as a single morphological category (absolutive). Ergative languages differ in the extent to which they are morphologically and syntactically ergative, many being both accusative and ergative on the morphological level and others being 'entirely accusative at the syntactic level' (Dixon 1979:59).

Languages with ergative case-marking systems represent a different (vis-à-vis accusative languages) model for a language-acquiring child. In the majority of cases, the child is exposed to a morphological system that is completely or partially ergative–absolutive but to a syntactic system that is predominantly nominative–accusative. In terms of the acquisition process, the child must become competent in using two sets of grammatical distinctions on the morphological and/or syntactic level. One could reasonably predict that this situation would present cognitive difficulties for a young child, difficulties not faced by a child acquiring a language with nominative–accusative case marking.

Two studies of the acquisition of ergative case marking have recently been completed – Schieffelin on Kaluli (1979, 1986a) and Pye on Quiché Mayan (1979, 1980). Both of these languages are split ergative in the sense that both ergative and accusative distinctions are made on the morphological and syntactic level. The results of both studies show that ergative case marking is productively acquired before the age of three, with Kaluli case marking acquired as early as twenty-seven months (Schieffelin 1979:293). Ergative distinctions, then, do not appear too difficult for a young child to acquire and express.

Samoan is predominantly a morphologically ergative language, with most syntactic operations sensitive to nominative–accusative distinctions (see section III below). Unlike the acquisition studies mentioned earlier, the present study indicates that ergative case marking appears quite late in Samoan child language, with children between the ages of three and four using the case marking in less than 5 percent of the obligatory grammatical contexts and younger children not using the case marking at all.

To account for the difference in rate of acquisition, two possible sources are considered. One concerns perceptual features of Samoan ergative case marking. Here a comparison is made between Kaluli (the study for which detailed information is available) and Samoan ergative case marking in terms of acquisition-facilitating and acquisition-delaying physical attributes (Slobin 1973, 1975, 1982, 1986).

The second source concerns the sociolinguistic status of ergative case marking within traditional Samoan communities. A comparison with Kaluli indicates major differences (from Samoan) in usage patterns. The most important of these differences is that in Samoan the ergative case marker is used variably, constrained by social identity of speaker and degree of social distance between speaker and addressee. In particular, the case marking is relatively rare in the speech of household members and other intimates.

These results are consequential for (1) *language typology*, in that they indicate that the expression of ergative–absolutive distinctions may not only be grammatically constrained in a language, but sociologically constrained as well, i.e. sociolinguistically variable; (2) *acquisition studies of case marking*, in that they indicate that registral status of particular inflections is an important variable (along with perceptual constraints) in an account of acquisition strategies; and (3) *studies of input*, in that they indicate that caregiver speech may form part of a larger speech register – in the case of Samoan, the register of intimates, particularly women.

II.   ERGATIVE CASE MARKING IN SAMOAN

As noted in Chapter 3, ergative–absolutive distinctions in Samoan are expressed through nominal case marking. The transitive subject (A) is preceded by the particle *e* only when the transitive subject follows the verb (VAO, VOA, OVA). Intransitive subjects (s) following the verb and all direct objects (o) receive no case marking. The difference in marking is presented in (1) and (2) below:

(1) *Transitive sentence*

VAO:	Na	fasi	e	le	tama	Sina.
	PST	his	ERG	ART	boy	Sina
VOA:	Na	fasi	Sina	e	le	tama.
	PST	hit	Sina	ERG	ART	boy

'The boy hit Sina.'

(2) *Intransitive sentence*

VS:	'olo'o	moe	le	tama.
	PRES PROG	sleep	ART	boy

'The boy is sleeping.'

Another restriction on the expression of ergative case marking in Samoan concerns the type of transitive construction in use. Chung (1978) has distinguished two types of transitive constructions in Samoan. The first contains *canonical* transitive verbs and marks the subject with the ergative particle *e*.[1] Canonical transitive constructions are formed from such verbs as *fai* 'make', *fasi* 'hit', *ave* 'take', *tape* 'to kill (an animal)'.

The second category of transitive construction Chung refers to as containing middle verbs, such as *va'ai* 'see', *mana'o* 'want', *tano* 'touch', *tilotilo* 'gaze at', *fa'alogologo* 'listen to', *alofa* 'love'. Middle verbs are generally (but not exclusively) verbs of perception, cognition, desire, and emotion. Middle-verb constructions, without modification through suffixation (transitive suffix) (see Chung 1978), do not mark subjects with the ergative particle. Further, unlike objects of canonical transitive verbs, middle-verb objects are marked by the preceding particle *i* (if common noun), *iaa* (if

---

[1] In Hopper and Thompson's (1980) framework, canonical transitive clauses tend to be characterized by more features of transitivity than do middle-verb constructions, e.g. expressing actions that are volitional, punctual, telic, whose agents are high in potency, and whose patients tend to be individuated and highly affected by the action specified. Samoan distinguishes agents of such constructions with the particle *e*.

proper noun or pronoun), or *iaa te* (if pronoun).[2] The one outstanding exception to this grouping is the verb *iloa* 'to know', which behaves like a canonical transitive verb in that its subject is marked by the ergative particle *e*.

Middle-verb constructions

VSO:	E	alofa	le	tama	i		lona	tinaa.
	PRES	love	ART	boy	PRT		his	mother
VOS:	E	alofa	i	lona	tinaa	le	tama.	
	PRES	love	PRT	his	mother	ART	boy	

'A/the boy loves his mother.'

In Samoan, certain syntactic processes operate on a nominative–accusative basis while others operate on an ergative–absolutive basis. Thus, syntactic operations such as subject-to-object raising and cliticization (Anderson & Chung 1977; Chung 1978) as well as verb conjunction do not distinguish between intransitive and transitive subjects, as in a nominative–accusative system:

Verb conjunction

Intransitive and	La		e	oo	ma
transitive verb:	they DUAL		PRES	go PL	and

'a'ai   le   suka.
eat PL   ART   sugar
'They are going and eating the sugar' or 'They are eating the sugar while they are going.'

Other processes, such as nominalization, however, distinguish ergative from absolutive constituents (Chung 1978):

Nominalizations

Intransitive:	le	o'o	mai	o	'oulua
	ART	arriving	DEICT	GEN	you two

'your (two) arriving'

Transitive:	le	faiga	e	'oulua
	ART	doing	ERG	you two

'your (two) doing'

III.   SOCIOLOGICAL CONSTRAINTS ON ERGATIVITY IN SAMOAN

A good deal has been written on the morphological and syntactic scope of ergativity across languages, but little is known about the sociological scope

---

[2] The preposition *i* in Samoan also marks temporal or spatial location, instrumentality, and comparison (Milner 1966; Tuitele & Kneubuhl 1978; Tuitele, Sapolu & Kneubuhl 1978). Tuitele et al. treat middle verbs as intransitive verbs, based on the uses of *i* specified above.

Table 5.1. *Ergative case marking in adult Samoan speech*
(AG = agent; V = verbal; ECM = ergative case marking)

Situation	AG/ Total (%)	POSTV AG (%)	Total ECM (%)	POSTV ECM (%)
Informal language of women to female adults & children (family members) (150 clauses)	40.0 (60)	20.0 (30)	4.0 (6)	20.0 (6)
Informal language of men to female/male adults & children (family members) (60 clauses)	40.0 (24)	30.0 (18)	5.0 (3)	16.6 (3)
Informal language of women to female adults (nonfamily members) (120 clauses)	52.5 (63)	29.2 (35)	13.3 (16)	45.7 (16)
Informal language of men to male adults (nonfamily members) (50 clauses)	40.0 (20)	32.0 (16)	24.0 (12)	75.0 (12)
Formal language of titled men to one another in discussion portion of village council meetings (56 clauses)	55.3 (31)	39.3 (22)	28.6 (16)	72.7 (16)

of ergative morpho-syntax within a language. That is, little is known about the extent to which speakers mark ergative–absolutive distinctions and the extent to which use of the case marking is sensitive to variation in social context (Gumperz 1972, 1977; Hymes 1972, 1974; Labov 1963, 1966, 1972).

A study of adult Samoan speech across several socially significant contexts indicates that the ergative nominal case marker *e* is used variably across these contexts. The use of the marker is sensitive to the social distance obtaining between speaker and hearer and to the sex of the speaker.[3]

The range of variation in the use of ergative case marking in adult Samoan speech is presented in Table 5.1. Five social situations are represented. In the *first situation*, women of the same extended family are talking to one another and to their children within the household compound. In the *second situation*, men are speaking to both male and female family members, adult and child. In these two situations, speech to child was not distinguished from speech to another adult, because, first, in all these situations there were many persons participating in the interaction, and

[3] As noted in Chapter 3, the social distribution of the ergative case marker is characteristic of other morphological elements in Samoan. That is, the ergative marker is one of a set of morphological features that vary across social contexts. Assessment of the distribution of these features is the object of ongoing research.

second, typically assertions are not directed to one particular addressee but rather to the participants as a group. In this sense, assertions differ from directives, which are typically addressed to a single recipient and are often preceded by a vocative. Many fewer utterances of men (versus women) inside households were collected. This difference is a result of the fact that men do not spend much of their time in this context. They will, rather, spend most of their waking hours working on the plantation, working in the capital, participating in formal gatherings of titled men within the village, or relaxing with their village peers. The data used here are drawn primarily from those men who stopped by their houses unexpectedly to report an incident, who were ill and not able to work, or who were passing by between tasks. The fourth and fifth situations are more representative of men's speech. The *fourth situation* is that of relaxed informal talk among male peers (outside the family) and includes both untitled men's speech and titled men's speech. The *fifth situation* is situated in the highly formal village councils in which only titled persons can participate. In this sample, only titled men were participants. The data are drawn not from the more conventionalized oratory (*lauga*) within these meetings, but rather from the discussion portions (*talanoaga*) that follow oratorical speeches (Duranti 1981a, b). These data are drawn from a larger analysis by Duranti (in progress) of word order and case marking in these social situations. The *third situation* represented in Table 5.1 contrasts with the other situations in that it displays informal women's speech to nonfamily members. The data are drawn from a group of village women who are seated outside picking weeds on the compound of their pastor and gossiping with one another.

What do these data indicate? There are two important patterns of variation. The first is that there is a major difference in percentage of ergative case marking in speech of family members and in speech of nonfamily members. Ergative case marking rarely appears when speakers are addressing members of their own household. Out of the entire corpus of canonical transitive assertions and yes–no questions in these contexts, women used the case marking 4 percent and 5 percent of the time. In those environments in which ergative case marking is formally required (postverbal agent expressed), women used the marking 20 percent and men 16.6 percent of the time. These percentages contrast with those characteristic of case marking in speech to nonfamily members. Women's speech to nonfamily members shows more than twice the percentage (45.7) of ergative case marking in postverbal environments as that of women's speech to family members; men's speech to nonfamily members shows nearly five times the percentage of ergative case marking (75 and 72.7) in postverbal environments as that of men's speech to family members.

From these data, we can infer that social distance between speaker and audience is an important constraint on the use of ergative case marking. The greater the social distance, the more likely it is that a speaker will use the marking.

A second important pattern of variation is linked to sex of speaker. While both men and women exhibit low frequencies of usage of ergative case marking in intimate settings, men appear to use the marking a much higher percentage of the time in other contexts. In the intimate settings, men and women do not show much difference in their percentage of use of ergative case marking in postverbal environments: men, 16.6 percent; women, 20 percent. In informal speech to nonfamily members, however, there is a large gap between the two groups of speakers: men, 75 percent; women, 45.7 percent.

Combining the two patterns just presented, we can predict that ergative case marking will be used more between speakers in more socially distant relationships; furthermore, in less intimate settings, it will be used more by men than by women.

Instances in which speakers omit the ergative case marker are illustrated in examples (1) and (2) below.[4]

(1) N50:131: Women's speech in household Niulala (N) and his sister (S).

Context	*Speech*
(N goes out of house)	

Ak (to N): Niulala,   sau   i –!
                Niulala   come here!
                'Niulala, come here!'

Ak (to S): Kago mai   i.
                touch bring here
                'Get and bring him here.'

(S follows N out)

N: le   ke –   le   alu
    NEG TENSE/ASP NEG go
    koe   fo'i mai// ii /   S: // Ia   savali
    again return   here   okay walk

---

[4] As noted in Chapter 3, spoken Samoan has two major speech varieties, one relying on /t/, /n/, and /r/ and the other on /k/, /ŋ/, and /l/. These are referred to as Samoan in the 't' and Samoan in the 'k' or 'good Samoan' and 'bad Samoan'. Household interaction and most spontaneous language use takes place in the 'k' register, but occasionally there are switches to the 't' register. We use conventional orthographic symbols adopted by Samoans to express these varieties. In particular, the velar /ŋ/ is expressed in the transcripts as 'g'. Aside from these conventions, transcription procedures used in conversation analysis (Schenkein 1978) are employed here. The reader should note that examples of speech phenomena are primarily colloquial Samoan, in which features of formal or literary Samoan (such as tense/aspect marking, complementizers, glottal stops, vowel lengthening) are variably present. In transcribing the children's speech behavior, the 'focus' child's speech is placed to the left of the speech of others participating in the interaction.

'I'm not going, I'm coming back   kogu   fale   ma   pisa.
here.'   inside house   CONJ   noise
                                          'Okay, go inside the house
                                          because you're making a
                                          rumpus.'
((N whines))   Sau   loa.
                                          come   now
                                          'Come now.'

                                          Ia   'ai   loa   Ko'oko'o   falaoa.
                                          okay   eat   now   Ko'oko'o   bread
                                          'Okay, Ko'oko'o (is going to) eat now
                                          (your) bread.'

(2) P10–300: Women's speech in household

S is with her daughter's daughter, Pesio (P), and another child (N).

Context   *Speech*

(P puts
plate of rice at back edge
of house and begins to eat.
N goes to P holding
pussy cat. P cries. N cries.
P goes to S, who has witnessed this
event. S wipes P's tears and nose,
rhythmically comforting P by
repeating:)

                                          S: 'uma   loa.
                                              finish now
                                              'It's finished now.'

                                              'uma   loa.
                                              finish now
                                              'It's finished now.'

                                              'uma   loa.
                                              finish now
                                              'It's finished now.'

                                              'o   le   aa?
                                              TOP   the   what
                                              'What is it?'

                                              'o   le   aa?
                                              TOP   the   what
                                              'What is it?'

                                              'o   le   aa?
                                              TOP   the   what
                                              'What is it?'

P: 'uma   ai   au/
    finish bite   me
    'The biting me is finished.'

                                          'ua   'ai   oe. ((pause))
                                          TENSE/ASP   bite   you
                                          'It has just bitten you.'

=〉
'ua		'ai	oe	le	pusi?
TENSE/ASP		bite	you	the	pussycat

'The pussycat has just bitten you?'

=〉
'ua		fela'u	oe	le
TENSE/ASP		scratch	you	the

pusi?
pussycat
'The pussycat has just scratched you?'

=〉
'ua		fela'u	oe	le
TENSE/ASP		scratch	you	the

pusi?
pussycat
'The pussycat has just scratched you?'
((soft))

Ia	'uma	loa.
PRT	finish	now

'Okay, it's finished now.'

Ia	'uma	loa.
PRT	finish	now

'Okay, it's finished now.'

Ia	'uma	loa.
PRT	finish	now

'Okay, it's finished now.'

Examples (3) through (6) illustrate the use of the ergative marker in spontaneous adult speech.

(3) Young men are talking about a boy, Pegi, who was put in jail.

T:
... auaa	faimai	ua		falepuipui	lesi	kama.
because	say	TENSE/ASP		put in jail	the other	boy

'Because they say the other boy has been put in jail.'

Loka.	P.
locked.	P

'Locked up. P.'

S: Oi.
'Oh.'

T:
Ke	iloa	P?
TENSE/ASP	know	P?

'Do you know P?'

S:
Ke	iloa	P?
TENSE/ASP	know	P?

'I know P.'

S: Aiseaa?
'Why?'
(1.0)

T:
O	le	sala	le	ka'avale.
TOP	the	fine	the	truck

'It was because of the fine of the truck.'

=〉
Ia	'ua		koe	kakala	e	S	ma	–	ma	U.
PRT	TENSE/ASP		again	release	ERG	S	and	–	and	U

'Now S. and U. have just released him.'

(4) Young men are talking about a Dracula film, which only T has seen.

    T: Leaga   leaga   le   amio   o   le   kama,   sole.
         bad   bad   the   character of   the   guy   brother
         'The character of the guy is bad bad, brother.'

         Gai   keige,   sole.
         poor dear girls   brother
         'Poor dear girls, brother.'

 =〉 S: 'ai   e   le   kama   a?
         bite   ERG   the   guy   right
         'The guy bit them, right?'

(5) *Fono* 'meeting' in the village about the elections

 =〉 M: Soli   e   Lufilufi   le   kakou   mavaega.
         violate ERG   Lufilufi ART our (INCL PL) promise
         'Lufilufi violated our promise.'

(6) *Fono*, April 7, 1979 – third speech of the day

 =〉 F: Ia.   O   gei   lava aso   uma o   aso   uma   a
         PRT TOP these very days all   TOP days all   PRT
         ga   fa'apa'ia e   Ieova.
         TENSE/ASP blessed   ERG Jehovah
         'So. All these very days, *all* these days, were blessed by Jehovah.'

IV.   ACQUISITION OF ERGATIVE CASE MARKING SYSTEM

A.   Results

The most outstanding result of the longitudinal study is that Samoan children between the ages of two and four rarely use the ergative marker *e* in their spontaneous speech. The frequency with which the ergative marker appears in canonical transitives of the five sample children is displayed in Table 5.2.[5] We can see that the three youngest children, Matu'u, Iakopo, and Pesio, use no ergative case marking whatsoever. The next-oldest children, Naomi and Niulala, used the inflection in one utterance (each) only, representing 0.9 percent and 0.7 percent respectively of the total canonical transitives and 10.1 percent and 13.5 percent respectively of the transitives with postverbal agents in their corpora. These extremely low percentages led me to examine the speech of an older sibling, Maselino, who was not one of the focal children in the study and was present only

     [5] A list of canonical transitive verb types used by each child in each session is listed in Appendix II. As can be seen, children use a wide range of such verbs. Those verbs whose agents received the nominal ergative marker are followed by 'ERG'. These verbs are so few in number that no generalizations can be made (for the use of the case marker) based on semantic properties of verbs.

Table 5.2. *Agency and ergative case marking in spontaneous novel canonical transitives*

(v = verbal; AG = agents; ECM = ergative case marking)

Child/age at onset	Total utterances	Utterances with AG (%)	POSTV AG (%)	Total ECM (%)	POSTV ECM (%)
Matu'u/2:1	76	22.4 (17)	14.5 (11)	0	0
Iakopo/2:1	50	30.0 (15)	12.0 (6)	0	0
Pesio/2:3	113	13.25 (15)	4.42 (5)	0	0
Naomi/2:10	109	15.6 (17)	10.1 (11)	0.9[a] (1)	9.1 (1)
Niulala/2:11	148	21.7 (32)	13.5 (20)	0.7 (1)	5.0 (1)
Maselino/3:3	86	36.0 (31)	33.7 (29)	4.6 (4)	13.8 (4)

[a] Partial repetition.

intermittently during the recording sessions. The percentage of ergative case marking was higher in the speech of this child – 4.6 percent of the total canonical transitives and 33.7 percent of these with postverbal agents. However, these figures are still extremely low and fail to provide evidence that ergative case marking is part of the productive competence of the child.

An instance in which the ergative case marker *e* is both omitted and expressed is presented in example (7).

(7) Niulala, three years and four months
(N has noticed and talked about a
tractor moving along the road. He
then begins to scare and threaten
the others present.)
N: sua   okou ((error))
     strike down you PL
     'It's going to strike you down.'
=>   sua   oukou e   maakou   lol'/
     strike you   ERG our EXCL   truck
     'Our truck is going to strike you down.'
     sua   okou ((error)) maakou   loli   fou/
     strike down you   our EXCL truck   new
     'Our new truck is going to strike you down.'

Examples (8) through (10) illustrate instead instances in which children use the ergative case marker in their speech.

(8) Na, two years and eleven months.

Context   *Speech*

(Na hits mother; asks where her
mango is)

Na: ikae   uma   mago
     shit   finish mango
     'Shit, the mango is finished.'

     uma   mago   a'u/
     finish mango   my
     'My mango is finished.'

     tae   tae   uma   mago/
     shit shit finish mango
     'Shit, shit, the mango is
     finished.'

     uma   mago   a'u/
     finish mango   my
     'My mango is finished.'

     uma   ai/
     finish eat
     'The eating is finished.'

                                    MOTHER: Ai   e   ai?
                                             eat   ERG   who
                                             'Who ate it?'

        (?)   fea?
                                             where
                                             'Where?'

     uma/
     finish
     'Finished.'
=>   'ai   e   oe.
     eat   ERG   you
     '*You* ate it.'

(9) Maselino, three years and eight months

Context   *Speech*

     (Pesio (2; 7) is crying, looking at
     her father. Another child, K, has
     hit her, though this has not been
     mentioned. Her father wants her
     to stop crying.)

PESIO ((crying))

                                    FATHER: ((soft)) (alu
                                                         go
                                             loa)/
                                             now
                                    OLDER SISTER: Pesio
                                                   Pesio
=>   MASELINO: Fasi // (a)   K
                                               hit   (ERG)   K
                                               'K hit her.'
                                    ELENOA: //K
                                             'K'

     =>   MASELINO: Fasi   e   K.
                       hit   ERG   K
                       'K hit her.'

(10) Maselino, three years and six months

     (Maselino decides to scare
     another child by using a
     common scare expression about
     mother's absence. He turns to this
     child, G.)

     =>   M: G! G!   le   ua   ai   e   le //   pua'a   K.*
                       DEICT   TENSE/ASP   eat   ERG   ART   pig   K
                 'G! G! Now the pig ate K.'

* G's mother.

         .
         .
         .

         fiu   e   sue
         tired   COMP   search
         'They are tired of searching.'
         fiu   e   kue*   aku
         tired   COMPL   search   DEICT
         'They are tired of searching around.'
         * Phonological error.

     =>   le   ua   'ai   e   le   pua'a
         DEICT   TENSE/ASP   eat   ERG   ART   pig
         'Now the pig ate her.'
         le   ua   'ai   e   le   povi   Gike
         DEICT   TENSE/ASP   eat   ERG   ART   cow   Gike
         'Now the cow ate her, Gike.'

         .
         .
         .

     =>   //ua   'ai   e   le   povi   a   K.
         TENSE/ASP   eat   ERG   ART   cow   PRT   K
         'The *cow* ate Koe.'

B.   Discussion of results

Several factors could account for the infrequency of the ergative particle *e* in the speech of young Samoan children.

1.   Expression of agents (as major constituents)

We can see from Table 5.2 that these results are linked to the low frequency of agents expressed in transitive assertion and yes–no questions (average percentage of agents expressed as major constituents: 21 (117 utterances)).

This explanation would not account, however, for why the case marker is not used when agents *are* expressed as major constituents and appear after the verb. Young children appear to use constructions in which ergative case marking is required (according to speakers' judgments of 'good Samoan' – *tautala lelei*), yet they do not use it.

2.   Perceptual characteristics of ergative case marking

A second possible determinant for the low expression of the ergative case marker in children's speech concerns the perceptual saliency of the marker in Samoa. Slobin (1973, 1975, 1982) has argued that the acquisition of grammatical morphemes is sensitive to whether or not the morphological items are postposed, syllabic, stressed, obligatory (rather than optional), tied to the noun, consistent with word-order patterns, rationally ordered, nonsynthetic, used exclusively for grammatical (versus pragmatic) functions, regular, consistently applied to all pro-forms, and distinct (i.e. without homonymous functors). If the morphological system of a language is characterized by the presence of these features, children do not find difficulties in acquiring it and do not, for example, prefer word order as an initial strategy for encoding semantic roles. A system of grammatical morphemes that displays these features, such as that of Turkish, is acquired more quickly than one that does not, such as that of Serbo-Croatian. Nonetheless, Slobin argues, these morphological systems are all usually learned during the preschool period, with Turkish children competent at the two-word period (1982).

The ergative particle in Samoan has a number of perceptually distressful characteristics (in terms of Slobin's list). As Table 5.3 shows, it is characterized by only five of the twelve features of perceptual saliency (i.e. it is syllabic, consistent with word-order patterns, regular, applied to all proforms, and has no homonymous case markers).[6] This fact could certainly affect the acquisition of the case marker by Samoan children.

However, if we examine features of Kaluli case marking, acquired much earlier than Samoan case marking, we find that it too has few acquisition-facilitating features. Table 5.3 shows that, like Samoan, it is characterized by only four of these features. In both languages the ergative marker is not

---

[6] Whether or not the morphological marker *e* should be considered as a lexical item distinct from the noun that follows is a relatively difficult issue, as is generally the case with unstressed morphemes in languages. As partial evidence of this independent nature, one may mention that lexical modifiers of the agent noun can appear between the particle *e* and the noun, e.g.:

Na   fa'a'ai   e   lenei   'aiga   le   nu'u.
PST   feed   ERG   this   family   ART   village
'This family fed the village.'

Table 5.3. *Features of Samoan and Kaluli ergative case markers*

Feature	Samoan	Kaluli
Postposed	–	+
Syllabic	+	+
Stressed	–	?[a]
Obligatory	–	–
Tied to noun	–	+
Rationally ordered	N.A.	N.A.
Consistent with word order	+	+
Nonsynthetic	N.A.	N.A.
Only grammatical functions	–	–
Regular	+	–
Applied to all pro-forms	+	–
No homonymous case markers	+	–

[a] The prosodic system of this tone language has not been worked out.

obligatory in that it is subject to morpho-syntactic constraints. As noted, in Samoan the marker appears only on transitive subjects that follow the verb; in Kaluli it appears only when the transitive subject immediately precedes the verb (OAV). In Samoan, the marker appears on all pro-forms except clitics (and these always appear before the verb). In Kaluli, the restriction is much more severe in that no personal pronoun can be marked with the ergative suffix; the ergative marker appears only with full nouns and demonstratives. Further, unlike Samoan, Kaluli has homonymous case markers. The same particle is used to mark the genitive and instrumental cases (Schieffelin 1979, 1986a).

With the knowledge that Kaluli ergative marking is acquired earlier than Samoan, it is plausible to infer that the acquisition-facilitating features that distinguish Kaluli have a greater impact on the acquisition process than those that distinguish Samoan. That the ergative marker is postposed and tied to the noun in Kaluli whereas the Samoan marker is preposed and independent of the noun may account for the differential rates of acquisition between these two groups of children.

3.   Sociolinguistic characteristics of ergative case marking

However, one of the most important differences between Kaluli and Samoan case marking concerns the feature 'obligatory'. This difference is not captured in Table 5.3, in which both case markers are characterized as 'not obligatory'. The difference is, rather, in the nature of the restriction constraining the use of the ergative marker in each of the languages. Kaluli and

Samoan both impose syntactic and semantic constraints on the appearance of ergative case marking. In this sense, the case marking is sometimes there and sometimes not in both languages. On the other hand, Samoan and Kaluli differ in the extent to which the case marking is used, given that the appropriate grammatical conditions are met.

As discussed so far in section IV, the use of ergative case marking is situationally restricted in adult Samoan; it is used more by men than by women and is more frequent in speech to nonfamily members than in speech among household intimates. If we then relate this to Samoan child language, we can see that the ergative case marking is statistically most salient in those environments to which the child is least exposed. Children up to the age of three or three and a half spend nearly all of their time within the household compound. The large bulk of discourse structures to which they are exposed are those between family members. Further, as noted earlier, it is women rather than men who spend time in the house during daylight hours. Thus, it is women's speech that provides the primary adult input to the language-acquiring Samoan child. Children do not acquire the ergative case-marking system rapidly primarily because it is not characteristic of the speech behavior of those around them.

The use of the ergative case marker in Kaluli, on the other hand, is not constrained by the social status of the speaker nor by the social relationship between speaker and others present. When the transitive subject appears immediately before the verb (OAV) and meets the necessary semantic criteria, Kaluli speakers must and do use the ergative case marker. Pye (1980) notes that Quiché Mayan speakers also use the ergative case marker with relatively high frequency.

The difference in the sociolinguistic status of the ergative marker between Samoans on the one hand and Kaluli and Quiché Mayan on the other provides an important source for understanding why Samoan children use the ergative case marker less frequently and later in developmental time.

V.   IMPLICATIONS OF THIS STUDY

A.   Acquisition of morphology

This study indicates that in assessing why particular morphological features are acquired when they are, researchers need to attend to their social salience. In the case of Samoan ergative case marking, perceptual factors, e.g. the fact that the ergative particle *e* appears before the agent rather than postpositionally, enter into the acquisition process. However, such perceptual characteristics of morphological features are relevant to the extent that the features themselves are actually in use in the speech environment of the language-acquiring child. If two languages under comparison share similar sociolinguistic and grammatical constraints on the expression of ergative case marking, then differences in other perceptual characteristics of the marking in each language play a very important role in accounting for acquisition patterns. However, where significant differences exist in environments and frequency of use, the differences emerge as the significant factors in influencing when a child will productively use the case marking. In comparing Samoan and Kaluli acquisition patterns, the fact that ergative case marking is sociologically constrained (variable) in Samoan but not in Kaluli mature speech best accounts for why Samoan children acquire the marking later than do Kaluli children.

B.   Caregiver register

In the past fifteen years, there has been considerable interest in the speech of those providing care for the language-acquiring child. Typically, in isolating features of caregiver speech, the researcher compares caregiver speech to the child with caregiver speech to the researcher (e.g. Garnica 1977; Newport 1976). This comparison focuses only on the status of the researcher as a member of the same generation as the caregiver and the child as a member of the next lower generation.

From a sociological perspective, such a comparison evidences major flaws. In particular, it fails to consider other relevant characteristics of the social relationships under analysis. The researcher may be of the same generation (an adult), but the researcher is not typically an intimate of the caregiver. The child may be of a lower generation than the caregiver, but the child shares an intimate relationship with the caregiver. Given this, it becomes difficult to sort out whether differences that exist between caregiver–researcher and caregiver–child speech are functions of age and/or maturity factors or of social-distance factors or of both. To sort out these effects, the analysis should minimally compare language among intimates of the same generation with language of intimates across generations (intimate adult–child relationships) and language of nonintimates of the same generation with language of nonintimates across generations (nonintimate adult–child relationships).

In the case of Samoan, the low frequency of ergative case marking in the speech of women with children is not a defining feature of the caregiver register. It is not a feature exclusive to adult–child communicative contexts. It is, rather, a feature that characterizes the language used between family members in relatively casual moments at home. The language of adult family member to child family member is part of a larger 'household register'. Intimacy rather than generation is the significant constraint on the use of ergative case marking in Samoan. Similarly, the increase in frequency of use is not a function of same-generation status between speaker and hearer; it is a function of increased social distance on the one hand and male status of the speaker on the other. That is, in speech to a nonfamily member, ergative case marking is far more frequent in the speech of men than in the speech of women.

C.   Typology of ergative languages

In the past several years, we have come to know much more about the distribution of ergative languages and their characteristics. Many descriptions of ergative languages have been produced. (See, for example, the contributions to the volume on ergativity edited by Plank (1979).) And such scholars as Comrie (1978), Dixon (1979), Chung (1978), Plank (1979), and Silverstein (1976b) have been analyzing ergative languages to isolate typological features and processes associated with this group of languages. Ergative languages have been typed according to how ergativity is expressed or marked and the extent to which syntactic and semantic factors constrain the expression of ergative distinctions. As a result of these studies, it is now apparent that ergativity is usually present only to a degree (see Comrie 1978, 1979; Dixon 1979; Plank 1979). Ergative systems may co-occur with accusative systems in the same languages.

The study at hand brings to this literature yet another dimension that constrains the expression of ergative distinctions in a language. This dimension is *sociological* in nature. It types ergative languages in terms of the extent to which the expression of ergative distinctions is constrained by social context of use, i.e. by speech register. For many ergative languages, given appropriate semantic and syntactic conditions, ergative distinctions are always or nearly always expressed by native speakers. Social setting and social relationship obtaining between speaker and hearer, for example, do not affect the expression of ergativity (in grammatically feasible environments). Such a language can be characterized in this sense as a *socially invariable* ergative language. On the other hand, other ergative languages are *socially variable* in the expression of ergative distinctions. Social definitions of setting, of speaker, of hearer, influence the extent to which ergative distinctions are overtly marked by speakers. Samoan is such a language.

6. Word-order strategies: the two-constituent bias

I. INTRODUCTION

In the preceding chapter, the focus was on the impact of social norms and sociolinguistic variation on the acquisition of case morphology. This chapter also examines these social phenomena, focusing on word-order strategies. Additionally, the discussion pursues the fit between adult and child word-order strategies and semantic and pragmatic functions. In this sense, this chapter is more strictly psycholinguistically oriented and relates to the central concerns of current language-acquisition research, i.e. the conceptual underpinnings of linguistic structure. The chapter will consider the notions of subject and predicate, formal strategies for encoding experiencer and instrument; and the relationship among grammatical structure, presupposition, and focus in Samoan child and adult language.

The chapter will also address certain issues that relate to formal properties of Samoan itself. In particular, it will relate word-order strategies to the ergative–absolutive distinction discussed in Chapter 5. The discussion will also address the relation between word order and deletion in adult and child language use. It will demonstrate that, like many languages, Samoan allows widespread deletion of major constituents. This fairly common characteristic of languages should be considered in assessing the linguistic competence of children. We have come to think of acquisition in terms of increased articulation of major constituents. Looking at this practice from the point of view of Samoan, it appears appropriate to only a subset of languages, ones like English, in which deletion of major constituents is rare and highly predictable in main clauses. For these languages, it makes sense to look at children's deletions of agents and patients as indicative of incompetence. In languages like Samoan, however, such deletions in main clauses are possible, even common. Unlike the acquirer of a language like English, the acquirer of Samoan may be displaying competence in producing utterances without reference to agents and/or patients.

The most important argument of the chapter will be that Samoan, as spoken by both adults and children, has a 'basic utterance type' or canonical sentence schema (Slobin & Bever 1982) consisting of two constituents – a verb and an absolutive NP (O, S; see Dixon 1979). This basic utterance type has been reported not only for Samoan (Duranti 1981a; Ochs 1982b, 1986a) but for other languages as well, such as Sapultec (DuBois 1981, 1984) and French (Lambrecht 1985). In Samoan, the absolutive NP typically follows the verb (VO, VS), with young children showing the strongest tendency to make it do so. This pattern suggests that ergative–absolutive distinctions are expressed through word order. Adults in informal settings and young children generally show a preference for word orders that keep the VO unit intact (VOA, AVO) and disprefer orders in which agents are expressed immediately following the verb (VAO, OVA).

A study of semitransitive constructions containing verbs of feeling and perception in the adult Samoan corpus indicates that there may be a more general semantic principle underlying word order in Samoan – a preference for encoding consecutively action/change of state and then entity affected by that action/change of state (e.g. experiencer, patient). The dispreference is, then, not only for agent NP in this postverbal position but more generally for the NP that encodes who or what causes/caused etc. that effect (e.g. instrument NP, evoker of experience NP). This pattern leads to the following surface word-order preferences: transitive clauses: (x)VO; semitransitive (verbs of perception and affect): (x)VS(x); intransitive: (x)VS(x).

In adult Samoan speech, the distinction between transitive and intransitive clause is not always clear (Hopper & Thompson 1980). For example, the deletion of agent in utterances containing (potentially) transitive verbs often renders them ambiguous as to whether the utterance is intransitive (e.g. 'The house is locked up') or transitive ('The house has been locked / (He) locked the house'). In children's speech at the early stages there is little evidence that children distinguish between transitive and intransitive constructions. In the latter portion of this chapter, I suggest that language development in Samoan could be understood as the gradual manifestation of this distinction in morphology and syntax.

As with most of the chapters in this book, the discussion will first concentrate on adult speech patterns and then turn to children's strategies over developmental time.

II.   WORD ORDER IN ADULT SAMOAN

A.   Word-order possibilities

Chapter 3 presented the word-order alternations possible in Samoan. I shall now briefly review this information. Samoan allows a number of word

Table 6.1. *Adult word-order preferences: canonical transitives with three full constituents (percentages)*

	VAO	VOA	AVO	OVA
Women Family (23)	21.7 (5)	34.8 (8)	34.7 (8)	8.7 (2)
Men Family (15)	26.7 (4)	66.7 (10)	–	66.7 (1)
Informal women Nonfamily (14)	28.6 (4)	35.7 (5)	28.6 (4)	7.1 (1)
Informal men Nonfamily (6)	66.7 (4)	16.6 (1)	16.6 (1)	–
Men Formal *Fono* (17)	52.9 (9)	17.6 (3)	11.8 (2)	17.6 (3)
Total (75)	34.7 (26)	36 (27)	20 (15)	9.3 (7)

orders, but the preferred orders are verb-initial (verb–subject–object, verb–object–subject).

(1) Verb–subject–object

Na 'ai   e   a'u le   keke.
PST eat ERG I   ART cake
'I ate the cake.'

(2) Verb–object–subject

Na 'ai   le   keke e   a'u.
PST eat ART cake ERG I
'I ate the cake.'

Constituents may precede the verb (subject–verb–object, subject–object–verb, object–verb–subject), but in standard Samoan these constituents are preceded by the topic particle *o*, indicating their more marked status.

(3) Subject–verb–object

O   a'u na   'ai   le   keke.
TOP I   PST eat ART cake
'I ate the cake.'

(4) Object–verb–subject

O   le   keke na   'ai   e   a'u.
TOP ART cake PST eat ERG I
'The cake I ate.'

Table 6.1 presents the frequencies of these word orders in adult speech across five social contexts. These contexts match those used for the ergative-case-marking study in Chapter 5. On the average, subject-initial and object-initial word orders account for only about 30 percent of the three-

Table 6.2. *Word-order preference and gender of speaker (percentages)*

	VAO	VOA	AVO	OVA
Men (38)	44.7 (17)	36.8 (14)	7.9 (3)	10.5 (4)
Women (37)	24.3 (9)	35.1 (13)	32.4 (12)	8.1 (3)

constituent transitives in the corpus. The table indicates as well that verb–subject–object order is used more by men than by women and more in talking to nonfamily members than in talking to family members. The relation of linguistic strategies to gender identity is displayed in Table 6.2.

The differential use of verb-subject-object according to speaker–hearer relationship is displayed in Table 6.3. This table indicates that verb–subject–object and verb–object–subject orders are in complementary distribution in terms of usage settings. Verb–object–subject is twice as frequent as verb–subject–object in speaking within the extended family. Verb–subject–object is twice as frequent as verb–object–subject in speaking to nonfamily members.

All five contexts in this study are characterized by speech in which more than two persons participated. Further, talk both to family members and to nonfamily members covers a range of speech activities, including reporting past events and advising others concerning future events, but it does not include formal oratory. The preference for verb–subject–object or verb–object–subject does not appear to be bound to this variable, i.e. the speech activity/genre. To understand why verb–object–subject is preferred over verb–subject–object order in more intimate situations, we turn to semantic and pragmatic considerations.

B.　　Focus and deletion

1.　　The unusual status of three-constituent utterances

In this and the following sections, I shall be drawing on research carried out by A. Duranti and myself jointly and independently on Samoan discourse and grammar (Duranti 1981a; Duranti & Ochs 1983; Ochs 1982b, 1986a).

As discussed in the introduction to this chapter, Samoan allows subjects and objects to be deleted. Indeed, deletion is not unusual. Table 6.4 indicates the percentage of canonical transitives in the corpus in which both subject and object are expressed. On the average, three-constituent transitives account for only 22.5 percent of the transitive declaratives and yes–no

Table 6.3. *Word-order preferences: speech to family versus nonfamily (percentages)*

	VAO	VOA	AVO	OVA
Speaking in (men & women) (38)	23.7 (9)	47.4 (18)	21.1 (8)	7.9 (3)
Speaking out (men & women) (37)	45.9 (17)	24.3 (9)	18.9 (7)	10.8 (4)

Table 6.4. *Three-constituent canonical transitives (percentages)*

	Full A+V+O	Clitic A+V+O	Total A+V+O
Women Family (150 total)	15.3 (23)	4.7 (7)	20 (30)
Men Family (60 total)	25 (15)	6.7 (4)	31.7 (19)
Informal women to nonfamily (120 total)	11.7 (14)	2.5 (3)	14.2 (17)
Informal men to nonfamily (50 total)	12 (6)	6 (3)	18 (9)
Men to men in formal village council (56 total)	30.3 (17)	10.7 (6)	41 (23)
Total average (436)	17.2 (75)	5.3 (23)	22.5 (98)

interrogatives in the corpus. This figure includes clitic as well as full pronoun/noun constituents. If we look at the three full-constituent transitives, we see that they account for only 17.2 percent of the transitive corpus.

Table 6.4 indicates as well that the percentage of three-constituent utterances does not appear to rise as social distance increases between speaker and hearer, as might be predicted. This pattern can be seen more clearly in Table 6.5, which shows that the percentage of three-constituent utterances is generally stable over the two contexts, but drops slightly in talking to outsiders. These figures suggest that the dispreference for three-constituent utterances is not confined to situations in which speaker and hearer are intimate. In other words, this dispreference is not registrally restricted.

Table 6.5. *Three-constituent canonical transitives: speech to family versus nonfamily (percentages)*

	Full a+v+o	Clitic a+v+o	Total a+v+o
Speaking in (to family) (210)	18.1 (38)	5.2 (11)	23.3 (49)
Speaking out (to nonfamily) (226)	16.4 (37)	5.3 (12)	21.7 (49)

2.   The two-constituent preference in adult discourse

In terms of major constituents, clauses in spoken Samoan contain characteristically either only a verb or a verb and no more than one major NP constituent. In this discussion, we are considering principally direct, full NP constituents, i.e. subject and direct-object nouns and full pronouns. Verbs appear of course with a variety of NPs in oblique syntactic roles. In the case of intransitive clauses, the expressed NP is by default the major argument of the intransitive verb (s). In the case of transitive clauses, this NP tends to be the direct object (o) of the verb. In other words, the major pattern is a clause with a verb and an absolutive NP.

Agents tend not to be expressed in transitive clauses. Instead, the referents (that might be expressed as agent NPs) tend to be expressed in other linguistic contexts. For example, the agent referent may function in some other semantic role in a prior clause, e.g. as the major argument of an intransitive verb, or as a possessor or benefactor or patient. This discourse pattern is illustrated in the example below:

(5) Three guys

Teenagers discussing a Dracula film

=> T: Ga   alaku   a   le   koea'iga   ma   –   ma   le
PST   go DEICT   EMPH   ART   old man   with   –   with   ART
pigisipa'u   ma   le   mea   –   h
?   and   ART   thing   –   h
'The old man went there with – with the (?) and the thing – uh . . .'
(1.5)
T: Ma (l–)
And (th–)
(1.2)
S: Kolosisi?
chisel
'Chisel?'
T: Ma   le   kolosisi   kolosisi   ai ((laugh))   le   kei(h)g(h)e
and   ART   chisel   chisel   CLIT   ART   gi(h)r(h)l

```
        he    he!
        heh   heh
        'And the chisel chisel (to him?) ((laugh)) (for) the gi(h)r(h)l heh heh!'
    s:  Kolosisi  fa'afea?
        chisel    how
        'Chisel how?'
=> T:  //Ku'i   le     magava.
         strike  ART    stomach
         '(He)* strikes the stomach.'
=> s:  //Ku'i   fakafaka   a?
         strike   chest      right
         '(He)* strikes the chest, right?'
=> T:  Mh.     Ku'i
        Hmm.    Strikes
        'Hmm. (He)* strikes (it).'
        'ee'ee.
        screams
        '(He)† screams.'
(0.2)
```

         * The old man.
         † Dracula.

In this example, the agent ('the old man') in a series of transitive clauses is referred to earlier in the discourse as a subject of an intransitive clause.

Alternatively, the agent referent may be referred to within the same clause (i.e. the agentless clause) in some other role, for example as a genitive or as a possessive adjective, or as an oblique object (benefactive, source, goal, etc.). It is common in spoken Samoan for utterances to be of the form (a) rather than the form (b):

```
(6a) 'ua    fai    le    lauga   o     Loa.
     PERF   make   ART   speech  GEN   Loa
     'Loa's speech has been delivered.'

(6b) 'ua    fai    e    Loa    le    lauga.
     PERF   make   ERG  Loa    ART   speech
     'Loa has delivered his speech.'

(7a) 'ua    fai    tatou        fala.
     PERF   make   our INCL     mats
     'Our mats have been made.'

(7b) 'ua    fai    e    tatou        fala.
     PERF   make   ERG  we INCL      mats
     'We have made the mats.'

(8a) Na    avatu       lau          api?
     PST   take away   your ALIEN   notebook
     'Was your notebook taken away (by you)?'
```

(8b) Na   avatu   e   oe   lau   api?
     PST take away   ERG   you   your ALIEN notebook
     'Did you take away your notebook?'

(9a) 'ua   'aumai   le   mea alofa   iaa   Lua.
     PERF bring   ART   gift   from   Lua
     'The gift from Lua has been brought (by Lua).'

(9b) 'ua   'aumai   e   Lua   le   mea alofa
     PERF bring   ERG   Lua   ART   gift
     'Lua has brought the gift.'

These alternative usages are not semantically equivalent. We are simply indicating preferences for encoding. Information tends to be expressed in one fashion rather than in another.

In addition to the two patterns mentioned, there is a third, related manifestation of the preference for a verb and a single NP. Very commonly transitive and semitransitive (see Chapter 3) verbs are nominalized (Duranti 1981a). Rather than finding a transitive or semitransitive verb with its direct constituents, it is common to find the verb nominalized as the NP of another verb (transitive, semitransitive, or intransitive). Utterances of the form (a) are more typical than utterances of the form (b):

(10a) 'e   tele   le   alofa   o   Elenoa   iaa te   'oe.
      PRES much   ART   love   GEN INALIEN Elinor   PREP   you
      'Elinor's love for you is considerable.'

(10b) 'e   alofa   tele   Elenoa   iaa te   oe
      PRES love   much   Elinor   PREP   you
      'Elinor loves you considerably.'

(11a) 'ou   te   'ofo   i   le   tagata   lea
      1ST PERS CLIT   PRES   surprise   PREP   ART   person   this
      i   le   mafai   ona   nofo   ave 'ese   nofoa.
      PREP   ART   able   COMP   sit   without   chair
      'I'm surprised at this person, at the ability to sit without a chair.'

(11b) 'ou   te   'ofo   e   mafai   ona   nofa
      1ST PERS CLIT   PRES   surprise   COMP   able   COMP   sit
      le   tagata   ave 'ese   nofoa.
      ART   person   without   chair
      'I'm surprised that this person can sit without a chair.'

(12a) 'e   manaia   le   faina   e   Sio   o   le   mea.
      PREF nice   ART   making   ERG   Sio   GEN INALIEN ART   thing
      'Sio's making of the thing is nice.'

(12b) 'ua   fai   e   Sio   le   mea   manaia.
      PREF make   ERG   Sio   ART   thing   nice
      'Sio made a nice thing.'

Looking at these patterns helps us to understand how information is expressed in Samoan. It also indicates why we have so few examples of three-constituent transitive utterances in our corpus. Indeed, the examples in 10a–12a indicate why we do not have more transitive constructions generally in our study (with or without an expressed agent): very often the would-be transitive clause is nominalized and functions as a constituent within an intransitive clause. An understanding of these preferences is fundamental to understanding the pragmatics of word order in both adult and children's speech.

3.   Word order, focus, and ergativity in two-constituent utterances

The word order of these two-constituent clauses is predominantly verb-initial (verb–absolutive NP), although this is more the case for transitive clauses than for intransitive clauses.

In Duranti & Ochs (1983), we suggest that the usual or unmarked position for an NP that expresses textually new information in Samoan is immediately following the verb and that the typical clause pattern is a verb followed by a single focused NP. By focused NP, we mean the NP that is the most informative or most salient element in a predicate (see also Lambrecht 1985).

Putting together the statements above, we have a picture of the typical two-constituent clause in spoken Samoan as a verb followed by a textually new NP, which is typically absolutive.

s – – –⟩ verb (absolutive NP)

Ergative NPs (agent NPs) may appear in this position and in this pragmatic role (focused NP), but do so less frequently than absolutives. When they appear, these NPs are often responses to 'Who?' questions, in accusations and in praises, where the focus is on who did something.

Notice here that the ergative–absolutive distinction has a pragmatic and syntactic counterpart. Absolutives are distinguished from ergative NPs by their likelihood to be expressed and, if expressed, by their likelihood to be the NP in postverbal, focus position. The similarity between patient NPs and NP arguments of intransitive verbs is apparent when examining V–NP clauses out of context. Under these conditions, it is unclear whether many V–NP clauses contain a transitive verb and direct object or an intransitive verb and major argument. A sentence like (13) below displays this ambiguity.

(13) Verb-NP sentence

'ua   loka   le   fale.
PERF   lock   ART   house
Reading 1: 'He/she locked the house.'
Reading 2: 'The house has been locked.'
Reading 3: 'The house is locked up.'

The sentence has three possible interpretations. Not only is there ambiguity as to whether 'the house' (*le fale*) is a major argument of the predicate 'is locked up' (reading 3) or is the patient of the verb 'lock' (readings 1 and 2), there is also an ambiguity between two readings of the transitive construction. In reading 1, the sentence is about the agent, and the deletion of the agent NP in the sentence is a case of zero anaphora. In reading 2, the sentence is about the house, as in reading 3. This reading differs from reading 3 in that an agent is implied. It differs from reading 1 in that the identity of the agent is not relevant or necessary to the semantic interpretation of the sentence. The agent here is elided, comparable to ellipsis of the agent in agentless passives in English. As has been noted for other languages (Dixon 1972, 1979; Hopper 1979; Hopper & Thompson 1980), there is a continuum of sentence types from intransitive to transitive.

The reader should not get the impression that direct objects and intransitive subjects are never distinguished formally (see Chung 1978 for extensive discussion of the syntactic properties of those two constructions) or disambiguated contextually. The point I am stressing is that when an agent is not expressed, the status of the verb as transitive or not and the status of the single NP as direct object or subject are not always clear. Since agents are often not expressed, this means that for a good deal of spoken Samoan such distinctions are not formally expressed.

When we discuss the notion of predicate generally, we think paradigmatically of either an intransitive verb or a transitive verb and patient NP. When a patient NP is not part of the predicate, a language usually indicates this marked status morpho-syntactically, as do passives in many languages. In a language like Samoan, the shift in status is not often structurally manifest in the basic clause type – a verb followed by an absolutive NP. For these constructions, then, the status and scope of the predicate are not grammatically encoded. And this, in turn, may have implications for the psychological reality of the predicate for Samoan speakers. This is not to say that the predicate does not have a psychological reality but that it may have different characteristics than in nominative–accusative languages.

4.   Word order: a more general semantic principle

In the view presented in section 3 above, Samoan has a verb-focus NP core, and there is a ranking of constituents to fill this focus-NP position. In the case of canonical transitives, NPs that express entities affected by some action are preferred over agents in this position. The semantic pattern seems to extend beyond canonical transitive constructions. The more general principle seems to be a preference for following the verb with an NP referring to an entity that has been affected by some state or action rather than making the NP refer to the entity that causes that transformation. The cause may be an agent (in which case the NP is preceded by the ergative particle *e*) or an instrument or stimulus (in which case the NP is preceded by the particle *i* (nonhuman), *iaa* (human noun), or *iaa ke* (human pronoun)). These NPs generally appear after the verb-affected NP core.

s − − − ⟩ verb (affected NP) (cause NP)

or

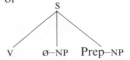

This semantic order helps to explain why certain semitransitive or middle-verb (see Chung 1978) constructions in Samoan display different surface word-order characteristics: in particular, semitransitives containing verbs of perception and feeling (hate, love, detest, like, etc.) tend to be v–s–middle o, seemingly in direct contrast with canonical transitives, where the o usually appears right after the verb. There are very few three-constituent middle-verb constructions in our sample; their distribution is shown in Table 6.6.

This word-order preference in clauses containing middle verbs of perception and feeling reflects the general semantic principle of ordering the affected entity (in this case, the experiencer) right after the verb. In these constructions, the middle-object NP (the NP referring to the entity that evokes the experience) is marked by the particle *i*, *iaa*, or *iaa ke*, but the subject receives no case marking. This is illustrated in the example below:

(14) 'e   alofa kele   Pesio iaa   Maseligo.
     PRES   love   much   Pesio PREP   Maseligo
     'Pesio loves Maseligo very much.'

Semantically, the NP marked by the particle *i/iaa/iaa ke* has something in common with the NP marked by the ergative particle *e*. Both encode cause. Morphologically, they are distinct from absolutive NPs in that they are both preceded by case-marking particles, whereas absolutive NPs are not. In terms of word order, they also have in common the fact that they are dispreferred in the position immediately following the verb. For canonical transitives, this produces a preferred two-constituent word order of vo, and for semitransitive constructions with verbs of feeling, this produces a preferred two-constituent word order of vs.

5.   The relation between two- and three-constituent utterances

We are now in a better position to evaluate the word-order preferences for three-constituent clauses discussed earlier. In particular, we have a reason-

Table 6.6. *Word-order preferences: three-constituent middle verbs of perception and feeling*

	VSO	VOS	SVO	OVS
Women Family (informal) (7)	6	0	0	1
Women Nonfamily (informal) (8)	7	0	1	0
Men Nonfamily (informal) (6)	5	0	0	1
Men Nonfamily (formal) (10)	5	0	3	2

able (but not complete) hypothesis for why adult Samoan speakers tend to prefer VOA over VAO word order in casual, intimate social interactions. This preference is tied to the more general preference for absolutives/affected NPs (here in patient role) being expressed in the position immediately following the verb.

An agent NP in this position (VAO) violates the canonical sentence schema of spoken Samoan (Slobin & Bever 1982) by 'superseding' the patient NP as the primary predicate focus. An agent NP that follows the verb–object sequence (VOA) does not supersede the object but itself also comes into focus, if only because it is relatively unusual to have an agent expressed in a transitive clause. Quite often, in fact, these NPs are 'afterthoughts' or affect-loaded descriptions of someone, added to the VO sequence to indicate the speaker's attitude toward a referent. In the latter context, the referent itself is not discourse-new; rather, the affective qualities are the new information. Indeed many of the VOA utterances have functions that are characteristic of right-dislocations in other languages.

A related hypothesis for the preference of VOA over VAO in intimate speech contexts draws from the general hypothesis proposed by Lehmann (1973) and Slobin (1973) that speakers will tend to preserve the predicate as an uninterrupted unit. In Slobin's view, VAO word order is cognitively distressful because it separates the verb from its patient, splitting the predicate in two. In this view, not only VOA but also AVO are cognitively preferable to VAO order. In many ways, this perspective more neatly accounts for why VAO orders increase in frequency as social distance between interlocutors increases. In this hypothesis, 'easier' word orders would show up where the speakers are least attending to their speech, and the more difficult order, if they were to appear at all, would appear where speakers are more careful and attentive to their speech. One might predict that speakers would be more careful in talking to outsiders than in talking to intimates.

In one sense, this hypothesis appears more general than the verb–absolutive NP core hypothesis: Lehmann's and Slobin's generalization is that speakers show a decided preference for keeping the verb and object together in a particular word-order sequence (where the object follows the verb).

In another sense, however, the generalization proposed here for Samoan is broader than the notion that the verb and object 'form a perceptual Gestalt that resists interruption' (Slobin 1975:13). I have indicated that not only transitive verbs and objects (VO) but also semitransitive verbs of perception and feeling and their subjects (VS) resist interruption. This broader pattern has implications for the notion of predicate. We cannot use the gestalt notion to argue for the psychological reality of the predicate in Samoan, because speakers also treat these semitransitive verbs and their subjects as a perceptual gestalt.

For Samoan, the verb and its patient NP are part of a larger set of semantic relations more generally characterized as verb and NP affected by the action/change of state expressed by the verb. In the case of canonical transitive verbs, this NP has the semantic role of patient; in the case of semitransitive verbs of feeling, this NP has the semantic role of experiencer. For Samoan, then, it is the verb plus affected NP that forms a gestalt and that resists interruption by an NP encoding cause. We would expect word orders that conform to this principle to be used more frequently, particularly in relatively informal speech settings.

III.   ACQUISITION OF WORD ORDER

A.   Expression of agent and patient

Given the bias toward two-constituent utterances in adult Samoan, what is the developmental pattern for young children acquiring Samoan?

One of the first things to notice about acquisition is that Samoan children infrequently produce utterances with agents and even more infrequently produce utterances with both agents and patients expressed as major arguments. Tables 6.7 and 6.8 provide information about the extent to which young Samoan children express major constituents in declaratives and yes–no interrogatives containing transitive verbs. Table 6.7 displays the extent to which agents appear as major constituents; Table 6.8 displays the extent to which children produce transitives with both patient and agent expressed as major arguments of the transitive verb.

Table 6.7. *Canonical transitives: children's utterances with agent*
          expressed as major constituent (percentages)

Child	Session I	Session III	Session V	Session VII	Average
Matu'u	16.7 (2)	42.9 (9)	30.4 (7)	18.7 (3)	25.6 (21)
Pesio	6.7 (1)	36.4 (4)	20.7 (6)	12.1 (7)	15.9 (18)
Naomi	12.9 (4)	41.2 (7)	3.8 (1)	17.5 (6)	16.5 (18)
Niulala	19.1 (4)	13.8 (4)	25.8 (16)	22.9 (8)	21.8 (32)

Table 6.8. *Canonical transitives: children's utterances with agent and patient*
          expressed as major constituents (percentages)

Child	Session I	Session III	Session V	Session VII	Average
Matu'u	16.7 (2)	38.1 (8)	30.4 (7)	18.7 (3)	24.4 (20)
Pesio	6.7 (1)	18.2 (2)	13.8 (4)	5.2 (3)	8.8 (10)
Naomi	9.7 (3)	5.9 (1)	3.8 (1)	–	4.6 (55)
Niulala	19.1 (4)	10.3 (3)	17.7 (11)	5.7 (2)	13.6 (20)

A second important pattern is that the frequency of expression of agents
and patients as major constituents of the verb does not increase over
developmental time between the ages of two and four years. There is no
gradual upward curve indicating that children go through stages comparable to R. Brown's (1973) stage I, stage II, stage III. Tables 6.7 and 6.8
show that developmental maturity is not matched by increased use of agents
and patients. Looking at each child, we can see that the use of these
constituents fluctuates from the first session to the last. In Table 6.8, we can
see that in the final taping session (session VII), three of the four children
actually display fewer three-constituent utterances than in the first session.
Further, in both tables, the youngest child in the sample, Matu'u (2;1 at
onset of study), shows the greatest percentage of utterances with agents and
patients expressed.

These patterns appear closely tied to adult norms. Like adults, children
disprefer three-constituent transitive utterances. Further, with such an
adult speech model, one would not expect a developmental pattern of
increasing mention of agent and patient.

We point out, however, that children do differ from adults in terms of the
percentage of two- and three-constituent transitives in the corpus. Though
both adults and children show a dispreference for these constructions,
particularly three-constituent constructions, children appear to use them
even less frequently than do adults. This difference resembles superficially
the results of other studies in which children's speech is seen as telegraphic

Table 6.9. *Three-constituent canonical transitives: summary
(percentages)*

Child	VOA	VAO	AVO	AVO CLIT	OVA	O[VA] relative clause	OAV
Matu'u	50.0 (8)	6.3 (1)	25.0 (4)	0	6.3 (1)	12.5 (2)	–
Iakopo	38.5 (5)	–	53.8 (7)	–	–	–	7.7 (1)
Pesio	37.5 (3)	12.5 (1)	12.5 (1)	37.5 (3)	–	–	–
Naomi	–	20.0 (1)	40.0 (2)	40.0 (2)	–	–	–
Niulala	25.0 (5)	30.0 (6)	5.0 (1)	25.0 (6)	10.0 (2)	–	–
Average	33.9 (21)	14.5 (9)	24.2 (15)	17.7 (11)	4.8 (3)	3.2 (2)	1.6 (1)

(R. Brown 1973) with respect to adult speech. However, the meaning of the results differs for each of the studies and speech communities examined: for languages in which expression of all major constituents is obligatory, the nonexpression of these constituents by young children reflects incompetence and counts as an error. This is the case for English-speaking children, for example. For a language like Samoan in which expression of major constituents is not obligatory and in which the norm is not to express all three constituents of a transitive clause, the children's deletion of agent or agent and patient much of the time does not in itself reflect incompetence or count as an error. In the Samoan study, differences between adult and child language are quantitative without being qualitative.

B.   Word order in transitive and intransitive utterances

Let us turn now to word-order strategies themselves. This section focuses on those transitive utterances that do contain all three constituents as well as on intransitive utterances that contain a major argument. The reader is reminded that these utterances represent only a portion of the utterances in the corpus.

1.   The verb-initial preference

In the discussion of adult speech, we noted that speakers prefer verb-initial word orders (see Table 6.1). The results of the longitudinal study indicate that children too show a preference for verb-initial constructions. This preference is summarized in Tables 6.9 and 6.10. Table 6.9 indicates the predominance of verb-initial constructions in transitive declaratives and

Table 6.10. *Intransitives (with major argument expressed): children's preferences for verb–major argument word order (percentages)*

Child	Session I	Session III	Session V	Session VII	Average
Matu'u	100.0 (9)	70.0 (7)	84.6 (21)	71.4 (20)	81.5
Iakopo	100.0 (1)	85.7 (6)	85.7 (18)	85.2 (23)	85.7
Pesio	96.1 (25)	80.0 (4)	78.9 (30)	86.5 (45)	85.4
Naomi	100.0 (16)	70.6 (12)	91.3 (22)	75.8 (25)	84.4
Niulala	90.9 (30)	77.3 (34)	88.9 (64)	65.8 (25)	80.7

yes–no interrogatives: roughly 61 percent of these constructions are verb-initial. Table 6.10 indicates the predominance of verb-initial constructions in intransitive declaratives and yes–no interrogatives: roughly 84 percent of these constructions are verb-initial.

These figures are augmented considerably when the entire corpus of transitive constructions, including those with only a single NP, is considered. The overwhelming preference for verb-initial order in two-constituent utterances is displayed in Table 6.11.

Combining the information concerning deletion and verb-initial preferences, we can see that in terms of major constituents, children's utterances characteristically consist of a verb (including the categories of predicate locative, adjective, etc.) only or a verb followed by one direct NP.

S – – – ⟩ verb (NP)

This pattern conforms to the adult basic utterance type (the two-constituent bias and the verb-initial bias).

2. The preference for absolutives

In the discussion of adult speech, we noted that typically in two-constituent utterances the NP expressed is absolutive. We can see the same preference in children's speech as well. Tables 6.7 and 6.11, for example, indicate that in the children's corpus most transitive utterances do not contain an agent NP.

The preference for absolutive NPs and the verb-initial preference lead to a general characterization of children's utterances as typically a verb followed by an absolutive NP. This characterization matches that of adult word-order strategies:

S – – – ⟩ verb (absolutive NP)

To understand Samoan language development, it is crucial to acknowledge the primacy of the verb–absolutive NP unit. The development of

Table 6.11. *Percentage of verb-initial canonical transitives*

Child	Session I	Session III	Session V	Session VII	Average
Matu'u	91.7 (11)	76.2 (16)	95.6 (22)	87.5 (14)	87.8
Pesio	100 (15)	54.5 (5)	68.9 (20)	91.4 (53)	78.7
Naomi	90.3 (28)	94.1 (16)	92.3 (24)	97.1 (34)	93.6
Niulala	80.9 (17)	82.8 (24)	85.5 (53)	94.3 (33)	86.4

linguistic competence has this unit as its core: at the single-word stage, children express typically either a verb or an absolutive NP. At the two-word stage, children can express both constituents. The next stage is one in which the child can use one-, two-, or three-constituent utterances. But the point of our discussion in section III.A was that there is no three-constituent level in the sense that from this point on all three constituents are always expressed. There is, rather, constant variation among one-, two-, and three-constituent utterances from this early point throughout life.

In Samoan, the major locus of language development is in the NP itself. While both adults and children have a two-constituent bias in spoken registers, the absolutive NP in adult speech can be far more complex than in children's speech. As specified in section II.B.3, the absolutive NP may make reference to an agent referent in the form of a possessive or genitive construction ('The chief's wish has been brought', meaning 'The chief has brought his wish') or may be a nominalized verb phrase of considerable length ('The man's driving of the car is slow'). Relative to a language like English, Samoan is a noun-oriented language. Ongoing research is investigating the development of complex NPs in the speech of Samoan children.

To recapitulate, the number of major constituents is an important criterion only at the earliest stages of language acquisition; however, for the period between two and four years there is a stable fluctuation among one-, two-, and three-constituent utterances. The notion of language development as a movement toward increased use of the three major constituents does not capture the dynamics of Samoan language development. The central locus of development is likely to be in the structure of the absolutive NP itself.

3.   Word order and ergativity

In this section, I propose that two- to four-year-old Samoan children distinguish ergative and absolutive NPs through word order rather than through case marking. This strategy is an instance of a more general strategy that has been observed of children: the use of word order as an initial formal means of encoding and decoding semantic relations. While it is not universally true (Slobin 1982, 1986), young children across a number of languages appear to prefer word order over case marking in the early stages of their grammatical development.

Slobin has indicated that children's opting for word order rather than case marking depends on properties of the morphological system being acquired. We noted in Chapter 5 the properties suggested by Slobin that lead to early or late acquisition of case marking. In that discussion, I pointed out a few properties of the ergative case marker in Samoan that may delay its acquisition by young children. The most important of these seems to be that the marker appears before the agent NP and that it is used variably in adult speech, being subject to both grammatical and sociological parameters.

In addition to these conditions, I am suggesting now that the basic utterance type in adult speech orients young children to make ergative–absolutive distinctions through word order. Another way of looking at this pattern is to see both adults and children preferring word order to case marking to distinguish ergative–absolutive constituents in certain registers of Samoan. However, we cannot maintain this position as strongly for adults as for two- to four-year-old children. In the speech of young children, the position of absolutives is far less variable than in the speech of adults. Specifically, young children even more strongly than adults tend to reserve the position immediately after the verb for absolutive constituents and exclude ergative constituents from this position.

This tendency is evidenced most strongly in the word-order strategies for three-constituent utterances. Table 6.10 indicates that the word order of verb–agent–patient (corresponding to the adult word order or verb–subject–object) is dispreferred by all but the oldest child in our study. Tables 6.12–16 show the word-order strategies for each observation period for each child in the longitudinal study. These tables indicate that the earliest word orders in children's speech are predominantly agent–verb–patient or verb–patient–agent. Table 6.17 focuses on the position of patient NPs. It shows how frequently these constituents appear immediately following the verb, so that a comparison can be made with the position of major arguments of intransitive verbs. The results indicate, with the exception again of the oldest child in the study, a strong tendency to place patient NPs immediately after the verb.

These results, together with those showing the high percentage of intransitive VS ordering, provide strong support for the notion that children through word order treat major arguments of intransitive verbs and patient NPs of transitive verbs (absolutive constituents) as a single category, distinct from agent NPs (ergative constituents).

These word-order patterns have implications beyond the expression of

Table 6.12. *Word-order preferences: Matu'u (2;1)*

Session	Total	VOA	AVO	OAV	VAO	OVA	O[VA]
I	2	1	1	–	–	–	–
II	4	–	4	–	–	–	–
III	8	5	2	–	–	–	1
IV	4	3	–	–	1	–	–
V	7	6	–	–	–	–	1
VI	7	3	4	–	–	–	–
VII	3	–	1	–	1	1	–
VIII	8	5	2	–	1	–	–
Total	43	23	14	–	3	1	2

Table 6.13. *Word-order preferences: Iakopo (2;1)*

Session	Total	VOA	AVO	OAV	VAO	OVA	O[VA]
I	–	–	–	–	–	–	–
II	–	–	–	–	–	–	–
III	–	–	–	–	–	–	–
IV	3	1	2	–	–	–	–
V	4	2	2	–	–	–	–
VI	3	2	1	–	–	–	–
VII	9	5	3	1	–	–	–
Total	19	10	8	1	–	–	–

Table 6.14. *Word-order preferences: Pesio (2;3)*

Session	Total	VOA	AVO	OAV	VAO	OVA	O[VA]
I	1	1	–	–	–	–	–
II	8	5	2	–	1	–	–
III	2	1	–	1	–	–	–
IV	3	1	2	–	–	–	–
V	1	1					–
VI	6	6	–	–	–	–	–
VII	2	1	–	–	1	–	–
Total	23	16	4	1	2	–	–

Table 6.15. *Word-order preferences: Naomi (2;10)*

Session	Total	VOA	AVO	OAV	VAO	OVA	O[VA]
I	1	–	–	–	1	–	–
II	5	2	3	–	–	–	–
III	1	–	1	–	–	–	–
IV	6	5	1	–	–	–	–
V	1	–	1	–	–	–	–
VI	4	4	–	–	–	–	–
VII	0	–	–	–	–	–	–
VIII	8	6	–	–	2	–	–
Total	26	17	6	–	3	–	–

Table 6.16. *Word-order preferences: Niulala (2;11)*

Session	Total	VOA	AVO	OAV	VAO	OVA	O[VA]
I	3	–	1	–	2	–	–
II	10	4	4	–	1	1	–
III	1	–	–	–	1	–	–
IV	7	–	5	–	1	–	1
V	9	5	–	–	2	2	–
VI	3	2	1	–	–	–	–
VII	1	–	–	–	1	–	–
VIII	6	2	2	–	1	1	–
Total	40	13	13	–	9	4	1

Table 6.17. *Children's preferences for verb–patient word orders*

Child	%	No. of instances
Matu'u (2;1)	86.0	37
Iakopo (2;1)	94.7	18
Pesio (2;3)	91.3	20
Naomi (2;10)	88.5	23
Niulala (2;11)	65.0	26

ergative relations. In particular, they indicate that what has been considered to be the basic word order of Samoan, namely verb–subject–object (Greenberg 1966), is not *developmentally basic*. This word order is relatively late to emerge and does not account for the majority of utterances in which both agent and patient are expressed.

These results also support the hypotheses noted earlier of Lehmann (1973) and Slobin (1975) that the verb and patient form a 'perceptual Gestalt which resists interruption'. Slobin would predict that verb–agent–patient word order would not be initially acquired by young children, and this is borne out by the Samoan data. Young Samoan children prefer to keep the verb and patient sequentially contingent, placing the agent either before or after this unit. We are unable to evaluate this hypothesis with respect to children's use of middle-verb constructions, as three-constituent constructions of this type were almost non-existent in the corpus.

4.   A speculation about ergativity

In this section, I want to comment more loosely on the material presented thus far in this chapter. My impression is that initially young children do not distinguish between intransitive verbs and their arguments and transitive verbs and their patients. In this sense, initially there is no evidence to suggest that the transitive verb and its patient form a predicate, i.e. a VP. Instead it is an information unit comparable to the intransitive verb and major argument (v + s). As Fillmore (1968) and later Dixon (1979) have suggested, there is a conceptual basis for this parallel. Both types of utterance typically express the information that something has happened or will happen etc. to some entity. Both have or will have undergone a change of state. Initially that the patient has undergone or will undergo etc. a change of state through the (usually intentional) actions of another entity is not attended to by the child in producing utterances containing a transitive verb and a patient NP. The child is oriented toward, i.e. focuses on, what happened/will happen to what rather than who/what caused/will cause etc. this to happen. Over developmental time, the causative dimension of these events becomes more attended to, more a focus in communicating. In this view, language development consists of a gradual separation of intransitive and transitive constructions, although, as noted in the discussion of adult Samoan, there will always be anomalous constructions, interpretable as either intransitive or transitive. In this sense, even in adult Samoan the verb plus patient functions sometimes as a semantic predicate and sometimes not.

The distinction between transitive and intransitive in adult speech has been described as a cline (Hopper & Thompson 1980). The transitive endpoint of this cline in Samoan is represented by verb-initial utterances not only with agent and patient NPs expressed but also with agent NPs marked with the ergative particle. Among other functions, the ergative particle appears to 'transitivize' the action encoded. It heightens the fact that action was/will be caused by some entity. In one story about an old woman attacked by dogs, for example, the storytellers repeated over and over throughout the story, *'ai e maile* 'bit ERG dogs', seemingly to heighten the transitive nature of the actions and stress that the dogs did something to the old woman. A common environment for the ergative particle is in accusations (see examples 4, 8, and 9 in Chapter 5) and praises (see example 6 in Chapter 5). Again, in both of these uses attention is directed to who did what. Further, when there is a two-constituent utterance consisting of a verb followed by an ergative case-marked NP, the existence of a specific patient is presupposed. The patient referent will have been expressed in prior discourse or is part of the immediate environment. A verb that can be either transitive or intransitive that is followed by an unmarked NP does not have this presupposition. Thus, a verb like *inu* 'drink' can be either transitive or intransitive. When the verb is followed by an ergative case-marked NP, as in *'ua inu e Sefo* 'PERF drink ERG Sefo', only the transitive reading is possible. When the verb is followed by an unmarked NP, as in *'ua inu Sefo* 'PERF drink Sefo', intransitive and transitive interpretations are possible. The sentence can mean either 'Sefo has drunk' or 'Sefo has drunk it', depending on the context. This property supports the notion that the ergative particle heightens or highlights the transitive quality of the proposition conveyed. This variation in case marking is a sociolinguistic phenomenon (see Chapter 5).

In the middle ranges of this continuum fall utterances in which agents are not expressed within the utterance as a major constituent. In some of these utterances, as noted earlier, the agent referent may appear in some other semantic role in the utterance (genitive or benefactor, for example). In these utterances, the agentive or causative dimension of the actions is not attended to; indeed, the producer of such utterances couches the information in such a way that some other role of the agent referent is articulated.

In Chapter 5, I presented sociolinguistic information concerning the use of the ergative case marker in adult Samoan and indicated that children simply do not often hear this marker in their social environment (household settings). This circumstance provides an immediate basis for the late acquisition of the case marker. Here I am suggesting that, beyond this sociolinguistic pattern, there are pragmatic patterns in adult speech that are shared by children. In particular, both adults and children tend to be absolutive-oriented, if one can put it this way. The causative (here agent) dimension of an action is typically not in focus (referent is deleted or in some other semantic role). The more marked strategy is to express the agent as a major constituent and mark it by the ergative particle *e*. In this instance, the causative/agent aspect of the action is in focus. (If the case-marked NP immediately follows the verb, it may supersede the patient NP as the major focus of information in the utterance.) The late acquisition of the ergative case marker by Samoan children may reflect these pragmatic norms of adult speakers and as well stem from conceptual difficulties in focusing on both the cause and the result of an action.

5. Implications for other acquisition studies

As discussed earlier, one of the issues in acquisition research concerns the extent to which children use word order in constructing grammatical systems. In languages with variable word orders, certain studies show that children do use a fixed word order initially, and others report that children vary word order. The Samoan materials are relevant. If one were to look at word order in the transitive *three*-constituent utterances of Samoan children, the results would indicate considerable variation. Young children use predominantly VOA and AVO and to a much lesser extent VAO and OVA. On the other hand, we have reported that for adults as well as children, three-full-constituent utterances are not the norm and the majority of *two*-constituent transitives have a fixed order of VO. Researchers working on other languages may also find that children do not typically hear three-constituent utterances. Children exposed to such input may use a preferred word order for a basic utterance type consisting of a verb and a single, direct NP. The researcher may find, as in the case of Samoan children, that this core order tends to be preserved in three-constituent transitives produced by language-acquiring children. In other words, children in certain speech communities may organize their early grammars primarily in terms of a two-constituent schema rather than a three-constituent schema (see Slobin & Bever 1982).

Secondly, ergative languages generally provide support for the conceptual similarity of patients and major arguments of intransitive verbs. In Samoan we can add experiencers (subjects of semitransitive verbs of feeling) to this list. It is quite possible that children acquiring nominative–accusative languages may develop in their own grammars ergative–absolutive categories, along the lines of Samoan children's grammars (cf. Goldin-Meadow 1975.) The semantic analysis used in other acquisition studies may be masking a regularity, marked through two-constituent word ordering (e.g. either intransitive v–s/transitive v–o or s–intransitive v/o–transitive v).

7.   Clarification

I.   INTRODUCTION

Chapter 1 introduced the notion that linguistic knowledge and sociocultural knowledge interface in the process of communication and in the process of children's intellectual development. Knowledge of one's language draws on knowledge of social expectations and cultural arrangements for understanding and evaluating events, relations, and entities. Knowledge of society and culture in turn crucially depends on language as a communicative tool and as a symbolic system. These two domains help to structure social life, in particular verbal activities or practices. That is, participants in verbal activities/practices draw on linguistic and sociocultural knowledge to create and define what is taking place. On the other hand, these verbal activities/practices are means through which aspects of linguistic and sociocultural knowledge are created and/or maintained. This two-way relationship between structure and practice is emphasized by Bourdieu (1977) and Giddens (1979) and is a crucial principle of the language-socialization approach of Ochs and Schieffelin (Ochs & Schieffelin 1984; Schieffelin & Ochs 1986a, b).

This chapter illustrates the relationship between structure and practice by discussing the relation between a particular type of verbal activity/practice, the clarification sequence, and sociocultural orientations. A major point of the chapter is that the verbal activities such as clarification sequences are organized by sociocultural as well as by linguistic principles. Strategies for clarifying unintelligible utterances are linked to local conceptions of social order, knowledge, and communication. When caregivers engage in clarification activities with their young charges, they too are guided by these conceptions. It is important for those analyzing caregiver–child communication and children's communicative development to see communicative activities of children as socially structured and culturally grounded and to link these activities to other activities in a local community.

I am grateful for the helpful comments of Elaine Andersen, Yigal Arens, Niko Besnier, Alessandro Duranti, and Edward Finegan, and for the long discussions with Emanuel Schegloff on earlier drafts of this research paper.

A second major point of this chapter is that the intellectual development of young children is impacted by their participation in verbal activities such as clarification sequences. Here the chapter illustrates the notion that intrapersonal psychological processes emerge not only in but through interpersonal or social activities (Leontyev 1981; Luria 1976; Vygotsky 1978; Wertsch 1985a). Like the sociohistorical school, this chapter emphasizes that activities vary in content and structure across societies and that this variation impacts members' cognitive orientations.

Heretofore the emphasis in sociohistorical research has been on the impact of literacy and schooling activities (see Chapter 10) on cognitive development. The well-known research of Scribner and Cole, for example, indicates that the development of cognitive skills in an individual is not so much the effect of literacy per se as the effect of engaging in particular types of literacy practices. This chapter illustrates that the impact of language practices is not limited to formal or institutional experiences, such as schooling, but rather extends to everyday, routine sorts of verbal activity. This chapter is interested in the kind of verbal activity that goes by unnoticed but is plentiful and recurrent in everyday social life. The clarification sequence is one such activity. These sequences pervade communication. They appear in a vast range of social situations, have a systematic and complex discourse organization (Schegloff, Jefferson & Sacks 1977), are interactionally negotiated, and yet are accomplished almost without notice by participants in an interaction.

This kind of 'nothing special' verbal activity is an important locus of investigation in analyzing the impact of activity on thought. Unlike schooling and literacy practices, such everyday, ordinary conversational activities (like clarifications) are part of children's earliest communicative experiences universally. Long before formal schooling experiences, infants and small children participate in hundreds of informal conversational activities, including clarification activities. Given that these activities are partially organized by society and culture, such activities are ideal loci for understanding how different sociocultural preferences for engaging in these practices affect thought in the early years of children's development.

This chapter promotes the idea that the organization of conversational activity carries with it basic information concerning social relationships, roles, events, values, preferences, beliefs, and the like. Conversational activity is, then, a critical means of socializing young children into this domain of knowledge. It is not only what is said but, importantly, the discourse structure of what is said that socializes. Children receive important sociocultural information in part through turn-taking procedures and preferences and through ways in which conversational acts are formulated. In Chapter 4 it was suggested that the prevalence of multiparty versus dialogic turn taking in traditional Samoan households socializes young Samoan children into a view of social order and personhood. The sheer presence of different parties of different social standing indicates that persons at any one moment have multiple social identities. Local preferences concerning who may direct what kind of conversational act (e.g. order, announcement) to whom also conveys important information concerning status and rank. As indicated in the latter part of Chapter 1, Samoan children learn these preferences quite early in life. The present chapter illustrates how social and cultural information is carried in the preferential organization of clarification sequences.

The discussion also calls for a reconsideration of the notion of linguistic relativity. Sapir's classic statement on this topic is repeated here:

It is quite an illusion to imagine that one adjusts to reality essentially without the use of language and that language is merely an incidental means of solving specific problems of communication or reflection. The fact of the matter is that the 'real world' is to a large extent unconsciously built up on the language habits of the group . . . We see and hear and otherwise experience very largely as we do because the language habits of our community predispose certain choices of interpretation. (Sapir in Mandelbaum 1949:162)

Sapir here speaks of language habits. Whorf spoke of fashions of speaking. What we need, to update this notion, is to strip the linguistic-relativity hypothesis of its undesirable deterministic elements and preserve Sapir's notion that language habits predispose to certain choices of interpretation. The notion of predisposition is akin to phenomenological views that experiential frames influence construction of interpretations. It is also akin to the sociohistorical view that habitual participation in language activities enhances the emergence of certain psychological skills. We want to make certain that we allow for creativity and individual difference in our reconsidered theory of linguistic relativity. We want to say that persons are oriented to ways of viewing the world through habitual participation in language activities, but that this process is open-ended. World views developed through verbal interactions can be transformed through further participation in language activities. The extent to which such transformations occur depends on personal and social conditions, but for all members of society socialization (including language socialization) is a lifelong process.

II.   CLARIFICATION

A.   Clarification and culture

Making clear our own and others' behaviors is a universal communicative activity, necessary for social order and survival. However, while clarification is a universal activity, preferences for how clarification is accomplished vary from situation to situation within a social group and (for some specific social situations, e.g. speaking to higher- or lower-ranking persons) may vary from one social group to another. More specifically, I want to suggest that both the conditions under which clarification takes place (what gets clarified, who participates in the activity of clarification in which roles) and the discourse procedures speakers prefer to use index (see Chapter 1, section I.B) members' views of knowledge, particularly members' views on the limits of knowledge (what can be known) and the paths to knowledge (how knowledge is acquired). Another way of looking at this is to say that when members engage in the activity of clarification, they display and construct tacit guidelines and principles for creating knowledge. These guidelines and principles in turn are tied to local theories of meaning, of learning, and of self.

I am interested in those cases of clarification where the participants are caregivers and young children. Clarification sequences have been a major focus of interest in research on caregiver register and its impact on communication involving young children and on language acquisition more generally (see Golinkoff 1983 for discussion of this point). Some of the research on clarification is incorporated in larger studies of questions directed to young children (see Corsaro 1977, 1979; Gallagher 1981; Garvey 1977; Petersen, Danner, & Flavell 1972), while other discussions of clarification are part of analyses of expansions (see R. Brown & Bellugi 1964; Cazden 1965; Cross 1975, 1977, 1978). These studies emphasize either social or cognitive effects of children's participation in such activities. All studies indicate that clarification pervades caregiver–child interactions in the Western middle-class homes observed.

The emphasis in this chapter will be the point that as caregivers involve infants and small children in clarification exchanges around the world, they are displaying and constructing with them more general, socially valued ways of understanding the world. In Sapir's terms, the language habits of their particular communities predispose children to view the world in a certain light. In the following discussion, I shall examine patterns of clarification between children and caregivers and their relation to folk epistemologies and concepts of the child–caregiver relationship. While this analysis will focus on traditional Western Samoan society, Western Samoan preferences will be compared with those observed in American white middle-class society.

B.   Structure of clarification sequences

Let us now try to formulate a working definition of the activity of clarification. A clarification sequence contains a verbal or nonverbal behavior that is seen as unclear by at least one participant to an interaction. Unclarity may involve both surface expression and/or underlying meaning. An utterance, for example, may be unintelligible because it has been poorly articulated, because it has not been heard, and so on. On the other hand, even when the surface form of an utterance is intelligible, its meaning may not be clear.

Using the terminology of conversation analysis, we can say that the unclear behavior is a trouble source for some participant and that the clarification sequence attends to the work of repairing or attempting to resolve that trouble (Jefferson 1974; Schegloff, Jefferson & Sacks 1977). That is, clarification is a goal of at least one participant.

As a type of repair sequence, the clarification sequence has the structural options that have been noted for repair sequences generally. Clarification may be self-initiated (i.e. initiated by the party that produces the unclear behavior) or other-initiated. Attempts to clarify may also be carried out either by self or by other.

C.   Other-initiated clarification

1.   Introduction

As noted earlier, it is the other-initiated type of clarification sequence that has received considerable attention in the language acquisition literature, because transcripts are laced with children's utterances and nonverbal behaviors that are followed by caregivers' initiations of clarification, as illustrated in the following examples:

(1) Jordan, a fourteen-month-old male infant, being served his lunch

1.   Jordan: (Vocalizes repeatedly until his mother turns around.)
2.   Mother: (Turns around to look at him.)
3.   Jordan: (Points to one of the objects on the counter.)
4. – ⟩ Mother: Do you want this? (Holds up milk container.)
5.   Jordan: (Shakes his head 'no.')
       (Vocalizes, continues to point.)
6. – ⟩ Mother: Do you want this? (Holds up jelly jar.)
7.   Jordan: (Shakes head 'no.')
       (Continues to point.)
8, 9, 10, 11. (Two more offer-rejection pairs.)
12. – ⟩ Mother: This? (Picks up sponge.)
13.   Jordan: (Leans back in highchair, puts arms down, tension leaves body.)
14.   Mother: (Hands Jordan sponge.)

(from Golinkoff 1983:58–9)

(2) Allison, sixteen months and three weeks

1.   Mother: What do you see?

2.   Allison: (A leans forward; looking at bag) pig/
       (A stands up.)
3. – 〉 Mother: What?
4.   Allison: pig/
5. – 〉 Mother: Play? Is that what you're saying? Play?
6.   Allison: oh/ pig/ —/

                                                    (from Bloom 1973:152–3)

For some researchers, these caregiver responses have been taken as evidence that caregiver speech facilitates the acquisition of grammar (Cross 1977, 1981). For others, these responses have been treated as a means by which caregivers are able to sustain communication with a young baby or child (R. Brown 1977; Golinkoff 1983; Snow 1972).

2.   Two types of other-initiated clarification

In societies around the world, speakers appear to rely on (at least) two strategies for clarifying an unintelligible utterance of another speaker in their presence. The two strategies are universal; however, the contexts in which the two strategies are used and the preference for one strategy or the other or both vary along cultural lines.

2.1.   *The minimal-grasp strategy*
The first strategy is to exhibit minimal or no grasp of what the speaker has said or done and to rely primarily on the speaker to resay the utterance or redo the gesture. Let us call this strategy the *minimal-grasp strategy*.[1]

In the case of caregiver–child interaction, getting the child to resay or redo the unintelligible may be accomplished indirectly by the caregiver expressing nonunderstanding, e.g. through a quizzical expression or through a verbal statement such as 'I don't understand' or 'I can't understand what you are saying.' Otherwise the caregiver may directly ask the child what she or he said or ask the child to supply a piece of what she or he said, using WH interrogatives such as 'What?', 'Who?', 'He went where?', and the like (see example (2), line 3). Examples (3) and (4) illustrate this strategy among Samoan caregivers with young children.

(3) Pesio 8–54

Pesio (P) two years and three months old, is with her mother's mother (SA) and father's sister (I).
1.   P: la ia oke*/
            '(there (?) a hibiscus)'/

_____

[1] I am indebted to E. Schegloff for providing this term.

2.–> I: Mai e aa?
          '(You) said what?'
3.   P: oke!/ oke!/
          'hibiscus!'/'hibiscus!'/
4.   SA: Fea?
          'Where?'
5.   P: ((P points toward road, where a titled man is walking along, wearing
          a hibiscus on his ear))
          (iie)/((=lale?))
          '(there)'/
          * *Aute* or *auke*.

(4) Maselino P21–62

Maselino, four years, is with his brother (S), sixteen years, his mother's
brother's daughter (O), five years, and his mother's brother's wife, A.

1. M (to S): Mai U le kusia sou igoa le kegi
              'U said (they) are not going to write your name (on the list of
              workers for) the gang.'
2. S: E aa?
              'What?'
3. O: ((laughs))
              [
4. M: Mai U lee kusia e sau igoa le kegi ee.
              'U said (they) are not going to write ((hesitation particle)) your
              name (on the list of workers for) the gang ((warning particle)).'
5. A (to S): Mai e aa?
              '(She) said what?'
              ((pause))
6. S: Mai lee kusia so'u igoa le kegi.
              '(She) said (they) are not going to write my name (on the list of
              workers for) the gang.'

Caregivers may also get children to say again unintelligible utterances by
saying to them, 'Say it again' or 'Show me another time' or 'Could you say it
once more?' and so on. Samoan caregivers rely on teasing and shaming to
get a clearer utterance from a child. Children who speak unclearly are
referred to in their presence as having *guku Saiga* (or *gutu Saina*) 'Chinese
mouth' or may be said to talk like a horse or may be called by the name of an
adult who doesn't speak or act normally.

2.2.   *The expressed-guess strategy*
A second strategy for clarifying unclear utterances of other speakers is to
articulate a guess at what the speaker's unclear utterance or gesture could be
or could mean. Let us call this strategy the *expressed-guess strategy*.[2]
    In contrast to the minimal-grasp strategy, here someone other than the
original speaker attempts a reformulation of the unclear act. In the case of

---

[2] This strategy is roughly comparable to the notion of 'candidate understanding'
within the paradigm of conversation analysis (Schegloff: personal
communication).

caregiver–child interactions in which the child produces an unclear utterance, the child's task is merely to confirm or disconfirm the caregiver's guess. This strategy is illustrated in example (1), lines 4, 6 and 12, and in example (2), line 5. In the case of disconfirmation, the child may resay his utterance or redo his gesture and the caregiver may continue to supply new guesses, as illustrated in example (1).

The speech act of guessing covers a range of uncertain knowledge. A caregiver or any speaker may formulate a guess when she or he is not at all certain of her or his knowledge. In interactions with infants, this is often the case. Caregivers often find themselves articulating wild guesses at what the infant could be signaling. On the other end, caregivers and others may formulate guesses when they are fairly certain of what an infant is saying or doing. In these cases, the caregiver is using the guess to make certain or to double-check her or his understanding.

III. CULTURAL PREFERENCES FOR OTHER-INITIATED CLARIFICATION

I have emphasized that cross-cultural differences are not necessarily categorical, i.e. 'These people do x; those people don't do x.' Instead, many cross-cultural differences reside in the preferential organization of acts and events. Many differences are differences of statistical frequency, i.e. 'These people do x much more frequently than those people'; other differences are context-sensitive, i.e. 'These people do x under these circumstances; those people do not do x under the same circumstances but they do x under different circumstances'; 'These people prefer x as an initial strategy; those people do x when other strategies are unsuccessful', etc. Differences across social groups in the use of other-initiated clarification strategies are of this sort.

Quantitative analyses of clarification strategies across contexts have not been carried out in either white middle-class (WMC) or Western Samoan society, but we can nonetheless see that there are major differences in the way the two strategies figure in social interactions in these two social groups. WMC caregivers, like WMC speakers generally, rely heavily on both minimal-grasp and expressed-guess strategies to resolve unclarities in the utterances and actions of others. WMC speakers generally have been observed to prefer as an initial clarification strategy constructions that display the maximum of what they understand of a problematic utterance (Schegloff, personal communication 1984). Relevant to our concerns here, the preference of WMC speakers, where conditions of hearing and understanding permit, is for the expressed-guess strategy over the minimal-grasp strategy. In using the expressed-guess strategy, speakers prefer specific interrogative pronouns ('Where?', 'Who?' etc.) over the weaker construction 'Huh?' and prefer partial repetitions that include an interrogative pronoun ('He went where?' etc.) over the interrogative pronoun on its own.

Samoan speakers use both the minimal grasp and the expressed guess to clarify but overwhelmingly prefer the first strategy. Nowhere is the preference for the minimal-grasp strategy more preferred than in interactions involving caregivers with infants and young children. In these contexts, expressed guesses are exceedingly rare.

In village households, caregivers initiate clarification of children's utterances through quizzical expressions, statements of nonunderstanding, wh questions, and other directives, to elicit from the child a reformulation of all or part of the unclear utterance or gesture (see examples (3) and (4)). In the corpus of interactions that we recorded in the course of our fieldwork, we rarely found cases in which caregivers – either sib or adult – formulated an explicit guess at what an unclear utterance or gesture of the child might be. This dispreference was also manifest when members of the family or others listened with me to recordings of children's unclear utterances. Almost everyone found my own enterprise of explicitly guessing at a garbled or telegraphic utterance of a child puzzling and not worth the time. They engaged in this activity primarily in deference to me. Similarly, in the household interactions recorded, the one or two cases of explicit guessing of children's utterances by caregivers were explicitly for my benefit, done in the knowledge that I needed clear speech for the recording. This variation will be accounted for below in a discussion of the relation of clarification to social rank.

The reluctance to use expressed guesses in clarification does not mean that these caregivers and others listening to and watching children may not guess *silently*. However, it is important to note that silent guesses differ from expressed guesses. First, expressed guesses make explicit a possible proposition. Expressed hypotheses, conjectures, and speculations all commit their makers tentatively to the possibility that some state of affairs may hold. Second, expressed guesses elicit the involvement of the original speakers in the process of understanding, whereas the silent guess does not. In the case of caregiver–child interaction, the expressed guess of the caregiver gives the child a role in the assignment of meaning; the child is given veto power, so to speak, over the caregiver's understanding. In the expressed guess, then, meaning is negotiated before it is assigned. In the silent guess, any negotiation of meaning that may occur takes place after the caregiver's initial assignment of meaning.

A.   Clarification strategies and modes of instruction

The Samoan preference for clarifying through eliciting a repeated performance (minimal-grasp strategy) is manifested more generally in situations in which instruction is taking place. As in many societies, Samoans rely heavily on repeated, often passive, observation of behaviors as a means of transmitting and acquiring knowledge and skills. Dance practice, for example, consists of one person modeling entire dances over and over in front of learners, who imitate the dance movements or watch to one side. As Samoan caregivers engage young children in clarification sequences, they are then socializing them through language into broader, socially valued methods of education, namely that the path to knowledge is through repeated exposure, i.e. through listening and watching over and over.

In WMC society, repetition of information is also an important strategy in the transmission and acquisition of new information. However, the tradition of clarifying through Socratic, dialogic methods is also strong in WMC society. In the Socratic method, knowledge is pursued through formulating and pursuing initial hypotheses, that is, through laying out for others explicit guesses. WMC caregivers who initiate clarification of children's utterances or gestures through yes–no interrogatives or other forms of guessing are socializing children into this socially valued procedure for gaining knowledge, just as when they elicit resayings or redoings they are socializing them into the alternative procedure whereby knowledge is enhanced through repeated observations.

B. The situational scope of explicit guessing

Explicit guessing is dispreferred among rural Western Samoans in most social situations. However, there are situational variables that influence the likelihood that explicit guessing will occur.

1. Social rank

E. Goody (1978) has noted that among the Gonja of northern Ghana the use of questions is socially constrained. In adult–child interactions, questions are appropriate speech acts of adults but not of young children. In Samoan society, the speech act of explicit guessing is also affected by social status.

As noted in Chapter 4, Samoan society is highly stratified. Rank is assessed in terms of political title (e.g. chief, orator, and positions within each of these statuses), church title (pastor, deacon, etc.), age, and generation, among other variables. Titled persons have higher rank than untitled persons, and older, higher-generation persons have higher rank than younger persons. Among the demeanors associated with distinctions in social rank is that of *perspective taking*. Lower-ranking persons are expected to assume the perspective of higher-ranking persons more than higher-ranking vis-à-vis lower-ranking parties in a social situation. Lower-ranking persons are expected to notice and anticipate the wishes of higher-ranking persons. They stand in a service relation to those of higher status.

As I have noted elsewhere (Ochs 1982a; Ochs & Schieffelin 1984), young Samoan children are socialized early in their lives to a *sociocentric* perspective. As infants, they are often held and fed facing outward toward others in a group. When they begin to speak, much time and effort is devoted to instructing the young child to notice others and to repeat their personal names. In Samoan society, sib and parental caregivers work hard to get children, even before the age of two years, to take the perspective of others. This demeanor is a fundamental component of showing respect, a most necessary competence in Samoan daily life.

The process of communication is affected by these social expectations concerning perspective taking. It is obvious that communication requires degrees of perspective taking by all participating parties, i.e. degrees of what has been called intersubjectivity (Trevarthen 1979).

In Samoan interactions, the extent to which a party is expected to assume the perspective of another in assigning a meaning to an utterance of another varies with social rank. In speaking to those of lower rank, higher-ranking persons are not expected to do a great deal of perspective taking to make sense out of their own utterances or to make sense of the utterance of a lower-ranking interlocutor. Higher-ranking persons, then, are not expected to clarify and simplify for lower-ranking persons. For example, caregivers are not expected to simplify their speech in talking to young children (Ochs 1982a). And exactly the reverse is expected of lower-ranking persons. They take on more of the burden of clarifying their own utterances and the utterances of higher-ranking interlocutors.

Of the two clarification strategies discussed earlier, the expressed-guess strategy involves more perspective taking than the minimal-grasp strategy. One reason we do not see caregivers making explicit guesses at what their charges are saying is that such a response demands an orientation that is generally inappropriate to the social role of caregiver. Only in situations in which a small child is speaking on behalf of someone of high status (e.g as when the child is a messenger) is this degree of perspective taking expected. Typically, when very small Samoan children produce unintelligible utterances, they are disregarded or addressed with a construction indicating noncomprehension and are directed to redesign their utterances to meet the communicative needs of others. Through such procedures, children develop early in life a sensitivity to the demands of their social environment and the communicative skills to meet them.

Looking at transcripts of interactions across many contexts (adult–adult, adult–child, child–child), I found few instances of explicit guessing. Of those instances located, most occur in interactions among peers, and a few occur in interactions in which a higher-ranking person has produced an unclear utterance. Explicit guessing appears across several speech activities in peer interaction; explicit guessing directed at a higher-ranking person is much less frequent. As audience to personal narratives, gossip, or speeches of higher-ranking persons, lower-ranking persons do not typically explicitly guess at the meaning of utterances. However, when a higher-ranking person directs a lower-ranking person to do something, then the lower-ranking person may clarify by directing a guess to the speaker. In this case, the explicit guess is part of serving the higher-ranking party. Even under these conditions, however, this strategy is not highly frequent. It is generally dispreferred for lower-ranking persons to explicitly guess at the utterances of higher-ranking persons. The expectation is that the lower-ranking person should be attending (and therefore not need to clarify on grounds of not having heard the utterance) and should understand.

In multiparty situations involving persons of different social rank, lower-ranking persons may get out of this bind by asking a *peer* to respond to an explicit guess concerning part or all of an unclear utterance of a higher-ranking person. This strategy is illustrated in the following example. In this example, a group of boys of differing ages are playing on the beach, pretending to be preparing a meal. In their play, the older boys do the directing of preparation and the younger boys carry out the directives (just as in daily life). In the case below, the oldest boy (Boy 1) directs a younger one (Sesi, Boy 3) to make *saka* 'boiled taro'. The younger boy then turns to a boy close to his age and requests confirmation of his understanding of what was said.

(5) Boys playing on the beach

BOY 1: Sole, alu Sesi fai saka ee!
'Mate, go Sesi to make saka ((EMPH PRT))!'
Ke iloa fai –
'You know (how) to make –'
BOY 2: ((Hums)) . . . eli ma'a.
((Hums)) . . . dig stones.
BOY 3: Fai mai "Fai saka"?
'(He) said "Make saka"?'
BOY 1: Sole, alu oe e e ((pause)) koli mai ulu.
'Mate, you go to to ((pause)) twist off and fetch down breadfruit.'

2.   What gets clarified

It is important to emphasize that explicit guessing is a viable activity in Samoan social life, but it is an activity that is situationally restricted. In addition to social rank, the object of clarification is an important variable constraining the use of explicit guessing in Samoan interactions. When explicit guessing occurs, the focus of clarification tends to be the nature of some external event or state of affairs rather than some internal psychological event or state (e.g. personal intention of speaker). Indeed, Samoan has a set of evidential particles indicating degrees of certainty with which a speaker knows or believes some external event or state to be the case. These particles may be used in talking about past, present, and future situations. For example, in the course of a lengthy narrative about an old woman who was attacked by dogs, one listener speculated that perhaps it was spirits and not dogs who attacked. This is an instance of explicit guessing. The bulk of the speculations concern whether or not some account of an event or state of affairs is true or accurate.

This object of concern contrasts with the object of concern where interlocutors are presented with unintelligible utterances. In the WMC caregiver–child interactions observed, the goal of clarification sequences is not only to obtain an utterance that is intelligible but assign a reading to that utterance that is compatible with the child's *intended meaning*. Here the object of clarification is some internal psychological condition, what the speaker (here the child) is thinking. In all speech, but particularly in children's speech, utterances may have several meanings. In WMC caregiver–child interactions, as in WMC interactions generally, a major problem is to sort out which meaning is the 'correct' one, where correctness is based on the caregiver's assessment of the child's intentions (what Grice (1968) calls 'utterer's meaning'). So important is the understanding of the child's intention in WMC society that caregivers will check with the child whether their understanding of the child's intended meaning is correct or not. This job is accomplished through the expressed guess. In guessing, the caregiver displays a tentative reading before a final interpretation. The child has an option, indeed is directed, to influence the caregiver's understanding of some particular utterance or action before a meaning is assigned.

In so doing, WMC caregivers are conforming to a cultural theory of communication in which speakers' personal intentions are critical to the interpretation of an utterance or action. Certain philosophical theories of meaning, such as that of Searle (1969) and Grice (1968), articulate the system of knowledge that underlies this folk theory. In the work of both Searle (following Austin 1962) and Grice, the issues taken up focus on the relation between convention and intention, locutionary and illocutionary meaning, sentence and utterer's meaning, evaluating the relative importance of each in a theory of meaning and language use.

Recently several sociolinguists and anthropologists have discussed this orientation to meaning in relation to cultural beliefs and orientations (Duranti 1984b; Kochman 1983; Ochs 1982a; Rosaldo 1982; Shore 1977, 1982). All of these discussions have focused on the concept of person that emerges from language behavior and from folk and academic theories of meaning. The emphasis on personal intentions in Western white middle-class society and scholarship is tied to a cultural ideology in which persons are viewed as individuals, i.e. as coherent personalities, who have control over and are responsible for their utterances and actions.

Personal intentions are important in a vast range of situations in WMC society. Members of WMC society seek to clarify an individual's personal intentions for a range of purposes. For example, members of this society usually base their assignments of responsibility and appropriate sanctions on the speaker/actor's particular intentions behind an utterance or action. This society distinguishes, for example, between inadvertent and planned behaviors, and between accidental and purposeful behaviors. In legal and other contexts, if it is established that a negatively valued behavior was consciously intended, then sanctions are usually more severe than if the speaker/actor 'didn't mean to do it' or couldn't help doing it or otherwise was not in control. Note that establishing intention is not always critical to sanctioning. In many situations, members of this society say, 'It doesn't matter whether you meant it or not.' The important point is that in Anglo-American WMC society, what a person *means* or *meant* to do or say is an important cultural variable. For this social group, what a person means to do is distinguished from what he does. This orientation leads members to take seriously and pursue establishing an individual's motivations and psychological states.

This concern with and emphasis on personal intentions is not matched in other societies. In societies such as American black working-class (Kochman 1981, 1983), Ilongot (Rosaldo 1982), Ifaluk (Lutz 1982), and Samoan (Duranti 1984b; Ochs 1982a), the *consequences* of an utterance or action play an important role in assigning meaning.

In certain accounts, the emphasis on consequences takes the form of the society focusing on the *social ramifications* of a behavior (rather than on the speaker/actor's intentions). Lutz, for example, notes that the Ifaluk focus on the 'wake' of an action. In Ochs (1982a), I discussed the primacy of consequences of action in Samoan evaluations of actions. In Samoan households, children are sanctioned according to the negative effects of their behaviors. This is also the case in the legal arena, where actions are assessed almost exclusively in terms of social and economic losses and disturbances. In the context of assessing misdeeds in Samoan society, the focus is much less on personal intentions behind an utterance/action. In this context, it is not terribly important whether the wrongdoer did something by accident, inadvertently, or on purpose. Indeed, Samoans see persons as not in control of their misdeeds (Shore 1977, 1982). Samoan children may try to get out of punishment by denying that they did that culpable act, but they do not try to worm out of it by saying, 'I didn't mean it', 'It was just an accident', 'I did it by mistake', 'I didn't do it on purpose', as do WMC children almost by routine.

Other accounts, following a more phenomenological approach to communication, have focused on the importance of the hearer's role in the assignment of meaning. Kochman, for example, has commented that for the community of black speakers in the United States, very often the perlocutionary effect on the hearer takes precedence over the speaker's intended meaning. Indeed, here, as in other societies, including Samoan society, speakers often leave ambiguous what is meant, waiting to see how a hearer will take it up. In this sense, meaning is in the hands of the audience more than in the speaker's; the audience has the final word.

Taking these accounts altogether, I might propose that we have found a variable in terms of which societies contrast. There are societies like the WMC in the United States that focus primarily on the *personal psychological sources of utterances/actions* and other societies, such as the Ilongot of the Philippines, the Ifaluk of the Caroline Islands, the Samoans, and the working-class blacks in the United States, that focus primarily on the *social consequences of utterances/actions*.

This distinction, however, is too simplistic. For example, we have theories supported by scholars in WMC society in the United States that argue against the primacy of personal intentions in establishing meaning. Sociohistorical theories of meaning such as that held by Bakhtin (Voloshinov 1973), deconstructionist theories within literary criticism (Derrida 1977), hermeneutic perspectives (e.g. Gadamer 1976), and conversation-analysis theory (see Sacks & Schegloff 1979; Sacks, Schegloff & Jefferson 1974; Schegloff 1984) are alive and popular in this country. This observation along with ethnographic observations of Samoan interaction suggests that within each society both orientations persist. The difference between societies lies in the contexts in which these two orientations prevail, the relative importance given to each, and the frequency with which these orientations mark social interaction.

In Samoan society, personal intentions are a focus of concern in a restricted set of contexts, primarily when the speaker/actor is of high social status and/or of higher social rank than the hearer/audience. For example, Shore (1977, 1982) and Duranti (1981a) have noted that in the context of political meetings of titled persons, only high chiefs and high-status orators are entitled to voice personal opinions. In this sense, high-status speakers in this situation are treated more as individuals than are others present, and their personal intentions are attended to. In addition, when a higher-ranking person orders a lower-ranking person to carry out some action, the personal intentions of the speaker are also of primary importance. The lower-ranking party cannot assign his own interpretation but rather must grasp that intended by the higher-ranking speaker.

Where the speaker is of low status and/or of lower rank than the hearer, then his or her personal intentions tend to assume low priority in assigning meaning, and the interpretation of the higher-ranking hearer takes precedence. Notice that whether the higher-ranking party is speaker or hearer, the higher-ranking party controls meaning.

Given that explicit guessing is tied to the pursuit of the speaker's intentions, it is somewhat understandable, given the comments above, that we would observe very little explicit guessing directed to lower-ranking speakers. The personal intentions of lower-ranking speakers, such as children talking to caregivers, do not count in the same way as those of higher-ranking speakers. It would be particularly improbable for caregivers to direct guesses at infants, since infants are seen neither as personalities nor as conversational partners. As noted in Ochs (1982a) and Ochs & Schieffelin (1984), Samoan caregivers refer to infants often but do not engage them as conversational partners in the way observed of WMC mothers with their young infants. Samoan caregivers cuddle and soothe and play with their infants, but they do not treat their gestures and vocalizations in the early months of life as necessarily intentional or social.

The two perspectives on personal intentions and meaning vary in importance in WMC and Samoan societies. The theory of meaning which Holquist (1983) calls the 'personalist' view of meaning (the view that 'I (the speaker) own meaning') is far more salient in WMC society than in traditional rural Western Samoan communities. When WMC caregivers attend very carefully to the unclear gestures and utterances of their infants and young children, when they explicitly guess at what the child means, they are socializing children into a prevailing view of meaning in which personal intentions are of primary importance. The absence of explicit guessing by Western Samoan caregivers is tied to the restricted relevance of this theory of meaning to Samoan social life, in particular to its inappropriateness in a wide range of contexts, including those in which children communicate with caregivers.

Samoans generally display a strong dispreference for guessing at what is going on in another person's mind. This dispreference has reflexes in a range of verbal activities and accounts for the rarity of activities such as test questions, riddles, and guessing games of the Twenty Questions and I Spy variety. These activities all involve explicit guessing at what the speaker has in mind. None of these activities are part of traditional instruction settings, nor are they common in informal adult–child, adult–adult, or child–child interactions. (As will be discussed in Chapter 10, they appear mainly in the context of formal classroom instruction in Christian church and Western-oriented public schools.)

IV.   Concluding remarks

This chapter has illustrated how the speech behavior of Western Samoan caregivers is congruent with traditional Samoan theories of knowledge, including their theories of learning and their theories of meaning. The major point was to indicate how children's conversations with peers and caregivers are socially and culturally organized. It is through participation in everyday conversational activities such as those described in this chapter that children in each society come to assume expectations concerning the world around them. Here our focus was on the clarification sequence as a type of verbal activity. Samoan children, like children in other societies, learn, through participating in clarification with different interactional partners, ways of acquiring knowledge, what counts as knowledge, what can be known, and rights of access to different paths to knowledge and to different kinds of knowledge. As for paths to knowledge, traditional Samoan speakers prefer to elicit repetitions of utterances rather than to explicitly guess at the intended meaning of utterances. The second path to knowledge, however, is more likely among peers than when there is a difference in social rank between interlocutors. As for limits of knowledge, generally Samoans disprefer guessing at the unclear thoughts of others. When explicit guessing does occur in Samoan interactions in village settings, the guessing tends to revolve around past actions of others, to be speculations concerning whether or not particular actions or events took place. We can see, then, that young children can be socialized through clarification activities into local epistemologies.

1. Mother with children and *matai* (sitting in the fashion only appropriate to high chiefs, with one leg over another) of the family.

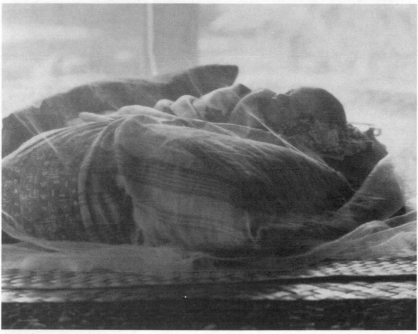

2. Infant under mosquito net.

3. Older children taking care of younger siblings and enjoying each other.

4. Girls returning from plantations with coconuts.

5. Preparing breadfruit.

6. Houses on family compound.

7. Learning to read and interpret the Bible.

8. First literacy experience: reciting letters and numbers.

8.   Affect, social control, and the
        Samoan child

I.   INTRODUCTION

A.   Goals of the discussion

In this chapter and in Chapter 9, the expression of affect in Samoan society and language will be discussed. Chapter 9 will focus on the linguistic means available in Samoan for encoding affect and the acquisition of these means by young Samoan children. The present chapter is concerned with the use of affect in family interactions involving infants and small children. The discussion will have two major foci. The first is the use of affect as a strategy for controlling the behaviors of youngsters. Here I shall consider previous considerations of anger and gentleness in Samoan society. In particular, I shall provide a developmental sociolinguistic perspective on the well-publicized Mead–Freeman debate (Freeman 1983; Mead 1928) concerning the emotional character of Samoan childhood. The reader is to keep in mind that the generalizations presented here are inferred from thousands of pages of transcribed speech of household members and from detailed notes on nonverbal behavior of these persons over the course of our fieldwork.

A second focus of the present chapter is to discuss affect in terms of the affective competence Samoan children are expected to acquire early in life. Thus, the second part of this chapter will be devoted to concepts of the Samoan child and patterns of communication with young children that may socialize young Samoan children into these concepts. Three affective dimensions of childhood are considered, including the qualities of boldness, respect, and a sense of performance.

B.   Affect: a working definition

Many of the discussions of emotion in the social-science literature have considered emotion as a physiological process associated with the nervous system. Several researchers have argued for the universality of a core set of emotional states, including fear, anger, grief, and embarrassment (Scheff 1977). Other research has focused on the expression and conceptualization of emotions within particular cultures. All human beings experience a core set of emotions sometime in their lives, but how they interpret and manifest those experiences differs across cultures. Levy (1984) suggests, for example, that certain emotions may be objects of considerable attention and knowledge. They are what Levy calls 'hypercognized', richly expressed within the culture. Other emotional responses may be underplayed or 'hypocognized'. Often a hypocognized emotion will be repressed and/or reinterpreted as some other experience, such as physical illness.

Concern with expression of emotion has led to an interest in a wide range of emotional processes, structures, and concepts; for example, feelings, moods, dispositions, attitudes, character, personality, masking, double binds, and undercutting (see Irvine 1982 for a review of this domain). To generalize, this semantic domain is often referred to as *affect*, and this is the term that I shall be using in the remainder of this chapter and in Chapter 9.

C.   Samoan concepts of affect

As discussed by Gerber (1975), Samoans have no word exactly corresponding to the English term 'emotion' but rather refer to the notion of *lagona* 'feeling'. Certain feelings corresponding to emotional feelings originate inside the *loto* 'chest'. Concepts of feeling are bound to concepts of person in all societies. As discussed in considerable detail by Shore (1977, 1982), Samoans do not see persons as having much control and are often held not to be responsible for their feelings and actions. Feelings are seen as reactions. This is encoded in the morphology of constructions using verbs of feeling. The objects of these verbs are marked with the preposition *i*, which also is a case marker indicating instrumental semantic role. Thus, a sentence such as *Fiafia Sina i le mea alofa*, literally 'Happy Sina instrument/middle-verb-object preposition the gift' can be loosely understood as 'Sina is happy because of the gift.' These constructions are also translated as 'Sina likes the gift', but this captures more the English than the Samoan concept of affect.

In line with the orientation toward external origins of feelings, in Samoan conversation there is explicit talk about the origins of a feeling within some person. However, there does not appear to be much talk about feelings as *origins of behavior*. One's actions are seen as evidence of one's feelings rather than consequences of one's feelings. Thus, for example, generosity, the giving of food and money and labor, indicates *alofa* 'love' more than it follows from *alofa*, from a Samoan point of view. Indeed, the meaning of verbs of feeling is more action (or reaction) -like than in other speech communities. As will be discussed later in this chapter, caregivers often control misbehaving small children by warning them that they or others will not love them. This is usually understood as meaning that they will not give things to or do things for the child. Withdrawal of love means in the most fundamental sense withdrawal of goods and services.

II.   AFFECT AND SOCIAL CONTROL

A.   The Mead–Freeman debate

A great deal of discussion has been generated recently by the Mead–Freeman debate over Samoan character, and much of it involves child-rearing practices of control. Freeman (1983) has portrayed Samoans as intensely violent and Samoan child rearing as highly repressive and restrictive; this portrayal is contrasted with statements by Mead (1928, 1930) to the effect that Samoans are relatively carefree and child rearing is rather an easygoing affair. One such statement is reproduced below:

The Samoan background which makes growing up so easy, so simple a matter, is the general casualness of the whole society. For Samoa is a place where no one plays for very high stakes, no one pays very heavy prices, no one suffers for his convictions or fights to the death for special ends.   (Mead 1928:198)

My own observations and understanding of Samoan child care lead me to see neither of these positions as comprehensive. Mead herself notes in other chapters of her 1928 volume that child care is indeed a demanding task and not at all a casual enterprise. Two such passages are noted here:

The weight of the punishment usually falls upon the next oldest child, who learns to shout 'Come out of the sun', before she has fully appreciated the necessity of doing so herself. By the time Samoan girls and boys have reached sixteen or seventeen years of age, these perpetual admonitions to the younger ones have become an inseparable part of their conversation, as monotonous, irritated undercurrent to all their comments.   (Mead 1928:23)

This fear of the disagreeable consequences resulting from a child's crying is so firmly fixed in the minds of the older children that long after there is any need for it, they succumb to some little tyrant's threat of making a scene, and five-year-olds bully their way into weaving parties where they will tear up the cooking leaves or get thoroughly smudged with the soot and have to be washed – all because an older boy or girl has become so accustomed to yielding any point to stop an outcry.
    This method of giving in, coaxing, bribing, diverting the infant disturbers is not only pursued within the household or the relationship group, where there are duly constituted elders in authority to punish the older children who can't

keep the babies still. Towards a neighbour's children or in a crowd, the half-grown girls and boys and even the adults vent their full irritation upon the heads of troublesome children.   (Mead 1928:24–5)

On the other hand, Freeman's description of Samoan children as 'from infancy on . . . subjected to quite stringent discipline' (1983:205) misrepresents relations between children and their caregivers and modes of control characteristic of their relationship. Harsh discipline does exist, but Freeman writes as if the most extreme physical punishment is given routinely:

The peculiarly Samoan way of administering punishment to children is illustrated in the following account from my field notes of 15 November 1942:

Punishment is almost always physical and severe. Despite the severity of the punishment the child is not permitted to show emotion . . .

In other words, Samoan children are early taught, through this particular mode of punishment, to accept without question the dictates of those in authority. This specifically Samoan system of discipline, which I had observed in the early 1940's, was still being practiced a generation later in the mid 1960's, as also in the 1980's, with those who had been thus treated during their childhood imposing the same form of punishment on their own young children. This method of dealing with the misbehaving young is used by all those in authority, however marginal; for example, in 1966, I witnessed a 10-year-old boy disciplining his 8-year-old brother in precisely this way.   (Freeman 1983:206–7)

There are several ways in which Samoan caregivers regularly control and negatively sanction their children. The harsh physical discipline to which Freeman devotes his attention is not the most common form of social control, although his writings give this impression.

In the following discussion and in the chapter to follow, I consider social control of children as a form of social behavior and relate it to the organizing principles and ideological underpinnings of Samoan society and culture.

B.   Control strategies of caregivers

In all societies, caregivers use a variety of strategies to stop a small child from doing something harmful, distasteful, or otherwise 'wrong'. These responses to wrongdoings differ in degree of severity. That is, certain responses are considered mild, whereas others are considered more severe. In Samoan society, severity or seriousness of a response can be evaluated on the basis of two features: (1) the type of control response and (2) the social identity of the person who executes the control response. Later on, I shall discuss social control in terms of social rank of caregiver. More immediately I consider representative types of control responses and their significance.

1. Bald imperative

By far the most common response to a child's wrongdoing is for a household member to address the child with an imperative utterance. Two negative imperatives, *Aua!* and *Soia!*, are commonly used in these contexts. These two imperatives are orders to stop carrying out some act; the imperatives presuppose that the act is undesirable. The imperatives differ in intensity: *Soia!* is an escalation of *Aua!*. *Aua!* can be roughly translated as 'Don't!', whereas *Soia!* is something like 'I said "Stop it!"' Typically caregivers start out using *Aua!*, but if the child does not pay attention, the imperative will be intensified to *Soia!* At times a caregiver may immediately respond *Soia!* indicating that the caregiver is irritated and wants the action terminated without further ado. *Aua!* is often used both as a single lexical item and with verbs and/or noun phrases that specify the action to be terminated, as in such phrases as *Aua le pisa!* 'Don't be noisy!' or *Aua le faie le tama!* 'Don't bother the boy!' *Soia!* is typically used as a single lexical item.

In addition to these constructions, caregivers may use a series of particles that convey the discontent of the speaker and direct the addressee to stop what he or she is doing. These particles include *A'a!*, *A'e!*, *Ei!*, and *Sh!*

These constructions are among the mildest forms used for social control within the household. They are also the most common, particularly the case of *Aua!*

2. Affect arousal

Another common control strategy of caregivers is to explicitly elicit or attempt to invoke certain feelings in the child who has performed the wrongdoing. This strategy typically but not always is a second-choice response, used if the simple imperative or other response fails. In the use of bald imperatives as control responses, the focus is on disapproval of the act. In the strategy of affect arousal, the caregiver tries to achieve compliance by getting the child to have a certain feeling.

In our transcripts, the feelings most commonly elicited by the caregivers were love, fear, and shame.

2.1. *Love*

Caregivers often try to evoke empathy or love in a small child, particularly when they want the child to behave in a certain way. These feelings are referred to generally by the term *alofa*. The caregiver will call attention to his or her love for the child or the child's love toward some other person, using one of several grammatical structures or lexical items that express this feeling. For example, caregivers often expand a negative imperative to include the address term *si a'u tama* or *si a'u kama* 'my dear child', as in the imperative *Aua le faia si a'u kama!* 'Don't do it, my dear child!' Or a caregiver may refer to another person affected by the child's actions with an affect-marked term. The most common of these is *si ou tei* or *si ou kei* 'your dear little sibling'. Caregivers often stop an older child from annoying a younger brother or sister by saying *Aua le faia si ou kei!* 'Don't bother your dear little sibling!' In so speaking, the caregiver presupposes that the child has a certain affective relation to either the sibling or the caregiver. Pragmatically, these constructions are used to create or evoke a feeling of *alofa* and to induce the child to act in ways that display this feeling, i.e. to act sympathetically or supportively.

2.2.   *Fear*

It has been noted by a number of researchers that Samoans (see Gerber 1975; Mead 1928; Shore 1982) as well as other Polynesians, such as Tahitians (Levy 1973), often use fear to stop children from carrying out a wrongdoing. After interviewing American Samoan teenagers in 1972–3, Gerber noted:

For Samoan informants, fear appears to be a major feeling connected with wrong-doing. The term is not, however, usually connected with fear of shame or fear of loss of status, etc. The fear which Samoans express is much more direct: they are afraid of being beaten by their fathers.   (1975:86)

Levy has noted that Tahitians also instill fear as a means of control:

The overt goal of management of children is to produce docility and 'fear'. By fear is meant a fear of trouble, a fear of something going wrong. People hope that children will obey because they are 'afraid' not to. The purpose of hitting a child, for example, is said to be so that he will become 'afraid', and then he will not have to be hit anymore; and in fact in time this will happen.   (1973:447)

In our sample of households, fear was indeed a major control strategy of caregivers. Among the ways in which fear is aroused, warnings and threats far outweigh physical punishment. In over a hundred hours of closely recorded and many more hours of casual observations specifically of infants and toddlers with caregiver, Platt and I never saw an infant under the age of one struck. Toddlers were spanked with a broom or with the hand, but caregivers did it with moderation. Like Tahitians, Samoan caregivers report that a child's head is never to be struck. The more severe beatings reported by informants in Gerber (1975) and Freeman (1983) are neither frequent nor preferred practices of caregivers with younger children.

As noted earlier, with these small children the far more preferred and frequent technique is to warn and threaten, using gestures or speech. The warnings and threats often refer to possible physical punishment. Nonverbally, the warning may be expressed by a raised arm or reach toward the broom or by a stone thrown in the child's direction (see also Gerber 1975; Mead 1928). Verbally, a caregiver warns and threatens, using a construction that predicates that some future action will take place, as in the elliptical predication *Sasa!* '(I'm going to) hit (you)!' One difference between a warning and a threat is that in warning, the speaker usually adds the affect particle *ee* to the predication of future action, as in the warning *Sasa ee!* '(I'm going to) hit (you) unless . . .!' Thus a caregiver may threaten by saying *Fa'akali!*, which roughly translates as '(You just) wait!' This implies that the caregiver or another authority figure is about to come and punish the wrongdoer ('You just wait: I am (or someone is) coming!'). The caregiver may warn by saying instead *Fa'akali ee!*, which roughly translates as '(You) wait, unless . . .!' This implies that the caregiver will come and punish the wrongdoer if he or she continues to act in some undesirable way. With the warning particle, the utterance is somewhat like 'Watch out!' in English.

Caregivers' warnings and threats also refer to possible withdrawal of love, in the form of withdrawing or denying desired items (like food). This notion is not frequently employed, but when it is mentioned it may be sustained for a long period, and a caregiver may involve a number of other household members, including other small children, in the listing of desired items that will not come the child's way if he is not cooperative. One such interaction is presented below. This interaction involved Niulala (N), three years and three months, with his mother (Ak) and his younger brother Fineaso (F). F has been sitting next to his mother; then N moves next to her. F tells N to go away. Ak and N respond with a series of statements concerning items that F will not be given. The example is a portion of a much longer sequence. In this example, Ak elicits from N a list of items that will be denied to F:

(1) N IV:3

Context	N	Others
N moves next to Ak; F puts head on Ak's lap/	ga'o Figeaso leai se – se faga ma ma saga lole/ 'only (for) Fineaso there is (not) any pistol and and not any candy for him/'	
		AK: Ia ia leai se faga Fineaso ma se aa? 'Okay, so there is no gun (for) Fineaso, and what else?'

Ak⟨=⟩F   ma se lole/
                          'and (not) any candy/'
F gets off
lap

                                                    AK: Ma se aa?
                                                    'And what else?'

                          ma se – ma – ma=
                          'and (not any) – and –
                          and'

F: ((Whines))

                            =se ma se ma saga GIU/
                          '=(not) any and (not
                                any)
                                (not) any COCONUT
                          for him/'

                                                    AK: Ma se aa?
                                                    'And what else?'

                          ma saga ta'avale/
                          'and (not) any truck for
                          him/'

                                                    AK: Oka! oka!
                                                    'Oh my! Oh my!'

                          ma saga se'evae/
                          'and (not) any shoes for
                          him/'

                                                    AK: Mmmmmmm.

                          ma saga se'evae/
                          'and (not) any shoes for
                          him/'

                                                    F: (?)
                                                    AK: Oka! Oka!
                                                    'Oh my, Oh my!'
                                                    Figeaso va'ai le la leai
                                                    sau ((pause)) sau sau
                                                    ka'avale, sau se'evae,
                                                    ma sau lole! Oka!
                                                    'Fineaso, see then,
                                                    there is (not) any for
                                                    you ((pause)) (not)
                                                    any for you, (not)
                                                    any truck for you,
                                                    (not) any shoes for
                                                    you, and (not) any
                                                    candy for you.'
                                                    F: ((Laughs))
                                                    AK: He! He! Le aka!
                                                    'Ha! Ha! (Look at)
                                                    the laughter.'

Ak puts on F's
shorts

> AK: Ia aua laia ke koe
> leaga ua e iloa
> Fineaso ((pause) ee!
> 'Okay now don't be
> bad again you know,
> Fineaso ((pause)) or
> else!'

Threats may specify either the speaker or some third party as the one to carry out the threat. Both are common subjects. A wide range of third parties may fill this role. If the wrongdoing has involved another child, then the caregiver may specify this child as the one who may retaliate. Very often a caregiver will tell the child who has hurt another to look at the other and at the anger of the other. Another common tactic is to specify an authority figure of high status, such as the child's father or the *matai* of the family. These threats usually begin with the clause 'When so-and-so comes here' and end with some specified action. Also common is the use of strangers, particularly non-Samoans (*paalagi*), prisoners, and ghosts (*aitu*) in these contexts. By definition, I as an outsider was a candidate for this role. For example, a caregiver would sometimes say to children, 'Elinor won't love you', meaning 'Elinor won't give you sweets if you act that way.'

It should be noted here that not all threats and warnings are serious from the caregiver's point of view. Many threats addressed to small children are keyed through facial expression and other ways as *bluffs*, as *mock threats*. Part of the child's linguistic and social competence is to recognize these keys. But like teasing everywhere, the key of 'play' may be suddenly transformed into 'serious' threats, and children must know when to shift their own responses from teasing replies to compliance.

In summary, by far the most preferred and pervasive strategy for instilling fear in children up to the age of five or six is to warn or tease them. In the households observed, punishments in the form of striking a young child or actually denying food or other goods usually occurred only when these techniques failed.

2.3. *Shame*
Like certain other societies (Gallimore, Boggs & Jordan 1974; Levy 1973; Piers & Singer 1971), Samoans tend to downplay feelings of remorse and guilt following an offense and foreground feelings of embarrassment and shame (Gerber 1975; Shore 1982). Fear of being publicly exposed and hence shamed is, Samoans feel, a deterrent against doing certain acts like lying, stealing, selfishly holding back food or money from others, or otherwise failing to show respect where appropriate.

Someone who is feeling ashamed or embarrassed is described as *'ua maa*. This feeling is elicited in very young children by their caregivers and their peers through two major speech activities: shaming and challenging (especially challenging the truth of statements).

2.3.1.   Shaming Shaming as a speech act has three major forms. The most direct and explicit form of shaming is to address the child with a *shaming formula* – either the lexical item *maa* (without its tense/aspect marker *'ua*) or any one of a series of shaming particles, such as *uee, uaa, uu*. These constructions are emphasized by drawing out the final vowel, e.g. *Maa::::!, Uee:::::!, Uaa:::::!* Very often a caregiver will repeatedly run the palm of his or her hand down the child's face as these words are spoken to the child.

This form of shaming is extremely common. It may be carried out by only one caregiver, but more typically several members of a household join in the shaming activity, with choruses of *Uee:::! Uaa:::!* and so on for several conversational turns. Older caregivers, particularly mothers, will explicitly direct very young children in the household to participate in shaming a sibling, saying *Kakou uee!* 'Let us (inclusive) shame!'

Another form of shaming is to *talk about the child or the act of the child in the child's presence*. In these predications, the child may be characterized as *leaga* 'bad', *mimita* 'prideful', *tautalaititi* 'cheeky', *fiamatua* 'bossy', *fiasioo* 'showing off', *fiapaalagi* 'acting like a European' (i.e. not wanting to do dirty work), or his behavior may be described as *maatagaa* 'unseemly, ugly'. This form of shaming is also quite frequent in day-to-day interactions among caregivers and their charges.

A third form of shaming is the use of *derogatory nicknames* (gao) *or other special names*. These names may stick with a child for a period of time, but usually those used for shaming are short-lived. In some cases, the names are topically related to the undesirable behavior. For example, children acting in a very silly way may be addressed with the name of a crazy woman. In other cases, a child will be called by one of a limited number of embarrassing names, like *moepii* 'bedwetter', to evoke that affect.

Like the use of threats, shaming can vary in seriousness. Just as threats may be mock threats or serious threats, so shaming can be mock shaming or serious shaming. That is, one can shame teasingly. As with threats, the nonserious nature of the shaming is signaled through facial expression (e.g. smiling), laughter, and prosody.

2.3.2.   Challenging Another means of getting children to feel ashamed is to demonstrate that one of their assertions is not true or that they have been otherwise acting in a deceptive manner. This is usually accomplished by directly confronting and challenging the child. In this way, acts such as bluffing, exaggerating, lying, and cheating are exposed to those within earshot.

Challenging a child is highly encouraged by adult caregivers. Very often a caregiver will bring some statement of a child's to the attention of another sibling and ask that sibling to assess its validity. Through participation in such interactions, children acquire knowledge of culturally preferred ways of evaluating and making claims. As discussed in Shore (1982), this knowledge is both crucial and complex in adult Samoan life. Competence in this society involves relating claims to evidence, both in challenging and in supporting them. Samoan language reflects this cultural orientation. There are, for example, several verbs and particles in Samoan that specify how certain a speaker is of the assertion he is making (e.g. *fa'apea, ailoga, mai*). Samoan children have to learn how to use these structures to distinguish speculation from fact and hearsay from direct personal knowledge.

C.   Summary of control modes

Samoan caregivers of all social positions use a range of verbal and nonverbal strategies to stop a young child from misbehaving. In this context, overwhelmingly caregivers prefer verbal techniques such as the use of negative imperatives, positive and negative affect terms of address and reference, warnings, threats, teasing, shaming, and challenging. These reactions are more common than punishment in the form of striking a child, withdrawing affection, or denying a child food and other goods. Further, these reactions typically precede such punishments. The order of preference is represented in an almost formulaic sequence following a child's wrongdoing. In this sequence, the caregiver first says *Aua!* 'Don't!', then *Soia!* 'I said "Stop it!"', then *Sasa!* 'I'm going to smack you', and if this fails, the caregiver smacks the young offender. In this case, the child gets smacked not simply because of the original wrongdoing but because the child has not respected the caregiver's directives. The offense has escalated and so the response.

D.   Control strategies and the caregiving hierarchy

I have observed two important patterns in the selection of personnel for admonishing and reprimanding a young child. The first was mentioned in Chapter 4. There I noted a preference for lower-ranking over higher-ranking caregivers to monitor the activities of young children. Part of the task of monitoring is to indicate to children what they must not do and, using the techniques listed above, to enlist cooperation. This does not mean that higher-ranking caregivers do not enter into these situations. The preference is to remain somewhat apart, but if a lower-ranking caregiver is not effective, then a higher-ranking one will respond. As I noted earlier, when a higher-ranking person becomes involved, the trouble is escalated to a more serious status. It is more likely in these cases that the negative sanctions will be more severe. Younger caregivers will use this knowledge to keep their sibs in line, telling them that they will be reported to someone else if they don't cooperate. This telling (*faitala*) is tantamount to threatening the child with severe repercussions (see the discussion in section 2.2 above).

In most day-to-day caregiving, the preference described prevails. However, lower-ranking caregivers sometimes tell on their charges to higher-ranking persons immediately following a wrongdoing. Or a sib close in age bypasses a somewhat older sib caregiver and goes straight to a parent or grandparent to report what the peer has done. Probably a universal, this kind of tattling is done to get the small child in a lot of trouble.

Higher-ranking caregivers respond to reports in several ways: they may ignore the report; they may turn against the lower-ranking caregiver and admonish him or her for incompetence (see Mead 1928); they may respond directly to the child; or they may involve the younger caregivers and the child's peers in reprimanding the child. The latter strategy is particularly common. Several examples of this strategy were mentioned earlier. Higher-ranking caregivers will get children to collectively shame, to list goods that will be denied, to report the child's act to still higher-ranking household members, or to spank the child on behalf of the caregiver.

Samoan children come to understand the social organization of responses to offenses. They may use the organization to escalate the severity of the response against one of their siblings or mates. On the other hand, they may protect one of these offenders by immediately shaming or even striking them. Although European eyes may see adversity, usually these reactions (if proportionate to the magnitude of the offense) are considered by Samoan children as supportive and protective acts; both sides know that as more household members up the social hierarchy are involved, the greater the shame and physical punishment experienced by the child.

III.   THE SAMOAN CHILD

A.   Boldness

In reading this account of caregivers' control strategies, one might gain the impression that Samoan children are powerless in their interactions with caregivers and others. In the following discussion, I shall indicate ways in which the child is culturally endowed with his own resources for controlling others. By 'culturally endowed' I mean that 'child' is a social status and that each culture defines the demeanor, rights, duties, capacities, and membership associated with this status. Cultural beliefs and expectations inform (structure and give meaning to) children's behavior just as they inform caregivers' behavior.

Far from being powerless figures in their day-to-day interactions with caregivers, Samoan children are often bold and defiant, even in the face of a string of controlling directives. This was noted by travelers and church emissaries who passed through the Polynesian islands in the nineteenth century. The following account illustrates such observations. The account is taken from an 1882 letter to London from the Reverend D. Tyerman and the Reverend G. Bennett, who had traveled throughout the Pacific. The letter refers to problems certain Christian families were experiencing living among Pacific people.[1]

> As a Christian parent he [Mr. Chamberlain] is naturally very anxious to preserve the minds of his offspring from the moral contamination to which they are liable from the inevitable exposure to the society (occasionally at least) of native children of their own ages, whose language they understand, and whose filthy talk they cannot but hear at time. The abominable conversation (if such it may be called) of infants as soon as they begin to lisp out words, in such a jargon of grossness and obscenity as could not be imagined by persons brought up even in those manufacturing towns of our country where manners are most depraved. And, so far from reproving the little reprobates, their fathers and mothers, both by voice and example, teach them what they are most apt to learn, the expression and indulgence at the earliest possible period, of every brutal passion. The subject is one of great delicacy and perplexity to faithful Missionaries in all stations among uncivilized heathen, but particularly in these islands.   (*Journal of Voyages and Travels*, vol. 1 pp. 465–6)

In Mead's (1928) description of Samoan child rearing, children are described as little tyrants, who 'oppress' their sib caregivers. Mead's account of why these young caregivers allow their charges to be overbearing is that punishing the children will make them cry; crying will disturb older persons in the area; the sib will be held responsible for this disturbance and be punished.

Although this may happen, such a string of cause–effect relationships does not provide a comprehensive account for the dominating demeanor that is regularly displayed between one and three years of age and caregivers' reactions to such displays. To mention just one further consideration, a willingness to let young children be sassy and assertive in family

---

[1] I am enormously indebted to Dotsy Kneubuhl for bringing this excerpt to my attention and to John and Dotsy Kneubuhl for their rich insights into the affective world of Samoan children.

contexts (i.e. with no guests present) is displayed by all ranks of caregivers, be they grandparents, parents, or sibs of the child. This attitude has apparently been maintained for quite some time. Krämer, for example, noted in his detailed monograph on Samoan life that

obedience to the parents is considered one of the first duties of a child, and disobedient children are often cursed by their parents [*manamatua*; Pratt]. On the other hand, the patience of the parents with their naughty children is often boundless. Those who have had the opportunity of seeing how willful children sometimes tyrannize over their elders must think that there are more weak fathers in this respect in Samoa than amongst us.

(Krämer 1902/3, vol. 2, pt. 1:95)

In other words, children are allowed to behave in this way even when the caregiver is of higher status and hence not likely to be punished. Fear of negative repercussions is not a strong enough rationale for this relation between child and caregiver.

Implicit in Mead's account is the notion that whereas the sib caregiver may be responsible, the child under care is not responsible for her or his actions. This notion is part of a larger conception of what it means to be a small 'child'. These ideas guide socialization practices and children's behavior, including those of concern here.

Notions about children need to be qualified in terms of developmental stage. Concepts of the newborn differ from concepts of the older infant and the young child. In Samoan, a newborn is referred to as *pepe meamea*, literally 'baby thing thing', more loosely 'little thing baby'. This stage lasts for the first several months of life. As in many societies, during this period, the child is seen primarily as a small, delicate, and needy creature. Newborns are highly attended to: they are held, cuddled, sung to, and bounced. They are fed on demand, soothed, and amused. Caregivers sing and coo to these young infants in a high-pitched voice. Children at this stage are never held accountable for their actions; they are not responsible. Somewhat in the way in which Shotter treated the 'natural powers' of infants (1974), the actions of young Samoan infants are treated by and large as natural actions. Their actions are not seen as intentional and personal. To this extent, the young infant is not a social being and, as was discussed in some detail in Chapter 7, is usually not treated as a conversational 'partner', i.e. as a 'speaker–hearer' in a 'proto'-conversational exchange (Bates, Camaioni & Volterra 1979). Children are talked about but not talked to or with (see Ochs & Schieffelin 1984).

On the other hand, toward the end of this period, when the infant is around four to six months of age, the demeanor of caregivers begins to shift. This shift is usually occasioned by the increased mobility of the infant. When the infant is able to sit up, reach, grab, and crawl, he or she loses the status of *pepe meamea* and is known as just *pepe* 'baby'. (Of course, a variety of other terms of reference and address are actively used at this time as well.)

At this time, the baby's caregivers change voice quality and speech activities. The pitch is dropped to the normal range and the voice quality is louder. During this period, children are not only talked about, they are talked to. They become recipients of a string of directives of the sort described earlier in this chapter. In both contexts, the children are represented as by nature mischievous and bold. Much as American caregivers speak of the 'terrible twos', Samoan caregivers describe the crawling, then walking, child as naughty, willful, easily angered, and cheeky, that is, generally hard to control.

This view of children is codified in notions about children's early language. As in many societies, Samoan parents have conventionalized ideas about children's first words. It is commonly believed that a child's first word is a curse. This curse is *Tae!* 'Shit!', which is part of the more complex curse *'Ai tae!* 'Eat shit!' but, at least as used by children, has the force of 'Damn!' or 'Damn you!' in English.

The interpretation of children's early vocalizations as this curse reveals as well as the ways in which the status of child takes shape. That is, in giving this meaning to children's first utterances, caregivers and others construct (or create) the social identity of the child (see Cicourel 1973). Although Samoan caregivers do not generally talk about their roles in this way, one mother in the study, a former schoolteacher, did present this perspective to me one day when we were talking about easy and difficult sounds for children to make. This mother knew some English, and in this discussion she switched from Samoan to English. I present a portion of this discussion below.

(2) N64–360ff.

Mother (Mo) and researcher (E) have just been talking about babbling, and E has just asked about first Samoan words.

MO: Oh, a Samoan word!
E: Mmm.
MO: ((Laughs)) Well I'm ashamed! ((Laughs)) ((Coughs))
E: Don't be ashamed! ((Laughs))
MO: They call a Samoan word ((pause)) a, you know, when the Samoan kids ((?//)) . . . =
E: //uh huh
MO: = then the Samoan ((pause)) WOMAN you know, =
E: Hmm.
MO: = or Samoan people// said 'Oh! she said "*Tae*".' ((Laughs)) *Tae!*
E: Hmm. Yeah.
MO: So maybe that's the FIRST word they know ((pause)).
E: Hmm.
MO: *Tae.* And so the people ((emphatic particle)), we – we as adults . . . =

MO: ((Laughs)) ((pause)) = then we know – then we know =

E: Hmm.
MO: ((soft)) = oh, my – my – my child is starting to first say the word *tae*// or ((pause)) stupid –
E: //Yeah ((pause)) swearing a lot ((Laughs))
MO: = stupid. That's a first word but ((pause)) but to a kid, =
E: Hmm. ((pause)) Hmm.
MO: = to a kid it is – ((pause)) he doesn't REALLY mean *tae*,
E: Hmm.
MO: He doesn't. We are translating // into that word *tae*// because we – we mean he says *tae*.
E: Hmm.
MO: But to a kid, NO!
E: Hmm.

.

.

.

MO: There's a time when they grow up and they know the ((pause)) *tae* is a BAD word.
E: Hmm!
MO: And they hear their parent. They are ((?)) then to say *tae tae* when they – when you get mad // you know
E: Hmm!
MO: And so the kid learns!
E: Hmm!
MO: When you get mad, you say *tae*. That's why ((pause))
E: Hmm mmm.
MO: uhh – when they call out, they know the word.

This mother articulates the role of the caregiver when she says that the child doesn't at first mean *tae*, but the caregiver 'translates' what the child is saying 'into *tae* because we – we mean he says *tae*'.

In much the same way as caregivers' understanding of children's vocalizations implies their ideology of children, so do other responses to children's behavior. In particular, the frequent laissez-faire response of caregivers to young children's actions in these contexts implies that children at this stage have a will that is difficult to tame. Similarly in both sets of responses, the responses provide the child with a social identity and a set of demeanors that are expected.

To follow up on this last point, let me emphasize that caregivers are not always displeased when their children act in a cheeky and defiant manner. They react negatively when the child acts this way for excessive periods of time or when guests are present, but very commonly the behavior receives covert support. Caregivers do not openly admit that the behavior is valued, but their own actions evidence that it is. A caregiver often giggles behind the palm of the hand when a two-year-old acts defiantly – swears, talks back, threatens, and so on. I have already mentioned that caregivers often respond to a child's wrongful act by playfully threatening or playfully shaming him or her. The message here is that the caregiver is not seriously directing the child to discontinue the 'wrongful' behavior. Further, caregivers often say that their young charges are *ulavale* 'naughty' and *tautalaititi* 'cheeky' with grins on their faces.

These behaviors convey that caregivers do indeed approve of boldness and assertiveness in small children. What Samoan children need to learn is the set of contexts in which this behavior is desirable and when it is not. In household interactions, caregivers try to steer the defiance toward a sibling, as in the provocation of challenges among siblings by a mother (see section II). As noted earlier, a strong and assertive character is needed later in life when siblings compete for *matai* titles. Further, in life there will be other occasions when assertive and defiant actions are called for. For example, it is often necessary to defend the name of the family if it has been challenged or insulted. There are a number of ways in which this may be accomplished, one of which involves physical retaliation. The *matai* of the household or village cannot carry out such a move; it is incompatible with expected demeanor. However, untitled members of the household or village can and do perform these acts on behalf of the group. This is an expected contribution of untitled persons, and when it is carried out successfully and under appropriate circumstances, it is greeted with pride as a brave act. Untitled persons are in part measured in these terms. Within a family, it is the incorrigible child, the troublemaker, who is often the darling and the favorite of the parents. The transcripts of village council meetings of *matai* show that even when one has become a titled person, acts of defiance in one's past are used metaphorically as a measure of one's worth. In one such meeting, one *matai* tried to shame another *matai* who had earlier offended him. Challenging the value of this *matai* in the eyes of the village, he asked, *'Ua kogi se ma'a legei kamaikiki?'* 'Did this little kid throw any stone?', meaning, 'Did he ever do anything for our village?'

Children the world over must learn that most demeanors and actions are evaluated relative to circumstances of performance. In the case at hand, Samoan children learn that what is bad in one set of circumstances may be good in another. Samoan caregivers very often voice the following logic. They say that fighting and defiance are bad, but they also say that bad may also be good and that good may also be bad. There are times to be bad, and to be bad at those times is good, and to be good at those times is bad. Samoan caregivers demonstrate the context-sensitive meaning of defiance and assertiveness in part through their evaluative responses to children's behavior. In so doing, they socialize children into cultural concepts of self and emotion through everyday language practices.

B.   Respect

Samoan caregivers feel that the single most important goal of child rearing is to teach children *fa'aaloalo* 'respect'.

The attitude of caregivers toward the demeanor of respect differs from their attitude toward the demeanor of defiance and assertiveness. I have already mentioned that caregivers are covertly supportive of defiance; in contrast, they are overtly supportive of displaying respect.

A second distinction is one of relative naturalness of the two demeanors. Caregivers generally treat aggressive behavior as natural and respect behavior as learned. Caregivers do not feel that they have to teach small children to be cheeky and assertive; they are born with the natural drive to be this way (see Schieffelin 1979, in press for a discussion of reverse attitudes among Kaluli caregivers). All human beings, but particularly small children, have difficulty in controlling these natural drives (Shore 1977, 1982). From a Samoan perspective, the major responsibility of caregivers (and more generally of all members of the society toward each other) is to monitor this drive, negatively sanctioning it where necessary and channeling it to appropriate contexts. On the other hand, the expression of respect has social origins. Once again in the Samoan perspective, whereas aggressive behavior takes its form from within, the form of respect behavior (postures, speech, actions) is both modeled and explicitly taught by those in the child's environs (see Shore 1977, 1982 for ways in which the distinction between natural and learned behavior is parallel to that between the Samoan concepts of *aamio* ('socially unconditioned aspects of behavior') and *aga* ('social conduct') – 1982:154).

The single most important quality of *fa'aaloalo* 'respect' is attentiveness to others. The word *fa'aaloalo* comprises two morphemes: *Fa'a* is a causative prefix meaning 'to make'; *alo* is a respect-vocabulary term meaning 'to face' or 'to recognize'. Two major expressions of respect (attentiveness) are greeting and serving. The greeting may be lengthy or brief, but typically recognizes the addressee through personal name, title, or other status terminology. Greetings themselves presuppose that the speaker is aware of the other's presence. The greeting is a preface to other displays of respect, such as serving. In both greeting and serving, one is attentive not only to the other's presence but to the other's wants, including his or her 'face wants', namely to be ratified as a person of particular status (Goffman 1967).

Respect, then, involves *awareness* of others (noticing), *perspective taking* or intersubjectivity (as in the case of recognizing wants), and *accommodation* (as in the case of satisfying wants). These three qualities are overtly socialized by sib and other caregivers through direct instruction.

Attentiveness to others in the form of noticing is encouraged quite early in life. As noted in Chapter 4, once infants reach the age of five months or so and are able to sit up, they are positioned so that they are facing outward toward those present in the immediate setting. Typically these infants are with a sib caregiver who may hold the infant on his or her lap or between the legs facing others. If there are others in the house, the child will be directed toward them. If there is no one in the house, the sib and the younger child will sit at the periphery of the house, with the gaze directed toward the road or other dwellings. From three to four in the afternoon, it is common to see groups of sib caregivers seated in a clearing near the road or central area of the village, with infants tucked in their laps facing either the others in the group or the goings-on in these public locations. Even feeding is carried out in this position. Sib caregivers are seated with the infant in front of them facing outward and spoon food into the mouth of the child from a bowl placed before both of them. Both the sib and the younger child are oriented toward some activity taking place in addition to that of feeding.

Occasionally while seated in this way, a caregiver may fold the legs of a small infant in the manner appropriate to public interactions. This way of folding one's legs is called *faitai* or *fa'atai* and involves sitting cross-legged, Native American style. This mode of sitting is the standard polite seating posture. It is considered impolite to show the bottoms of one's feet or to point one's feet in the direction of others. (In more casual, familiar interactions, stretching one's legs out is entirely appropriate. If one stretches out a leg in more public settings, one usually uses a mat to cover the leg.)

When children reach the age of eighteen months to two years, they are continually reminded to keep their legs folded (*Faitai le vae!* 'Cross your legs!'). This reminder is usually preceded by an instruction to sit down (*Nofo lalo!* 'Sit down!'). It is also considered impolite for one to be standing if another of higher rank is seated. Even when serving another, the serving is done crouching to minimize the difference in height between the served and the server.

The difference in attitude toward respect and boldness discussed earlier is manifest when children start using words. As noted above, the children's use of cursing is expected and part of human nature (even though one caregiver recognized the cultural construction of this expectation). Children's use of polite speech is not considered natural and is, rather, the object of explicit instruction. In these instructions, the caregiver produces the desirable utterance and directs the child to repeat it. In other words, polite speech behavior originates explicitly from the caregiver (whereas assertive speech is generally felt to express the child's natural willfulness).

At the single-word stage, children are explicitly instructed to recognize others by name. They are asked to *vala'au* 'call out' to persons who happen to pass on the road or who are somewhere in the household compound. This procedure is quite frequent in this period of language development. An example is provided below.

(3) Kalavini II:48

Kalavini, twenty months, with two young caregivers, Mese (Mes) and Menime (Men) sitting outside the house

Kalavini	*Others*
	MEN: //Vala'au Valasi.
	'Call to Valasi.'
	MES: //Vala'au Mareta.
	'Call to Mareta.'
	MEN: 'Valasi'.
	'"Valasi".'
	//Vala'au!
	'Call out!'
	MES: //Vala'au "Sauiluma"
	'Call out "Sauiluma".'
//((Coughs))	MEN: Vala'au Sauiluma,//loa 'ua alu.
	'Call to Sauiluma, now (she's)
	gone.'
	MES: Vala'au Sauiluma, loa.
'ua alu	'Call to Sauiluma, now.'
'(she's) gone.'	
	Vala'au.
	'Call out.'
hh?	MES: 'Sauiluma!'
'huh?'	'"Sauiluma!"'
Umaa!	MES: 'Sauiluma'.
'Sauiluma!'	'"Sauiluma".'
	Vala'au kele!
	'Call out a lot!'
	'Ke alu i Apia?'
	'"Are you going to Apia?"'
	((Laughs))
	.
	.
	.
	((Calling-out sequence
	continues))

Naming is a very important aspect of respect and at the heart of the more complex greetings. Subsequent instructions to repeat may include instructions to repeat greetings as well as naming.

In these sequences, the child is being socialized not only to be attentive to others, but to attend to and accommodate the caregiver as well. In elicited repetition, the child is directed to attend to what the caregiver is saying. When a child repeats what a caregiver has said, the child evidences that he or she has attended. Further, given that the elicitation is a directive, the child's repetition also satisfies a want of the caregiver.

These repetition-elicitation sequences anticipate more complex repetition tasks expected of older children. By the age of two and a half, children are given messages to be delivered to a third party not in the immediate vicinity. In the early repetition sequences, the caregiver remains with the child as the child repeats a message to some third party. When the child is somewhat older, the caregiver expects the child to keep the message to be repeated in his or memory and deliver the message without the presence of the caregiver. Well under the age of four, children are able to deliver complex messages from one part of the village to another. The delivering of messages is comparable to the carrying of objects for a higher-ranking party. That is, it is the kind of activity expected of lower-ranking persons, a form of serving and as such an expression of respect.

The overall impression I have of these early years is that caregivers are more concerned with the attentiveness of small children than with compliance. There is a strong expectation that children will notice what is happening around them, will recognize those in their environment by name, will attend to the words of others, will attend to the tone of the words (serious, teasing), will report what others are doing and saying, and so on. These forms of *fa'aaloalo* are emphasized more than absolute compliance in the first two and a half years of life.

C.   A sense of performance

Although much has been written on Samoan child rearing concerning assertiveness and respect, little has been said concerning another vital dimension of affective competence, that is, a sense of *performance*, a sense of theater.

In previous chapters, I noted that Samoan children grow up in an environment in which multiparty interaction is the norm. The absence of walled dwellings, the proximity of houses to each other and to the road, and the expectation that at least certain persons are to be attentive and responsive creates an environment in which talk and other social behavior are witnessed by a number of persons. In other words, in addition to a 'primary audience' a 'secondary audience' (Brenneis 1978) is an ever present dimension of the social situation. These terms are drawn from Brenneis's analysis of Fiji Indian political performances:

> The primary audience is composed of the individuals or group at whom the performance is chiefly aimed, i.e. those whom the performer hopes to influence directly. The secondary audience includes others who are present. It is not merely a residual category, however, as the secondary audience provides both evaluation and an element of control.   (1978:162)

The most striking instances of the participation of primary and secondary audience are found, of course, in formal events. Both verbal and nonverbal behavior is carried out with these two sets of recipients in mind. The giving or exchange of items, for example, is not only a transaction between two parties but a displaying of that transaction to others (the secondary audience). The display aspect may be evidenced through physical movement, such as when mats are held up and shown as they are transferred from one party to another. Or the display may be manifest through speech behavior, i.e. through the use of oratory. As with nonverbal behavior, these oratorical pieces are intended to be heard by those not immediately involved in the transaction. In these contexts, the manner of the actors will affect how the event is defined (e.g. formal/informal) and the degree of significance associated with the gift or exchange.

However, even in the informal surroundings of one's home, talk is overheard and movements noticed. While the style of the actor's behavior in informal settings may differ from that of formal contexts, the intention to address two sets of audiences is characteristic of both formal and informal interactions. This is not to say that informal interactions never include only two parties (an actor and one audience/addressee). The main point is, rather, that a secondary audience is an ever present potential party to an interaction. Actor–speakers very often exploit this potential by designing their speech or actions to two sets of recipients. When this occurs, the speech or action takes on the qualities of performance and display, much as formal speech and actions are understood.

When speakers or actors indicate through conventional markers (such as postures or prosody) that more than one audience is addressed, they indicate ways in which the behavior is to be interpreted. For example, a threat delivered in such a way as to include a secondary audience is less likely to be carried out by the speaker than a threat (of similar content) delivered out of earshot of others. Threats in full daylight differ from threats under cover of night. Many of the threats delivered by caregivers to children, children to caregivers, and peers to one another are of this sort. They expose publicly the feelings of the speaker (or others the speaker represents) and the object or cause of those feelings. These displays often invite others to respond to the situation. In other words, these displays have the effect of transforming the conflict from the personal to the public arena, letting the secondary audience participate in the construction of subsequent social interaction.

To summarize, affective competence involves evaluating the relationship between actor (speaker) and audience and the bearing of this relationship on interpretation of verbal or nonverbal behavior. Children come to understand the affective meanings of behavior with respect to this communicative relationship. Behavior that is meant to be witnessed or overheard will be interpreted differently from behavior that is meant only for a particular addressee. The first has a quality of performance and display in ways that the second does not.

As children develop, they engage in the different communicative roles discussed here. I have previously noted that caregivers, for example, actively encourage small children to watch and listen to the interactions of others in their surroundings. Where a public display has been enacted by a child, caregivers encourage the other children to respond to what they see or hear in action or voice, to activate their role as secondary audience. If one child threatens or curses another, a caregiver may elicit supportive or critical responses from these other children.

The major emphasis in the first two to three years of life is the skill of performance itself, that is, the ability to speak and act to an audience. Children are directed to perform before they can speak, as for example when they are asked to dance or to pose in a variety of postures, from that of respect to that of defiance or assertiveness in front of others. Almost any elicited behavior can be treated as a performance, including sitting cross-legged in a respectful manner, chasing a chicken out of the house, or miming karate gestures.

More formal performance contexts demand conventional postures and language. When children reach the age of about two years, they are instructed as to how they should stand, where they should place their arms, how they should move (if at all), and the quality of voice to be used in singing and reciting and dancing for others. Certainly by the time children reach the age of five and enter public school, they are at ease with performance itself. While children and adults differ in their performance competence, no one seems to experience stage fright. A sense of theater comes early in the development of social knowledge and social skills. This sense is vital to full participation in Samoan society, where performances and stages emerge in the flow of daily social life.

The importance of the concept of performance cannot be stressed enough. The sense of performance is a potential component of the meaning of any single action. Competent members of Samoan society are able to search for the keys of performance modalities to discern the seriousness of an action. Outside observers are very often unable to discern these keys themselves and apply more serious interpretive frames to the event taking place than perhaps do the participants in that event themselves. Distinguishing degrees of seriousness requires that participants and observers alike take note of the setting and audience, voice quality, speech acts, and affective particles used by speakers. These keys modulate the character of the event, and children are socialized early in life to use them in the production and interpretation of language behavior.

9. The linguistic expression of affect

I.   INTRODUCTION

In Chapter 8 we considered ways in which affect relates to social-control procedures and to concepts of the child. Through the use of affect-marked speech, Samoan caregivers socialize young children into local expectations concerning appropriate social behavior. They also socialize young children to distinguish degrees of seriousness of verbal and nonverbal acts through attention to linguistic and situational keys marking this dimension. In this chapter we concentrate on the linguistic characteristics of these keys and the pragmatic functions these keys serve. The discussion will examine how these keys are used among adult Samoan speakers. It will also document the acquisition of these features by young children. In considering adult language use, we shall examine the effects of social rank and gender on the expression of affect.

II.   AFFECT AS A COMPONENT OF COMMUNICATION

The meaning of a behavior is partially a function of the relation of that behavior to assumptions concerning the context of situation and other facets of sociocultural knowledge. Among other areas, affect is an important component of situational and sociocultural knowledge. It is essential for young children in all societies to acquire an understanding of the affective orientation of utterances and nonverbal actions. This is partly accomplished by attending to the linguistic and nonlinguistic features that index or cue particular affective frames or affective meanings. As will be discussed in the following section, attention to such features has been observed quite early in children's development and appears to be an accomplishment critical to their intellectual development.

168

A.   Social referencing

The growing literature on socialization and social development (see Bowlby 1969; Bretherton & Beeghly 1982; Bretherton, McNew & Beeghly-Smith 1981; Eibl-Eiblesfeldt 1970; Heath 1983; Hoffman 1981; Levy 1973; Much & Shweder 1978; Ochs 1986a; Ochs & Schieffelin, 1984; Schieffelin 1979, in press; Schieffelin & Ochs, 1986a, b; Zahn-Waxler, Radke-Yarrow & King 1979) indicates that caregivers are concerned with children's affective competence and that children quite early in their lives attend to, recognize, and act on displays of emotion by others in their social environment. Klinnert et al. (1983) report that by nine months of age infants can monitor the facial expression of affect of mothers and will act differently toward some third object according to the affect displayed. Through this type of monitoring, termed *social referencing* (Klinnert et al. 1983), infants are socialized into associating particular events (e.g. the copresence of a particular object, a change of state) with particular feelings on the one hand and particular expressions on the other. Infants come to know for particular situations what they should feel and how to display or mask that feeling (Schieffelin 1979). These frames lay the groundwork for attitudes, opinions, values, and beliefs that evolve over a lifetime. The process of social referencing indicates as well that affect is very much part of cognition. Children come to know objects in the world around them in part through the mediation of perceived affect.

Recognition and use of lexical and grammatical structures for conveying feelings are more sophisticated extensions of this early form of production and appraisal of affect expression. The work of Bretherton & Beeghly (1982), Dunn & Kendrick (1982), and Zahn-Waxler, Radke-Yarrow & King (1979), demonstrates that verbal competence in this domain is regularly displayed before the age of two. This research concerns primarily children's acquisition of lexical terms of emotion (in English only). If we include prosody, we can see the conventional linguistic expression of affect through intonation even before a child's first words, and certainly it is widely in evidence throughout the single-word stage (Cruttendon 1982; Halliday 1973; Peters 1977).

An important difference between the use of lexical terms of emotion and intonation is that typically the lexical terms assert or predicate a quality of self or others, whereas intonation presupposes or implies that quality. Relative to intonation, the adjectives of affect such as 'afraid', 'angry', 'mad', and 'happy' indicate more explicitly the nature of the affect communicated. These adjectives have considerable interest for developmental psychologists, because their use displays to a high degree an awareness among young children of their own and others' feelings. Dunn & Kendrick (1982), for example, have documented the capacity of two- and three-year-old children to notice and even anticipate the feelings of their younger siblings:

> The important point on the issue of perspective-taking is that the children commented on the baby's behavior in a way that certainly did not always represent a projection of their own feelings about their own situations. Sometimes the difference between the perspective of the child and the baby was made quite explicit. One boy watching his baby brother playing with a balloon, commented to the observer: "He going pop in a minute. And he going cry. And he going be frightened of me too. I LIKE the pop." (1982:46)

The interest in affect among development psychologists is growing by leaps and bounds, for it seems that a great deal can be learned about children's cognition from observing the affective behavior of children and others engaged in face-to-face interaction. These behaviors indicate the extent to which children can take a sociocentric perspective, their understanding of cause and effect, and their concept of person as distinct from other entities in their environment. It is apparent from existing studies that attitudes, emotions, moods, feelings, and the like are communicated and perceived in the first year of life and that this system expresses an understanding of the world, i.e. a world view.

B.   Affect in adult communication

Research in adult processing indicates further the essential role of affect in communication (see for example Mandler 1975; Norman 1979; Zajonc 1980). Among other phenomena, the processes of attention, memory, and recognition can be facilitated or impeded by an individual's emotional state. We have every reason to believe from this growing literature as well as from the writings of Burke (1962), Hymes (1974), and Jakobson (1960) that such a fundamental component of human nature will find its place in language beyond prosody and the lexicon. Speakers' affective dispositions are expressed through syntactic, morphological, and phonological structures, such as verb voice (Hopper 1979; Hopper & Thompson 1980), word order (Givon 1979; Halliday 1967; Kuno 1972; MacWhinney 1977, 1984), sentential mood (Searle 1969), right and left dislocation (Chafe 1976; Duranti & Ochs 1979), tense/aspect (Hopper 1979; Smith 1983), deictics and other determiners (Clancy 1980), quantifiers (P. Brown & Levinson 1978; Labov 1984; G. Lakoff 1972), focus particles (Dixon 1972), affect particles and evidentials (Besnier in press a, b; Clancy 1986a, b), phonological simplification, reduplication (Ferguson 1977), and phonological variation (Blom & Gumperz 1972; Ferguson 1977; Labov 1966).

In most arenas of daily communication, speakers convey not only information concerning some state or event but their feelings about some state or event as well, and languages have varying structures for encoding this level of information. As in the case of the social referencing of facial expressions discussed in the infant-development literature, adult listeners attend to these linguistic structures as keys (Goffman 1974; Hymes 1974) to an affective disposition a speaker is conveying. In certain contexts, the speaker is more highly constrained as to the affective frame he or she can communicate; both the affect and the grammatical structures to convey that affect are tightly bound to registral norms (Anderson 1977; Ferguson 1977). This is the case for many formal communicative contexts, such as, in American society, certain formal meetings, certain religious services, and certain literate genres such as scholarly writing and front-page news articles.

An important stand taken in this chapter is that all sentences expressed in context have an affective component. In certain contexts, the affect conveyed will be one of 'distance' from some other proposition conveyed. Thus a speaker or writer may convey an impersonal attitude or indifference or objectivity in expressing information. As noted, such an affect may be a registral defining feature. Indeed, much of current scientific communication is consumed with the idea that objectivity is an ideal disposition and formal style. It would be naive to see this disposition as exemplifying the absence of affect. The impersonal, objective style reflects and expresses cultural assumptions about the relationship among the communicator (scientist), the topic of the message (scientific research), and the audience of that message. This style renders the communication more valid and 'factual', deemphasizing the subjective dimensions of the proposition(s) conveyed. In other contexts, the personal, subjective response of the communicator to the information conveyed is more overtly expressed.

Distinct from the dimension of impersonal to personal is the notion of markedness of affect (see Irvine 1982). Speakers in different speech communities have expectations regarding the type of affect expression associated with particular events, settings, and social statuses of communicators. For example, speakers have expectations concerning the expression of affect by women to women, women to men, men to women, men to men, parents to children, judges to members of the jury, members of a funeral party to each other, and so on. When these communicators display a more marked form of affect, more complex interpretations of affective dispositions may be generated.

Although both our own experience and scholarly research confirm that affect does indeed penetrate the linguistic code, the precise nature of this penetration has not been clarified. Until recently, affect has not been a topic of concern among psychologists pursuing research into information theory. Shweder (1984) has argued that the concept of 'man' as a rational being, while having a long history in Western thought, has become the foremost concern of the social sciences generally since World War II, as evidenced by the emergence of cognitive psychology, cognitive anthropology, cognitive sociology. Linguistics has followed this pattern as well, with Chomsky's attachment to cognitive psychology as a theoretical paradigm. Now that the prominent figures in information processing have renewed interest in affect and incorporated affect in their models of communication, perhaps linguistics will follow suit and begin to ascertain the grammatical structures associated with affect and the pragmatic and sociolinguistic systems in which they participate.

III.   THE LINGUISTIC EXPRESSION OF AFFECT IN SAMOAN

A.   Grammatical encoding of affect

Table 9.1 displays some of the ways in which Samoan encodes affect. There are special affect particles, affect first person pronouns, and affect determiners. In addition, there are interjections, affect-loaded terms of address and reference, and a long list of affect descriptors. Like many other languages, Samoan uses prosody as well to encode feelings. More language-specific, as noted by Shore (1977, 1982), is the use of the front and back of the oral cavity to convey distinct affects, namely delicacy/propriety (in a Christian sense) versus earthiness/coarseness. Additionally, Samoans may switch back and forth between two different phonological registers and two lexical registers (respect vocabulary and unmarked vocabulary) to indicate a shift in mood or in intensity of feeling.

B.   Pragmatic functions of affect features

1.   Affect specifiers and affect intensifiers

I have found it useful to analyze these linguistic features in terms of two semantic roles. The first role is that of indicating *the nature of the affect being conveyed*. When a feature carries out this role, we shall refer to it as an *affect specifier*. The second role is that of indicating the *intensity of the affect being conveyed*. Linguistic features that carry out this role are *affect intensifiers*. All of the features listed in Table 9.1 are affect intensifiers in the same sense that they are affect-loaded alternatives to more neutral features. However, the features differ in the degree to which they function as affect

Table 9.1. *Linguistic expression of affect in Samoan*

Particles	Interjections		Pronouns	
ia (intens.)	*ota*		*ta*	
a (intens.)	*ola*	surprise	*ta ita*	
ee (intens.)	*oi*		*lota*	(1st pers. sympathy)
fo'i (intens.)	*uoia*	surprise/sympathy etc.	*lata*	
	tafiolae			
	otafefe			
	uisa	neg. surprise		
	oti			
	tch			
	ui			
	isa	annoyance		
	se			
	a'e	disapproval		
	a'e			
	talofae	sympathy		
	tae	anger		

Determiners		Phonology
si (sing.)	sympathy	loudness (intens.)
nai (pl.)		lengthening
		stress
		glottal stop
		reduplication (weaken/intensify)
		backing (earthiness)
		fronting (refinement, distance)
		switching registers between /t/ & /k/ (abrupt mood changes)

Address/reference terms	Adjectives
maile 'dog'	*'ita* 'angry'
pua'a 'pig'	*lotoleaga* 'jealous'
mataomo 'smalpox'	*lotomalie* 'agreeable
moepii 'bedwetter'	*fiafia* 'happy'
moeti'o 'bedshitter'	*mimita* 'proud'
lima pipilo 'smelly hand'	*fiapoto* 'conceited'
lou aitae 'your shittiness	*fiamatua* 'acts like bigshot
puu tele 'big hole' (to woman)	*fia autu* 'acts like boss'
avilu 'baby face'	
lou alelo 'your snake/eel eyes'	*fiasioo* 'showoff'
ali'i 'master'; 'little devil' (to child)	*fiapepe* 'babyish'
sole 'mate'	*fiu* 'fed up'
toea'iga 'old man'	*'ofo* 'surprised'
si + ref. term, e.g.	*fa'aaloalo* 'respectful'
si tama 'dear boy'	

Table 9.1 (*contd*)

Address/reference terms	Adjectives
suga 'lassie'	*fa'amaoni* 'faithful'
etc.	*popole* 'worried'
	fefe 'afraid'
	pala'ai 'cowardly'
	maulalalo 'humble'
	tautalaiti 'cheeky'
ulavale 'naughty'	
taea 'disgusting'	
	etc.

Respect vocabulary

afio mai 'come' (of a chief)
maliu mai 'come' (of an orator)
faletua 'wife' (of chief)
tausi 'wife' (of orator)
gesegase 'sick' (of chief orator)
silafia 'to know' (chief or orator)
etc.

specifiers as well. For example, the particles *a*, *ia*, and *fo'i* are unmarked with respect to type of affect. They can be used to intensify over a range of positive and negative affects. On the other hand, the affect particle *ee* is more specifically associated with negative feelings such as anger, irritation, disapproval, and disappointment. Other features even more narrowly specify affect, such as the first person pronoun *ta ita* 'poor me' and the determiner *si* 'the dear', both of which denote sympathy for the referent.

2.   Speech-act functions

In many cases, the affect specifier or intensifier may color the interpretation of the sentence as a whole, much like a sentence adverb. Among other effects, the feature may indicate to the hearer which speech act is being performed. For example, the particle *ee*, as just discussed, typically denotes anger, disappointment, displeasure, or irritation. Adding this particle to an assertion or imperative utterance usually signals that the utterance is a warning. For example, the utterance *Laku i oo* 'I'm going over there' is an assertion with several speech act functions. When the particle *ee* is added, as in *Laku i oo ee!* 'I'm going over there + neg. affect', the utterance is interpreted as a warning, with a rough gloss something like 'I'm going over there unless . . .' Similarly, the imperative utterance *Kamo'e!* 'Run!' is a neutral directive. The utterance with the particle *ee, Kamo'e ee!* 'Run + neg. affect' will usually be heard as a warning that the addressee should run, or else the speaker is going to take some specified action.

We can also carry out this analysis for the first person sympathy pronouns. When the neutral first person is used in the imperative utterance *Mai ma a'u!* 'Give (it) for me!', the utterance will usually be heard as a demand. When the sympathy pronoun is used, as in *Mai ka 'ika!* 'Give (it) for dear me!', the imperative will usually be heard as begging.

I have introduced here only the bare bones of the system. As more of the same type of affect specifiers appear, with or without affect intensifiers, the interpretation of the speech act changes. For example, warnings become threats and acts of begging become acts of pleading.

3.   Speech-genre functions

At this point, I suggest that affect features function not only to signal speech acts but *speech genres* and *speech events* as well. The use of these features over continuous discourse (or, indeed, their absence!) defines that discourse as a type of talk. Certainly, in Samoan the extended use of respect vocabulary is a key (Bauman 1977; Duranti 1981a; Hymes 1972) to the speaker's delivering a formal speech rather than being engaged in some other type of activity. Similarly, the use of affect features in narrative discourse distinguishes that discourse as *personal narrative* rather than as a narrative that might appear in a newspaper article. These features are not incidental to the genre or event. The use of affect in personal narrative, for example, is tied to the purpose of these discourses. They are primarily told to express a feeling, and if possible to secure an empathetic response from the audience (Langness & Frank 1981). For Samoans at least (and, I suspect, for most people in most societies), a telling of a personal experience without affect is a story without a point and a speaker without competence (see also Labov 1984).

4.   Constraints across turns and speakers

In examining personal narratives exchanged among adult speakers of Samoan, I have found that the domain of influence of affect features extends even beyond the discourse of a single speaker. To put this more precisely, there *is a sequential organization of affect across turns* and *speakers*. A narrator will use one or more affect features that indicate the attitude or feelings of the narrator toward the events discussed. These features clue the addressee as to the appropriate feedback response. Thus, in the course of a personal narrative, one can isolate sets or pairs of affect-linked turns. The existence of such an organization reinforces the notion that the point of telling stories is to express feelings and elicit sympathy. The selection of the appropriate empathetic response will be guided by the narrator's initial selection of affect specifiers and intensifiers. An illustration of the sequential organization of affect is provided in example (1).

(1) Women are weaving and talking about the funeral of another woman's mother.

F: Uhmm (pause) sa'o   a   le   mea   ga   ka   popole
                     right EMPH ART thing that I dear worry
   ai   le   lo'omakua   le   tagi.
   PRO   ART   old woman   ART   cry
   'It is true that the thing poor me worried about was the old woman crying.'

L: Kagi   kele   si   lo'o//makua.
   cry   much   the dear   old woman
   'The old woman cried a lot.'

F: Kagi   ia   le   lo'oma//kua.
   cry   EMPH   ART   old woman
   'The old woman really cried.'

L: Kalofa   ee, sh.
   pity   EMPH
   'What a pity.'

F: Le   mafai –   kau   alu   aku   ia(pause)
   not   able   –   try   go   DEIXIS EMPH
   falekua   gei   fo'i   ma   le   solosolo (pause)
   chief's wife   this   EMPH   with   ART   handkerchief
   solosolo   fo'i   o   le   keige (pause).
   handkerchief   EMPH   of   ART   girl
   'The chief's wife was not able – tried to give the handkerchief – the handkerchief of the girl ((= older woman whose mother had died)).'
   E   alofa   a   i   si   oga   kiga.
   PRES   love   EMPH   OBJ   ART dear   her   mother
   '(She) really loves her dear mother.'

In this example, one woman is telling two other women about a funeral. In the narrative, several features associated with feelings of sympathy are used. The narrator refers to herself with the first person sympathy pronoun *ka* in the phrase *le mea ga ka popole ai* 'the thing that poor me worried about'. The narrator refers to the woman whose mother had died with the sympathy referenced term *lo'omakua* 'dear old woman'. The intensity of this feeling is heightened by the narrator switching phonological register on the word *tagi* 'cries'. This word is spoken in the register that uses /t/ in contrast to the previous discourse, which is in the register /k/.

All of this conveys to the hearers what the narrator's attitudes are and suggests the appropriate response. The first response by L is a more intensive repetition of the narrator's description. L uses the sympathy determiner *si* as well as the sympathy reference term *lo'omakua* in referring to the grieving woman. The crying is emphasized not by code switching like the narrator's but by the use of the adverbial intensifier *kele* 'a lot'. The narrator subsequently paraphrases what L has just said, using the intensifier particle *ia* to emphasize the crying of the woman. This particle typically occurs in escalations or second sayings of utterances. After three utterances that focus on the poor woman's crying, L responds with the appropriate interjection of pity and sympathy *Kalofa ee!* In these lines and subsequently, the turns are systematically organized in terms of conventional expressions of affect. Each turn constrains the affect expressed in the next turn.

To summarize the points made so far, affect is richly encoded at many levels of Samoan grammar and discourse. The linguistic features that express affect fall into two nonexclusive functional categories – those that *specify* affect and those that *intensify* affect. These features enter into the literal meaning of propositions. Further, they signal the speech act performed by an utterance. Finally, there are co-occurrence restrictions on the use of affect specifiers and intensifiers within and across utterances and turns.

IV.   SOCIOLOGICAL VARIATION IN AFFECT EXPRESSION

A.   The expression of sympathy

In this section, I shall discuss the ways in which gender and other social features such as age and title interact as variables in the expression of affect. The discussion will focus on one particular dimension of affect, namely the expression of sympathy/love, what Samoans call *alofa*.

Much has been written about gender differences and affect expression in language. Many have observed that women are more polite generally (P. Brown 1979; R. Lakoff 1973). Brown's analysis of Tzeltal women indicates that women talking in private, in-group situations tend to use what P. Brown & Levinson (1978) call 'positive politeness' and use 'negative politeness' in public settings. Men, on the other hand, tend to speak more directly or 'bald on record'. Positive politeness is approach-based, addressing the face needs of a person to have his or her values, beliefs, and other facets of his or her social image appreciated. Much of positive politeness involves showing interest and involvement with another (complimenting; sympathizing; use of relatively friendly address terms, endearments, etc.). This aspect of women's behavior has also been thought of as women's tendency to empathize with another or at least to act in a sympathetic manner to a greater extent than do men.

As noted in section III, Samoan has a rich system of encoding positive affect. It has a number of affect particles that intensify and/or indicate the speaker's mood, and, like many languages, it has descriptive terms that indicate the speaker's feelings toward a referent (including love/sympathy). More unusual, Samoan has affect pronouns and determiners that express sympathy toward a referent. The affect pronouns express sympathy toward the speaker and are often used to get a listener to feel sorry for the speaker. Both affect and neutral first person pronouns can appear in a variety of syntactic roles. As possessive and genitive constituents, they may be inflected for both inalienable and alienable possession (see Chapter 3). These two pronominal systems are presented in Table 9.2.

The affect determiners *si* and *nai* express sympathy typically toward a third party but may also be used to express sympathy toward the addressee. Two prevalent situations in which these forms are used are begging and personal narratives. Begging is prevalent in children's speech but is not common in the adult–adult interactions recorded in our study. Personal narratives, on the other hand, are characteristic of adult conversation.

In the context of the narrative, affect forms alert the listener as to how the listener should respond to the narrative. The narrator's use of particular forms constitutes a type of affective first part, to which the listener should supply the appropriate affective second part. If we want to examine sociolinguistic variation in the expression of affect, and in particular expression of sympathy, these two contexts are appropriate. We can determine the extent to which gender and social rank affect narration and audience affective feedback.

Personal narratives were used as a basis for comparing the use of sympathy forms (including pronouns, nouns, determiners, adjectives, verbs, particles, and interjections) across gender and social rank. The narratives were concerned with either loss (including death) or danger, and all were told to listeners of the same sex and social rank (i.e. to peers). The social situations in which the narratives were conveyed were relatively informal; the listeners were not from the narrators' families but were close acquaintances.

Because of limitations of the data base, not all statuses could be represented in the comparison. Three different sets of narrator–listeners are represented. The first consists of untitled young men in their early twenties. (Men do not usually hold a title under the age of thirty.) The second consists of men in their mid forties to mid fifties who have chiefly titles (*ali'i*). The third set of narrator–listeners is a group of women above the age of fifty who are wives of titled men. Wives of untitled men and young unmarried, untitled women are not represented. Thus, the findings and generalizations associated with the following study should be taken as suggestive and tentative.

The narratives vary in topic. The narratives of untitled men include a

Table 9.2. *First person pronouns*

Category	Neutral form ('I, me, my')	Affect form ('Poor I, poor me, poor my')
Full pronoun[a]	*a'u*	*ta ita*
Subject clitic	*'ou*	*ta*
Poss. adj., sing., specific, inalienable	*lo'u*	*lota*
Poss. adj., sing., specific, alienable	*la'u*	*lata*
Poss. adj., sing., nonspecific, inalienable	*so'u*	*sota*
Poss. adj., sing., nonspecific, alienable	*sa'u*	*sata*
Poss. adj., pl., specific, inalienable	*o'u*	*ota*
Poss. adj., pl., specific, alienable	*a'u*	*ata*
Poss. adj., pl., nonspecific, inalienable	*ni o'u*	*ni ota*
Poss. adj., pl., nonspecific, alienable	*ni a'u*	*ni ata*

[a] These forms behave syntactically like nouns and can be used to express different grammatical functions, viz. subject, direct object, indirect object, oblique object.

speaker's telling of his going to see a film about Dracula and a narrative about a mutual friend in jail. The main narrative in the corpus of titled men's informal conversation concerns how one of the men (the narrator) lost his watch. The titled women's narratives include two narratives in which the narrator is the protagonist, and a third in which another village woman (an intimate of those present) is the major character. In our corpus we have more instances of women's narrative, given that domestic activities were a major focus of our research.

B.   Narrators' use of affect features

In these three sets of narratives, there are great differences in the narrator's use of affect forms. These differences (in terms of frequencies of occurrence)

Table 9.3. *Expression of sympathy in narrator's speech*

Affect form	Corpus 1 (77 clauses)	Corpus 2 (50 clauses)	Corpus 3 (146 clauses)
Address terms	16 (20.7%)	1 (2.0%)	0
Inclusive 'we'	0	1 (2.0%)	0
Sympathy 1st pers. pro.	2 (2.6%)	0	2 (1.4%)
Sympathy determiner	7 (9.1%)	1 (2.0%)	4 (2.7%)
Sympathy nominal ref.	8 (10.4%)	1 (2.0%)	2 (1.4%)
Sympathy adj./verb	7 (9.1%)	1 (2.0%)	8 (5.4%)
Particles	12 (15.6%)	13 (26%)	31 (21.2%)
Interjections	0	0	1 (0.7%)
Total	52 (67.5%)	18 (36%)	48 (32.9%)

Corpus 1 = untitled young men; Corpus 2 = titled (chief) older men; Corpus 3 = untitled older women married to titled men.

are codified in Tables 9.3–4. The differences are tied not so much to gender of speakers as they are to age and relative rank of the speakers. Women over fifty married to titled men and men who are chiefs show one pattern, and young untitled men show a different pattern of affect expression. More particularly, the young untitled narrator in the corpus used far more sympathy forms than the two other sets of narrators. This is demonstrated in two ways.

First, in Table 9.3 the number of sympathy forms is compared with the number of clauses in the narratives. If we disregard distinctions of title and age, that is, if we compare only women's speech (Corpus 3) with men's speech (Corpus 1, Corpus 2), then we find significant differences in use of affect forms at the .005 level, with men using more affect forms than women. However, when we incorporate into our analysis the variables of title and age, then we see that the difference is heavily influenced by the frequency of affect forms in the speech of untitled men (Corpus 1).

As can be seen in Table 9.3 and again more concisely in Table 9.6 below, the narrative of the young men (Corpus 1) contains such forms almost twice as frequently as do the other two sets (Corpus 2, Corpus 3) of narratives examined. Further, the difference in affect use between untitled and titled men (Corpus 1 vs. Corpus 2) and the difference in affect use between untitled men and older women married to titled men (Corpus 1 vs. Corpus 3) are also significant, whereas the difference in affect use between titled men and older women married to titled men (Corpus 2 vs. Corpus 3) is not.

We can also see the more effusive style of the young untitled narrator by examining the proportion of sympathy-marked to neutral first person pronouns, as displayed in Table 9.4. Here we can see that, while the young

Table 9.4. *Sympathy and neutral first person pronouns*

Pronoun	Corpus 1	Corpus 2	Corpus 3
Sympathy	2 (66.7%)	0	2 (13.3%)
Neutral	1 (33.3%)	24 (100%)	13 (86.7%)

untitled male narrator did not refer to himself often, in two out of the three instances he employed the sympathy form. In contrast, the older titled male narrator referred to himself often but never used the affect-marked form, and the older women used the affect form only 13.3 per cent of the time.

This pattern reflects expectations of Samoans concerning the demeanor of relatively high- and low-status persons. One would not expect relatively high-status persons, especially chiefs, to express (and thereby elicit) sympathy for themselves as often as lower-status persons. Relatively high-status persons are expected to conduct themselves in a more restrained and detached manner.

With respect to gender differences, these data tentatively suggest that title and age overshadow gender in accounting for affect expression in narration. The women in this corpus used slightly fewer affect features than titled men of the same age, but these two sets of narrators look quite similar when compared with the young untitled male.

C.   Listeners' use of affect features

Let us consider now the use of affect features by those listening to the narratives in the three sets of situations. The comparison here is somewhat flawed by a feature of the data collection. One of the two listeners in Corpus 1 (young untitled men) was also the one recording the interaction. No one else was aware of the recorder, but this person was and monitored his speech accordingly. This circumstance may have affected the frequency of sympathy features in listeners' speech in this situation.

Table 9.5 provides a comparison of listener usage patterns across the three contexts examined. We cannot rely on the results of Corpus 1, but we can make interesting comparisons between Corpus 2 and Corpus 3. The results show somewhat different patterns from the earlier analysis of narrator style. As in the earlier analysis, if we compare only men and women's speech (Corpus 1, Corpus 2 vs. Corpus 3) as listeners, we find a gender difference in affect use that is statistically significant (at .025 level only). However, the frequency of affect forms in the speech of older titled male listeners (Corpus 2) is significantly lower than that of either the young

Table 9.5. *Expression of sympathy in listeners' speech*

Affect form	Corpus 1 (33 clauses)	Corpus 2 (43 clauses)	Corpus 3 (59 clauses)
Address terms	2 (6.1%)	0	0
Sympathy determiners	1 (3.0%)	0	4 (6.8%)
Sympathy nominal ref.	2 (6.1%)	0	1 (1.7%)
Sympathy adj./verb	4 (12.1%)	1 (2.3%)	6 (10.2%)
Particles	11 (33.3%)	10 (23.3%)	18 (30.5%)
Interjections	1 (3.0%)	2 (4.7%)	4 (6.8%)
Agreement ('yes/right')	3 (9.1%)	1 (2.3%)	3 (5.1%)
Repetition/paraphrase of narration	6 (18.2%)	4 (9.3%)	13 (22.0%)
Total	30 (90.9%)	18 (41.9%)	49 (83.1%)

Table 9.6. *Proportion of sympathy features to number of clauses*

	Corpus 1	Corpus 2	Corpus 3
Narrator	1 : 1.5	1 : 2.8	1 : 3
Listener	1 : 1.1	1 : 2.4	1 : 1.2

untitled men (Corpus 1) or the older untitled women married to titled men (Corpus 3). On the other hand, there are no significant differences in the use of affect forms by young untitled men (Corpus 1) and the older titled women.

D.   Narrator–listener affect relations

Combining the results of narrators' and listeners' usage patterns, we can piece together the narrative interaction styles of our different sets of speakers. In Table 9.6 I have indicated the proportion of sympathy features to number of clauses for narrators and listeners in each corpus. This table suggests that untitled younger men use a moderate number of sympathy features as narrators and a large number as listeners, titled older men use very few sympathy features as both narrators and listeners, and untitled older women use few sympathy features as narrators but many as listeners. While speakers across all three corpora used more affect forms as listeners than as narrators, the women in Corpus 3 show the greatest increase in affect usage (from 1 : 3 to 1 : 1.2) and the titled men in Corpus 2 show the least increase (from 1 : 2.8 to 1 : 2.4).

To summarize, the analyses of affect features in the speech of narrators and listeners indicate that both gender and rank are important variables, but rank is more important. The statistical analyses indicate that women are more like titled men in the use of affect forms in narration, but they are more like untitled men in the use of affect forms as listeners.

V.   ACQUISITION OF AFFECT EXPRESSION IN SAMOAN

In sections III and IV, we considered the linguistic system for encoding affect in Samoan and ways in which affect features are used by speakers of different gender and social rank. In this section, we turn to the acquisition of affect morphology by Samoan children under the age of four. Two important themes of this section are that

(1) Affect once encoded is a powerful means of securing some desirable response from others, constraining what will be said next and what will be done next; and

(2) Young children understand this cause–effect relationship quite early in rural Western Samoa and use language to this end from the start.

A.   Developmental span

In this section, the order of emergence of grammatical forms expressing affect is presented. The data on which this ordering is based are drawn from utterances that express either anger, *'ita*, or sympathy/love, *alofa*. Table 9.7 presents construction types or areas of grammar and the time of their first appearance in the acquisition corpus. It does not indicate order of appearance of different forms within the same grammatical category (e.g. different interjections, focus particles).

One of the most general developmental patterns to emerge from the data is that most of the grammatical forms for expressing positive and negative affect are acquired before the age of four. The expression of affect through linguistic structures begins at the single-word stage. At that stage, the children in the study used a variety of curses and vocative insults, switched back and forth between two phonological registers for rhetorical effect, and used the affect first person pronoun ('poor I', 'poor me', 'poor my'). All this was supplemented by a variety of prosodic strategies for conveying affect. These prosodic strategies are recognized and named in Samoan. For example, there are terms for shouting (*e'ee*), screaming (*i'ii*), speaking softly (*leo vaivai*), speaking loudly (*leo kele*), whining (*fa'a'uu*), and so on, each conventionally linked to types of affect.

Table 9.7. *First appearance of grammatical forms of affect*

Age of child	Grammatical form (anger)	Grammatical form (sympathy)
1;7	Prosody Phon. alternation of /t/ & /k/ Interjection (*tae* 'shit')	Prosody Phon. alternation of /t/ & /k/ 1st pers. poss./obl. pro. (*ta/ta ita*)
1;10	Neg. existential (*leai*)	Focus particles (*a, ia*)
1;11	Neg. imperative (1st deg. intens.: *aua*)	
2;0	Vocative (*ise*)	Vocative (*sole*)
2;2		3rd pers. ref. term pred. adj. (*fiu* 'weary') Diminutive suffix
2;4	Neg. imperative (2nd deg. intens.: *soia*)	
2;5	Pred. adjective (*'ita* 'angry')	
2;11	3rd pers. ref. term (*le alelo*)	
3;7		Sing. determiner (*si*)

From a Samoan perspective, the acquisition of verbal affect expression begins not only at the single-word stage, but at the very first word, the beginning of recognizable Samoan itself. As noted in Chapter 8, all Samoan parents we questioned said that their child's first word was *tae*, a term meaning 'shit'. The term is a curse, a reduced form of *'ai tae*, meaning 'eat shit'. This conventional interpretation of a child's first word reflects the Samoan view of small children as characteristically strong-willed, assertive, and cheeky. Indeed, at a very early point in their language development, children use the curse frequently and productively to disagree, to reject, to refuse, and to prevent or stop some action.

B.   Presupposition and predication

As might be predicted from other developmental studies (Cruttendon 1982), linguistic forms that presuppose affect seem to be acquired before forms that predicate affect in the form of assertion. Thus, like English-speaking children, Samoan children use prosodic devices for conveying affect at the earliest stages of language development. Further, for both anger and sympathy, the explicit predication of these affects through predicate adjectives of affect (e.g. *fiu* 'weary/fed up', *'ita* 'angry', *fiafia* 'happy') is a relatively late development. Rather than saying 'I am angry', for example, children at first convey their anger through increased loudness, through a negative interjection, or through a vocative. Similarly, before children state, 'I am happy (about something or toward some person)', they will convey their feelings through phonological code switching or through a referential term of positive affect for self (*ta ita* 'dear me') or a vocative of endearment (*sole* 'mate/brother', *suga* 'lassie', etc.).

I want to note here that the children predicate feelings associated with their own and others' physiological conditions (hunger, thirst, tiredness, etc.) far more often than they predicate/assert affective feelings. These predications are formed by prefixing the verb *fia* 'want/feel like' to a verb denoting a physical action or activity, such as *'ai* 'eat' (*fia 'ai* = 'want to eat' or 'hungry'), *'inu* 'drink' (*fia 'inu* = 'want to drink' or 'thirsty'). The predication of these feelings begins at twenty-five months among the children in our study.

C.   Speech-act context

In a near parallel to the result above, children use the grammatical forms of affect first and more often in directions than in assertions. In the domain of sympathy/love, for example, first person sympathy pronouns first appear in the course of begging for objects. Whereas the affect pronoun is used in begging at nineteen months, when our recording began, this pronoun is not used in assertions until twenty-nine months.

Just as an adult uses these affect pronouns to obtain sympathy from the audience in the telling of a narrative, young children use them to obtain sympathy from someone who has some desired good. As discussed earlier, from a Samoan perspective sympathy/love is manifest when the audience/ addressee offers the desired good (in the case of begging) or the desired verbal expression of support and appreciation (in the case of a narrative about 'poor me', see example 1).

D.   Referents and subjects

Despite the sociocentric orientation of socialization, Samoan children show a decided egocentrism in their use of affect terms, determiners, and adjectives. Looking at Table 9.7, we can see that young children acquire or at least produce terms referring sympathetically to ego (first person pronoun of affect) before terms referring sympathetically to others (third person reference terms such as *toeina* 'old man') and before noun-phrase constructions that contain the sympathy determiner *si* 'the dear' (e.g. *si tama* 'the dear boy'; *si teine* 'the dear girl'). When children first use these third person forms, they use them to refer to themselves and much later apply them to other referents. For the domains of both anger and sympathy/love, reference to addressee, i.e. vocatives, precedes third person forms of reference. Finally, the egocentric bias is seen in subject referents of predicate adjectives. These predicates all refer to the speaker, i.e. the child, in our corpus of children under the age of four.

E.   Affect-marked versus neutral constructions

Perhaps the most interesting developmental pattern is that there is a strong tendency for affect construction to be acquired before the corresponding neutral constructions. With the exception of the acquisition of determiners, the affect-marked form is acquired before the neutral form whenever there are two alternative forms for carrying out a semantic function.

The best example of this is seen in the acquisition of first person full-pronoun forms. As noted earlier, Samoan has an affect full pronoun *ta ita* ('poor I', 'poor me'). In addition, it has a neutral full pronoun *a'u* ('I', 'me'). The first uses of the first person pronoun in the children's speech are as benefactives ('for me'), corresponding to indirect objects in adult speech, and as possessive adjectives. In both roles, the affect pronoun appears in children's speech several months before the neutral pronoun appears. For example, for one child, the affect pronoun appeared as a benefactive at nineteen months, whereas the neutral first person benefactive appeared at twenty-two months. For a second child, the possessive affect form appeared at twenty-one months, whereas the neutral first person possessive forms appeared at twenty-four months. An example of the affect pronoun taken from a child at the single-word stage is presented below.

(2) K, one year and seven months, asking his mother for food

K	*Mother*
((crying)) //mai/	//(Leai.) Leai.
bring	(no) no
'bring (it)/'	'(No.) No.'
((Calls name of mother))	
	'O le a
	TOP ART what
	'What is it?'
(i)ta/	
dear me	
'(for) dear me/'	

A very similar pattern is found if we look at the acquisition of negation. In this case, we find young Samoan children using their official first word *tae/kae* (the interjection meaning 'eat shit') to express negation in the way in which English-speaking children use 'No' and 'Don't!' The Samoan child at the single-word stage and later as well uses the negative affect term *tae/kae* to disagree, to reject, to refuse, and to prevent or stop some action. The use of this form for these functions appears long before the more neutral negative particle *leai* 'no' and the negative imperative *Aua!* 'Don't!' As stated earlier, the youngest children in our sample are using the affect term *tae/kae* at nineteen months. The use of the negative particle *leai* 'no' does not appear in the speech of one child until twenty-two months and in the other young child's not until twenty-four months. The use of the negative imperative *Aua!* 'Don't!' appears at twenty-three months for one child at twenty-five months for the second child. An illustration of how young children use *tae/kae* to refuse and reject is presented in the example below.

(3) K, one year and seven months, refusing to comply with his mother's wishes

K	*Mother*
	'ai muamua le talo a?
	eat first ART taro okay
	'Eat first the taro. Okay?'
tae/	
shit	
'shit/'	
	'ai muamua le talo lea.
	eat first ART taro this
	'Eat first the taro here.'
u tae/	
? shit	
'(?) shit/'	
	*'A'*a!
	NEG AFFECT
	'Don't!'
	Se 'ai muamua le talo lea.
	please eat first ART taro this
	'O please eat first the taro here.'
tae/	
shit	
'shit/'	

The basis for children's preference for the affect form over the neutral form appears to be rhetorical. As noted earlier, for example, the affect first person pronoun expressing sympathy for oneself is used to elicit sympathy from others for oneself. In adult speech, one finds this pronoun in narratives of complaint, for example, where minimally some sort of commiseration is desired. As discussed earlier, in the children's corpus the most common environment for the pronoun is in the course of asking for some good or service. In using the affect pronoun, the speaker appeals to the addressee to provide what is desired out of love or sympathy for the speaker. The neutral first person pronoun does not have this rhetorical force. Children apparently are sensitive to these rhetorical differences. The affective forms can 'buy' something that the neutral pronoun cannot.

VI.   IMPLICATIONS OF ACQUISITION PATTERNS

These and other findings strongly support the idea that children can express affect through conventional linguistic means from a very early point in developmental time. The Samoan materials indicate that small children are concerned with the rhetorical force of their utterances and that rhetorical strategies may account for certain acquisition patterns.

Affect strategies and goals, then, should be considered along with others that have been proposed as underlying children's emerging grammar. No matter to what use you put words – whether to request, to assert, or to question – you need to get the hearer to recognize dispositions that underlie and sometimes lend definition to those conversational acts and their propositions. All languages have conventional means of encoding this information. We can turn to the historian, the drama critic, and the clinical psychologist to tell us this. But we can also turn to our transcripts and our recordings of infants, small children, and caregivers. These materials reveal the patterned and conventional ways in which affect pervades both form and meaning in language.

10. Literacy instruction in a Samoan village

ALESSANDRO DURANTI and ELINOR OCHS

I. INTRODUCTION

This chapter reports on a study carried out by Alessandro Duranti and Elinor Ochs of literacy acquisition in a traditional Samoan community. The study concentrates on yet another environment in which socialization through language and socialization to use language take place, namely the classroom. Here our interest is in particular ways in which literacy instruction is organized in terms of Western-based expectations and norms and the possible socializing effects of this communicative organization on Samoan children.

This research is part of a growing number of studies that relate schooling and literacy instruction and practices in particular to cognitive and social development of children and others who participate in these activities (see for example Cook-Gumperz & Gumperz 1981; Heath 1982, 1983; Mehan 1979; Schieffelin & Cochran-Smith 1984; Schieffelin & Gilmore 1986; R. Scollon & Scollon 1981; Scribner & Cole 1973, 1981). This literature indicates that literacy acquisition and literacy activities display some variation across different communities. Research on psychological dimensions of literacy acquisition has considered the impact of such variation on the emergence of complex psychological skills such as perspective taking, hypothetical reasoning, abstract thinking, and complex memory skills (J. Goody 1977; Greenfield 1972; Olson 1980, for example). One theme of sociohistorical research in this area (see Luria 1976; Scribner & Cole 1981; Wertsch 1985a, b) is that, like other types of activity, literacy activities are culturally arranged and these arrangements enhance the development of certain cognitive skills. In this sense, higher psychological development is

An earlier version of this chapter was presented, with an accompanying film, at the Conference on Literacy and Linguistics, University of Southern California, November 1981, and at the Department of Anthropology, Pitzer College, November 1981. We thank the participants in both of those events for their stimulating questions and comments. We also thank Peg Griffin for reading an earlier draft of this chapter and providing helpful comments and inspiring criticism.

189

rooted in social interaction. It is through participation in culturally organized activities that individuals acquire new ways of thinking.

Ethnographic research on literacy acquisition has tended to focus on the relationship of literacy practices to local expectations concerning communicative and social competence. Heath's research, for example, enlightens us concerning attitudes toward written and spoken texts prevailing in different ethnic and class communities in the United States. Heath reveals how the earliest literacy experiences of young children are organized by these attitudes and other notions regarding language use in the local community. R. Scollon & Scollon (1981), too, have demonstrated how literacy practices are embodied in cultural notions of personhood and in expectations concerning interpersonal interaction – expectations concerning the task of message senders and recipients and concerning the explicitness of information conveyed.

The perspective of this study of literacy in a Samoan village is also ethnographic. The major point we wish to make is the following: in the course of transmitting literacy skills, the instructor exposes and socializes Samoan children to new expectations surrounding the adult–child relationship and the notion of task accomplishment.

The role and behavior of adult and child in the class of events we might call 'literacy classroom instructions' match those characteristic of many adult–child social interactions in Western middle-class society (Heath 1982). On the other hand, they do not match certain traditional Samoan beliefs, values, and social norms that underlie the relationship between adult and child. We posit that a global effect of literacy instruction is a change in the social identity of the child in Samoan society.

A more specific effect of literacy instruction concerns the notion of accomplishment or achievement. Instruction is organized in such a way that the child alone is pictured as having accomplished a particular task. Whereas the instructor has assisted the child, his contribution is not acknowledged by participants in the interaction. In contrast, traditional tasks outside the classroom setting are not organized along these lines. Tasks are seen as cooperatively rather than individually accomplished. In this chapter, we shall consider differences in these two notions of accomplishment through comparison of the acts of acknowledging and praising in literacy instruction and in a variety of social contexts in daily Samoan life.

The consequences of exposing young Samoan children to Western patterns of adult–child interaction and task accomplishment are difficult to document but are as dramatic and pervasive as the other facets of literacy and formal schooling that have been considered. In transmitting literacy skills, the instructor transforms the way in which these children view themselves with respect to others. The particular emphasis on *individual* achievement in literacy instruction is compatible not only with Western notions of classroom achievement but also with notions of economic achievement. We suggest that literacy instruction in this village provides the child with social and cultural knowledge necessary to participate in a Western-style economy: to obtain employment, carry out one's job, and be rewarded monetarily according to individual accomplishment.

The chapter is organized in the following way: in section II, we introduce the contexts of the use of literacy and the basic features of the written materials used in literacy instruction (viz. Bible reading). In section III, we describe the social organization of tasks and the concept of achievement in village settings outside the classroom. Section IV analyzes the discourse patterns of literacy instruction. These patterns reveal attitudes, expectations, and values not characteristic of social interaction in other village settings. In particular, we focus on the child-centered nature of the verbal interaction and the orientation toward individual rather than collective achievement. Section V summarizes our findings and our perspective on the effects of literacy instruction.

II.   CONTEXTS AND SOURCES OF LITERACY IN RURAL VILLAGES OF WESTERN SAMOA

In rural villages such as Falefaa, there are two main sources of written material in Samoan: (1) the Samoan version of the Bible, and (2) weekly newspapers that come from the capital, Apia. There are also a number of religious and educational publications put out, respectively, by various religious denominations and by the Education Department; the former are to be used in church activities and the latter in the public schools. Texts for secondary education are in English.

In everyday life, we find writing used for a number of reasons and in a number of social contexts. The most common use is probably for listing people, especially for the purpose of money collections and contributions and also for fines to be paid to the village judiciary committees. Writing is also used for corresponding with relatives who have gone to work (or to live) overseas, in New Zealand, in Australia, or in the United States.

There are also institutional records, for instance church records kept by local pastors and priests, who document dates of births, deaths, and special religious services for some family or group. Local hospitals also keep records of patients and treatments, births, deaths – it is worth noticing that in the hospital records people are listed under the name of the titled man (*matai*) who is the head of the extended family (see section III.A) rather than alphabetically by individual name.

Table 10.1. *The syllabary*

Table 10.2. *Key to Table 10.1*

Letter	Word (as written)	Word (as pronounced in reading)	
A	*ato*	'ato	'basket'
E	*'elefane*	elefane	'elephant' (loan)
I	*ipu*	'ipu	'cup'
O	*ofu*	'ofu	'dress'
U	*uati*	wati	'watch' (loan)
F	*fagu*	fagu	'bottle'
G	*gata*	gata	'snake'
L	*logo*	logo	'bell'
M	*moa*	moa	'fowl'
N	*nofoa*	nofoa	'chair'
P	*pusi*	pusi	'cat' (loan)
S	*solofanua*	solofanua	'horse'
T	*taavale*	ta'avale	'car, truck'
V	*vaa*	va'a	'boat, vessel'
H[a]	*Herota*	herota	'Herod' (loan)
K[a]	*kirikiti*	kirikiti	'cricket' (loan)
R[a]	*rapiti*	rapiti	'rabbit' (loan)

[a] Found only in loanwords.

Within the household, with the exception of the above-mentioned family correspondence and some secret books in which older men keep family genealogies and ceremonial greetings (*fa'alupega*),[1] writing is not a common activity.

A.   Learning how to read and write

Long before the age for public education, at the age of three or four, children are sent to the local pastor's school, where they first learn the alphabet, Arabic and Roman numbers, and the recitation of a few passages from the Bible. With the help of an illustrated alphabet table (see Table 10.1), young children recite the name of the letter and the name of the picture contained in the same box. Thus, for instance, they say aloud 'a *ato*, e *elefane*, i *ipu*', etc. for the vowels, and 'fa *fanu*, ga *gata*, la *logo*, mo *moa*', etc. for the consonants.

[1] There is a taboo, in fact, for anyone but the one who wrote them to read these lists of names and ceremonial greetings. The violation of such a taboo is believed to cause misfortune or even death to the transgressor. Such a restriction reinforces (reflects?) the basic Samoan belief that one should learn from direct experience, i.e. from watching and listening to competent people.

Given the age range of the pupils, the younger ones are immediately exposed to the more complex tasks and routines performed by the older children. They participate in such routines according to their competence. At first they may be able to perform only part of a given routine; as they mature, they perform in a more competent way, providing a model for younger and less experienced peers.

In Table 10.2 we have listed the words that correspond to the picture associated with each letter of the alphabet. For each word, we have listed the present spelling[2] and the actual careful pronunciation.

There are several reasons for wanting to consider in some detail the alphabet table reproduced in Table 10.1. It tells us some important things about literacy instruction in Samoa, and it also confirms what is already known about literacy in other societies. We shall focus on two aspects of the alphabet table: (1) the Western orientation of its content (by 'content' we mean both what is represented in the table and the particular way in which it is represented) and (2) the conventions for transcribing Samoan sounds and words.

1.   Western orientation of the alphabet table

Even without knowing much about Samoan culture, one can easily infer a Western orientation in the illustrated alphabet as shown in Table 10.1. More generally, however, there is a clear preference for an imagery that evokes nontraditional settings, referents, and values. Out of the seventeen pictures chosen to represent current Samoan words, none represents a traditional Samoan referent – traditional at least from a historic viewpoint: none of the pictures represents something that existed or was known to Samoans before contact with Europeans. – This could not have been avoided for the last three letters ('h', 'k', and 'r'), which correspond to sounds introduced by Europeans for borrowed words: we find 'Herod', Samoan *Herota* (from the Bible), 'cricket', Samoan *kirikiki*, and 'rabbit', Samoan *rapiti*. What is striking, however, is that even for those words that could have been represented by an image of something traditional or familiar to a Samoan child, a corresponding less familiar object or artefact is chosen. This is the case, for instance, for the first picture on the top right corner, where, for the Samoan word *ato* 'basket', we find a kind of basket that is sold to tourists in the capital rather than the traditional basket used in

---

[2] As can be seen by comparing the written version of each word and its corresponding careful pronunciation, current educational publications in Western Samoa tend not to use the glottal stop, despite the fact that the missionaries originally introduced a conventional sign for it, namely a grave accent (`). This sign is used, although inconsistently, in the Samoan Bible and in newspaper articles.

everyday activities for carrying goods or collecting garbage. To represent *ipu* 'cup', we find a china cup rather than the traditional Polynesian cup, that is, half a coconut shell. The dress, *ofu*, is an end-of-the-century British missionary's wife's dress (notice the short sleeves covering the shoulders, an unfitting feature for the hot and humid climate of Samoa). Finally, the picture of the boat, for the word *va'a*, is an ocean liner rather than the more familiar Samoan outrigger.[3]

These facts suggest that when a Samoan child is first exposed to literacy instruction he or she is taught something more than the alphabet. From the very first day of school, literacy is accompanied by an attention to a world of objects and values that either are removed from the immediate context of the child's everyday life or suggest Western alternatives within a range of possible choices that would include more traditional objects and values. We find reference to Western codes for dressing, Western products (viz. the bottle of cola), Western artifacts and technology (e.g. the sedan car rather than the more useful and familiar pickup truck, the big ship rather than the outrigger). Finally, some of the words anticipate unknown characters (e.g. Herod, the snake – there are no such snakes in Samoa) soon to be encountered in the reading of Holy Scripture.

2.   Features of the literacy register

To illustrate the main feature of the sound system portrayed by written Samoan, let us take as an example the word used to illustrate the letter/sound 't', namely *ta'avale* 'car' but also 'truck' (literally 'rolling thing').

Especially where a village is located along a road with trucks, buses, pickups, and cars passing by at all times of the day, the Samoan child must learn from his very first steps to watch for the often speeding motor vehicles. The word referring to 'car, truck' is thus often heard along and around the road, usually shouted as a warning to young children by older siblings or adult bystanders. *Va'ai ka'avale!* 'Watch (for the) car/truck!' one hears, or simply *Ka'avale!* 'Car/truck!' In these situations, the word is pronounced with a /k/ rather than with a /t/ (*ka'avale* instead of *ta'avale*). Such a difference between the way the word is written and read and the way it is pronounced in most of daily interaction reflects an important distinction between two sharply marked phonological registers.

---

[3] In making these remarks, we are not suggesting that imported artifacts or concepts be considered 'non-Samoan'. We do take sedan cars, china cups, European dresses, clocks, etc. to be part of the contemporary Samoan culture and environment. We are simply pointing out that the choices made in illustrating the alphabet reflect a bias toward those elements of contemporary Samoan culture that are still overtly bound to a Western lifestyle and its values.

As noted in Chapter 3, in Samoan communities these registers are called 'good speech' (*tautala lelei*) and 'bad speech' (*tautala leaga*). Figure 10.1 illustrates the differences between the two phonemic inventories.

As summarized in Figure 10.2, in 'bad speech' the alveolar segments /t/ and /n/ merge with the velar segments /k/ and /g/ respectively. (Given that Samoan does not have a velar stop, we have here adopted the Samoan orthographic convention of using the letter 'g' for representing a velar nasal – the voiceless velar segment replaces the voiced one in loanwords, e.g. English *gallon* = > Samoan *kalone*.) Furthermore, /r/ and /l/ merge into /l/, and /h/ is often not realized in 'bad speech' or is pronounced as a glottal stop (/ʔ/).

As pointed out by Shore (1977, 1982), the contexts in which 'good speech' predominates are strictly related to imported, Western-oriented activities. Typically, such activities or interactions involve or presuppose the use of literacy. Thus, we find 'good speech' used in writing, reading, school instruction, praying, singing, radio broadcasting, and talking to foreigners (who are prototypically seen as missionaries or teachers). 'Bad speech', on the other hand, is found in most of everyday spoken interaction, ranging over both formal (see Duranti 1981a, b, 1983) and informal situations (see Ochs 1982a, b; Platt 1982) (see also Duranti 1981a:ch. 8; Ochs 1986a, and Shore 1977, 1982 for a general discussion of the variation between the two registers).

'Good speech'   'Bad speech'

Consonants

```
p   t       k*  ʔ                          p           k   ʔ
f,v  s   l,r*                              f,v   s   l
m   n       ŋ   h*                         m           ŋ
```

Vowels

```
        i    u
        e    o
          a
```

Figure 10.1. *Phonemic inventories of 'good speech' and 'bad speech' (/g/ stands for a velar nasal).*

Note: *Letters marked with an asterisk are found only in loanwords. Short vowels are in phonemic contrast with long vowels, which can be analyzed as consecutive identical vowels (see Milner 1966; Pawley 1966). Although vocalic segments can be considered as one set for both registers, in 'bad speech', as noted by Shore (1977), the tendency to articulate everything farther back in the mouth affects vowel quality.*

III.   THE SOCIAL ORGANIZATION OF TASK
         ACCOMPLISHMENT OUTSIDE THE CLASSROOM

We want to focus now on one aspect of Samoan society and culture, namely the concept and practice of task achievement. To illustrate this concept, it is necessary to amplify certain basic information concerning Samoan social organization presented in Chapter 4 and to introduce local notions concerning collective responsibility for task accomplishment.

A.   Social stratification

As noted in Chapter 4, Samoan society has been characterized as 'stratified' (see Sahlins 1958), that is, as a society in which distinctions with respect to decision power and prestige are made not only in terms of the universal features of age, sex, and personal characteristics but also, and crucially, according to the rank of particular 'titles' that adult individuals may hold from a certain moment of their lives on, usually until death. A very basic distinction is thus made in Samoan society between titled people, called *matai*, and untitled people, or commoners, called *taulele'a*. A title is conferred on a person by a special session of the extended family (*'aaiga potopoto*) and gives its holder privileges and duties with respect to an extended family and to the village political structure. More specifically, a *matai* title gives its holder control over a plot of land and its products (taro, breadfruit, bananas, coconuts), decision power, and responsibilities both within the family and in larger contexts, e.g. village affairs. A *matai* title carries with it the right and duty to attend the meetings of the village council

'Good speech'	'Bad speech'
t, k	k
Ex.: *lota* 'my'	*loka* 'my' or 'lock'
loka 'lock'	
n, g	g
Ex.: *fana* 'gun'	*faga* 'gun' or 'bay'
faga 'bay'	
Ex.: l, r	l
kirikiti 'cricket'	*kilikiki* 'cricket'
natura 'nature'	*gakula* 'nature'

Figure 10.2.   *Correspondence between 'good speech' and 'bad speech'.*
   Note: *The number of minimal pairs for the /t/ and /k/ and the /n/ and /g/ oppositions is very low.*

(*fono*), where important decisions are made and solutions to social dramas are negotiated among the most influential members of the community (see Duranti 1981a).

Social stratification is seen in the division of labor within the family. Generally, untitled men and women are the ones who cultivate food on family land, go out fishing, or nowadays work in the capital and then bring the product of their labor back to be shared among all family members according to social status and the needs of the family at large. The highest-ranking chief in the family generally has first rights to choose the quality and amount of food; younger, lower-status adults and children share what is left.

High rank is associated with stationary behavior: controlled, dignified (*mamalu*) posture (the term used to refer to the ceremony of installation of a title is *saofa'i*, the respect-vocabulary word for 'to sit'). Low-rank people instead are movable, run errands, carry objects or messages. The dichotomy between high rank = stationary and low rank = active is realized in many different ways and across all kinds of situations.

For example, when we observe people remodeling an old house, we see young untitled men of the family move long and heavy posts, while a much older woman is weaving new blinds with leaves from pandanas trees. Similarly, a young titled man and his wife may be supervising closely those carrying out the heavy labor, giving advice and directing children to help; in the meantime, the oldest man of the house and highest-ranking orator in the compound sits silent in a nearby house, watching now and then the others working, while routinely making string from coir sennit (*'afa*). The string will be used to secure the new blinds and roofing to the house. Participation in the building task, then, is differentiated according to social rank.

As this description suggests, more than activity level distinguishes relative status. Generally, there is an expectation that low-ranking persons will attend to and accommodate those of higher rank. The accommodation is at the same time mental and physical, in the sense that lower-ranking persons are expected to take the perspective of others in order to serve them.

Throughout this volume a major emphasis has been that from a very early age young children are both explicitly and implicitly socialized into a disposition of attention and accommodation (see Chapters 1, 4, 7–9). Chapter 4 describes how caregivers often hold and feed infants and toddlers so that they face outward to others present. Children in the early stages of acquiring language are expected to notice the activity of others and report on it. Further, they are expected to speak intelligibly. Chapter 7 points out that unintelligible utterances will generally not be unraveled by older persons present in the manner described for middle-class Western caregiver–child interaction (Ochs & Schieffelin 1984). By the time children reach the age of three and a half or four years, they will be asked to transmit orally lengthy messages to persons in other compounds. This task will demand of them competence in politeness conventions and respect vocabulary appropriate to the social status of the addressee. Generally, in carrying out these tasks, children are not praised or complimented. The child's accommodation to older persons is part of showing *fa'aaloalo* 'respect', a crucial dimension of Samoan social life.

B. Collective accomplishment: the concept of *taapua'i* 'supporter'

Having briefly considered the organization of daily activities according to social rank and the socialization of children into such a system, we can start introducing a very important notion in Samoan culture, namely that of *taapua'i*, which can be translated as 'supporter' or 'sympathizer'.

In all kinds of daily activities, Samoans see other people as needing someone else to sympathize with them. Very rarely does a Samoan do something without someone next to him to provide recognition of his actions, attempts, or accomplishments. Whether building a house, singing a song, fixing a broken tool, driving a car, Samoans know that they can usually count on the company of one or more sympathizers. The relationship between the actor and the supporter is truly reciprocal rather than unidirectional. When someone's work or accomplishment is valued and recognized by a supporter, the supporter's work at recognizing the accomplishment is also recognized by the actor. This relationship is symbolically and routinely instantiated by the use of what we shall call 'a *maaloo* exchange'. If the driver avoids a collision with another vehicle, the passengers will recognize his presence of mind with a *maaloo*. The driver will then acknowledge the support by answering with another *maaloo*.

The exchange goes as follows:

(1) Context: Driver does something that shows skill, presence of mind
PASSENGER(S): Maaloo le fa'auli!
                        'Well done the steering!'
DRIVER: Maaloo le taapua'i!
                        'Well done the support!'

If the driver is able to see a hole in the road and avoid it in time, the exchange might be as follows:

(2)
PASSENGER(S): Maaloo le silasila!
                        'Well done the looking!'
DRIVER: Maaloo le taapua'i!
                        'Well done the support!'

This kind of routine is found in situations that at first appear more difficult for a non-Samoan to understand. Thus, as illustrated in (3), when a party of people who have been away on a trip return home, those who stayed home welcome them with a *maaloo* greeting, and those who just arrived reply with another *maaloo*:

(3)

PEOPLE AT HOME: Maaloo le malaga!
'Well done the trip!'
TRAVELERS: Maaloo le fa'amuli!
'Well done the staying back!'

To understand this exchange, we must realize that, in the Samoan view, the travelers' reply not only acknowledges the sympathy of those at home (some of whom might have worried about the outcome of the trip) but also recognizes the fact that a trip is made into something valuable, deserving recognition, by the very fact that someone stayed home and did not go on the trip. The same is true for the exchange between the driver and the passengers. The driver is skillful to the extent to which his supporters are willing to recognize his skills.

More generally, something is an accomplishment because of and through the recognition that others are willing to give it. Any accomplishment can then be seen as a joint product of both the actors and the supporters. In the Samoan view, if a performance went well, it is the supporters' merit as much as the performers'. This is so true that if the performer receives a prize or some previously established compensation, he has to share it with his supporters.

To conclude, the notion of 'supporter' and the *maaloo* routine reiterate the Samoan view of accomplishment as a collective and cooperative enterprise, in which the individual's competence is defined by his audience appreciation, and his merit is framed within the merit of his group. Being skillful (*poto*) at something does not mean to stand out with respect to everyone else as much as to be able to create the conditions for a successful collective endeavor (see Mead 1937). By sharing the products of his labor or his earnings (if any) with his supporters, a person gives goods back to those who gave him sympathy first.

IV.   LITERACY INSTRUCTION IN CLASSROOM SETTINGS

A.   The setting

As noted earlier, Samoan children generally first acquire literacy skills in a village pastor's school. They enter this school two or three years before entering the kindergarten class in the village public school. The classes meet in the late afternoon, and many children of the congregation attend until their early teens. The interactions analyzed here are drawn from both pastor's and public schools; however, our primary focus will be on literacy instruction in the pastor's school.

While the youngest children spend time learning the alphabet table, older children in the pastor's school concentrate on two important tasks: reading aloud from the Bible and interpretation of Bible passages. The children typically sit cross-legged on mats, facing the instructor (the pastor, the pastor's wife, the pastor's assistant), who is seated also cross-legged on a separate mat, facing the children. Every child holds a Bible in his or her lap or places it on the mat in front of him or her. The lesson begins with Bible reading. In this part, each child reads one verse from the Bible, with the pastor's assistance (see example 4). Following this, the pastor questions the children concerning their understanding of the written material they have just read. Three stretches of classroom interaction between a pastor and his students illustrate the character of these events.

(4) Pastor's school: reading aloud

Context: A child reading aloud from the Bible misreads the word *faaliu* 'to turn toward' – spelled *faliu* – as *fa'aliliu* 'to translate'. Such a mistake is probably related to the fact that in the Bible the glottal stop (?) is often left out; *fa'aliliu* could have been written *faaliliu*.

1 CHILD: 'a 'ua fa'aliliu* Iesu iaa ((* Error))
           'But Jesus translating to –'
2 PASTOR: Sipela le 'upu!
           'Spell the word!'
3   (3.0)
4 CHILD: Fa–a–la–i–u.
           'F–a–l–i–u.' ((NB: The word is spelled out one 'a'))
5 PASTOR: Ia. Le aa laa?
           'So. What is it then?'
6   (6.0)
7 CHILD: 'a 'ua fa'ai'u*. ((* Error))
           'But (he) ended.'
8 PASTOR: ('a 'ua –) (1.5) Sipela le 'upu!
           '(But he) – (1.5) Spell the word!'
9 CHILD: Fa–a–la–i–u.
           'F–a–l–i–u.'
10   (1.0)
11 PASTOR: Faa,
           'Faa,'
12 CHILD: Fa'aliliu*. ((* Error))
           'Translated.'
13 PASTOR: Leo kele!
           'Speak aloud!'
14 CHILD: Fa'aliliu*. ((* Error)
           'Translated.'
15 PASTOR: 'e lee se fa'aliliu! Fa'aliliu fa'afefea?
           'It's not "translate"! How come "translate"?'

16 Fa–a–la–i–u
    'F–a–l–i–u.'
17 (4.5)
18 PASTOR: 'o le "faa" ma le "liu." 'o le aa le 'upu?
    '"Faa" and "liu." What is the word?'
19 (2.0)
20 CHILD: ((Unclear))
21 PASTOR: Le aa?
    'What?'
22 CHILD: Faaliu.
    'Turn.'
23 PASTOR: Faaliu. Leo kele!
    'Turn. Speak loud!'
24 (1.0)
25 CHILD: a 'ua fa'al– faaliu Ieusuu i– iaa te 'i–
    'But Jesus transl– turning to –'
26 ia– iaa te 'i laatou 'ua fetalai (0.3) atu
    'up– upon them said'

(5) Pastor's school: discussion of Herod

1 PASTOR 'o ai Herota?
    'Who is Herod?'
2 TERESA: Tupu.
    'King.'
3 PASTOR: 'o le aa?
    '(It) is what?'
4 TERESA: 'o le tupu.
    '(He) is the king.'
5 PASTOR: 'o le tupu. Lelei.
    '(He) is the king. Good.'
6 E iai se si e 'ese sana tali?
    'Is there anyone else with a different answer?'
7 BOY: 'o le tagata lea na fia fasi fua iaa Iesuu.
    'The person who wanted to kill Jesus for no reason.'
8 PASTOR: Lelei fo'i.
    'Good also.'
9 'a 'o le aa lona – lona tofiga?
    'But what is his – his occupation?'
10 'o le tupu aa,
    'The king, isn't he?'
11 Tupu lea saa – saa lee fiafia iaa Iesuu
    '(The) king who did – didn't like Jesus'
12 ina 'ua fanau mai Iesuu
    'because Jesus was born'
13 ma 'ua folafola mai e tagata
    'and was proclaimed by the people'
14 'o ia 'o le tupu o tagata Iutaia aa,
    '(that) he is the king of the Jews, right?'
15 Saa – saa lee fiafia la iai
    '(he) did – didn't like him then'
16 'ona 'o le manatu o Herota
    'because Herod's idea (was that)'

17   na 'o ia lava le tupu aa,
            'only he himself is the king, right?'
18   e lee ai se si tagata e tatau
            'there is no other person (who) should'
19   ona – ona fai ma tupu.
            'become king.'
20   Se'i vaganaa 'o ia lava.
            'Except he himself.'

(6) Pastor's school: discussion of Barabbas

1 PASTOR: . . . Parapa saa fouvale i le – i le nu'u.
               'Barabbas had rioted in the – in the city.'
2   Saa tele fo'i ana amio leaga na fai.
               'Many were the bad actions he had done.'
3   'ona 'ave ai lea tu'u le fale– . . .
               'so that (he) had been put in the pri– . . .'
4 CHILDREN: –puipui
               '–son!'
5 PASTOR: Falepuipui!
               'Prison!'
6   Ia. 'o lona uiga 'a tu'u tagata
               'So. That is to say, if someone is put'
7   i le falepuipui 'o le aa le tagata egaa?
               'in a prison, what is that person?'
8   'o le paago– . . .
               'A priso– . . .'
9 CHILDREN: Paagota.* ((* Error: the last 'a' should be long, 'aa'))
               'Paagota.'
10 PASTOR: ((Correcting the pronunciation)) PaagotAA!
11   Po 'o le paagota?'
               'What is a *paagota*?'

B.   The role of literacy instruction in redefining adult–child social relationships

Examining the verbal interaction in these examples, we can see that the pastor/instructor enters into the activity of reading and interpreting at many points. Very much like contemporary Western pedagogues, the pastor in this village school grants permission to speak, selects topics, points out errors, corrects certain of them, and clarifies terms and passages.

Three constructions are heavily relied upon to introduce and clarify topics: *rhetorical questions* (example 5, line 9), *test questions* (example 5, line 1), and *incomplete sentence frames* (example 6, lines 3 and 8). Rhetorical and test questions are similar in that in both cases the speaker knows a possible answer to the question posed. They are distinguished in that the rhetorical question is intended to be answered by the speaker, whereas the test question is intended to be answered by a selected addressee. The incomplete sentence frame functions as a question as well in that the instructor elicits through prosodic means missing information in a sentence he has initiated. Both the test question and incomplete sentence frame involve the instructor and student in the expression of an idea. The instructor provides the first part and the student the second part of the idea.

These pedagogical procedures are very familiar to readers of this book. These constructions and strategies parallel those found in classrooms following the Western or European tradition of formal education (see Mehan 1979; Philips 1983). And the parallel is not coincidental. The pastor's school is organized through the Christian church. Training in Western pedagogical techniques is provided to pastors and their spouses over a four-year period in a theological seminary.

The procedures characteristic of teachers in Western classrooms are extensions of practices of caregivers in Western middle-class households. In other words, *teacher talk* (Cazden 1979; Coulthard 1977) has something in common with middle-class caregiver speech to young children. In both situations, speakers simplify and clarify for the child (Ferguson 1977). For example, rhetorical questions simplify a proposition by breaking it down into two separate utterances. The child's attention is drawn to certain information (topic) in one utterance, and then a predication (comment) concerning that information is made in a separate utterance (see Keenan (Ochs) & Schieffelin 1976; Ochs, Schieffelin & Platt 1979; R. Scollon 1976). Test questions and sentence frames simplify by helping the child to express an idea; typically caregivers/teachers produce the first part of the idea (topic), and the child completes the predication (comment) (Greenfield & Smith 1976; Ochs, Schieffelin & Platt 1979). In Western middle-class societies, these procedures are part of a broader set of simplifying features that distinguish language addressed to young children from language in many other sociolinguistic situations. When a middle-class child enters the classroom, then, there is quite a lot of continuity with his or her early experiences in talking to adults.

In contrast, these features are not characteristic of traditional Samoan caregiver speech. Whereas these features reflect and express in middle-class society the expectation that adults should adapt their language in relating to small children (Ochs & Schieffelin 1984), the traditional Samoan expectation is the reverse – that children, not adults, should adopt their behavior, including their speech (Ochs 1982b).

Samoan caregivers generally do not simplify their speech in addressing small children. Relevant to this discussion, they do not characteristically break down propositions into rhetorical questions and answers, nor do they jointly express propositions with children through test questions/answers and sentence frames/completions. As a rule, caregivers do not ask children questions to which they know the answers. For example, Samoan caregivers do not engage in labeling routines with small children, asking the child such questions as 'What's this?' to which the caregiver knows the answer. As noted earlier, in contrast to Western middle-class caregivers, Samoan caregivers place far greater responsibility for acquisition of knowledge with the child. Children are expected to watch and listen. Samoans say that the way to knowledge and power is to serve (i.e. attend).

When a three- or four-year-old Samoan child enters the classroom for literacy instruction, then, he or she participates in verbal interactions that differ in important ways from interactions with adults outside the classroom. Most critically, in the classroom the adult verbally accommodates (in terms of simplification and clarification) the child to a greater extent than do adults outside this setting. In the classroom, the interactions are more child-centered; in other village settings, the interactions are more adult-centered. The net result is a shift in social expectations surrounding the roles of adult and child.

C. The role of literacy instruction in redefining task accomplishment

In this section, we shall consider how accomplishment or achievement is expressed in literacy instruction and contrast this with expectations outside the classroom setting. We shall see that the notion of task accomplishment in the classroom further enhances the child-centered orientation of the interaction.

In the previous section, we indicated ways in which the pastor/instructor facilitates the tasks of reading and comprehending written material. Examining the transcripts, we can see that the achievement of these tasks has drawn on the efforts of both instructor and student. Indeed, in certain cases the instructor and student together have produced the correct reading or missing information. Curiously, however, these accomplishments are not seen as cooperative in this social context. Instead, tasks are treated as individually accomplished; specifically, as accomplished by a particular child.

Support for this claim comes from the set of positive assessments – compliments or praises – that can mark the successful completion of particular tasks. Before proceeding with a comparison of complimenting/praising in and out of the classroom, we need to point out that, across societies, these forms of verbal behavior codify perspectives on task and achievement. Complimenting and praising can indicate *that* something has been accomplished, *what* has been accomplished, *who* has accomplished it, and *in what manner*. They are, then, good sources for understanding how members of a society conceptualize a task. Where young children are involved, complimenting and praising socialize them into seeing a task from a particular perspective or 'world view'.

We noted earlier (section III.B) that the successful accomplishment of tasks in day-to-day village life is often acknowledged through a verbal ritual – the *maaloo* exchange. Task accomplishment in the classroom is also associated with a verbal ritual. The successful completion of a task is often acknowledged by the instructor uttering such praises as *Lelei* 'Good' or *Lelei tele* 'Very good'. Example (5) illustrates two instances of this pattern. Lines 5 and 8 contain the assessment *Lelei* 'Good'. In these instances, the pastor praises two children for successfully answering a question. Below we provide another example of these assessments. Example (7) is drawn from the kindergarten/first-grade class in the village public school. In this example the instructor acknowledges accomplishment through the predicates *Lelei tele* 'Very good' (lines 5, 12).

(7) Kindergarten/first-grade class

Context: It is the second week of school. The teacher has just taken the class for a walk around the school yard. Once back in the classroom, she asks the pupils questions about what they have just seen.

1 TEACHER:	Lima i luga lima i luga lima i luga!	
	'Hands up, hands up, hands up!'	
2	Si'i luga lima o le tagata	
	'Raise a hand the person (who)'	
3	e iloa ta'u mai se mea (iaa) te a'u!	
	'can tell me something!'	
4 ((A boy raises his hand.))		
5 TEACHER:	Lelei tele. 'o ai fo'i le igoa laa?	
	'Very good. What is the name there?'	
6 BOY:	Salani.	
	'Salani.'	
7 TEACHER:	'o ai?	
	'Who?'	
8 TWO GIRLS:	Salagi.	
	'Salagi.'	
9 TEACHER:	Salagi tama lelei Salagi. Tu'u i luga Salagi.	
	'Salagi, good boy, Salagi. Stand up, Salagi.'	
10	Ta'u mai se mea na 'e va'ai iai.	
	'Tell (us) something you saw.'	
11 SALAGI:	'ulu!	
	'Breadfruit(s)!'	
12 TEACHER:	Lelei tele. ((Continues))	
	'Very good.'	

We turn now to a comparison of *maaloo* and *lelei* in the different social settings in which they are used. *Maaloo* is used pervasively in social situations outside the classroom setting; it is rarely used in the classroom. *Lelei* is used consistently in the speech of instructors in the course of literacy instruction; it is rarely used as a form of praise in social situations outside this setting.[4] In our discussion we focus on one variable, the recipient of the compliment or praise (the one/ones who take(s) credit for the task accomplished).

Comparing examples (1), (2), and (3) with examples (5) and (7), we can see that *Maaloo* 'Well done' and *Lelei* 'Good' have different conversational consequences. As noted in section III.B *Maaloo* is part of a verbal exchange. In conversation-analysis terminology, the first utterance containing *Maaloo* (*Maaloo* 1: 'Well done') is the first pair part of an adjacency pair, and the second utterance containing *Maaloo* (*Maaloo* 2: 'And well done to you') is the second pair part (Sacks, Schegloff & Jefferson 1974). The important property is that once *maaloo* 1 is produced, there is a strong expectation that *maaloo* 2 will be produced.

Lelei 'good', on the other hand, is not a first pair part of an exchange/ adjacency pair. It is instead the last act of a three-part sequence, typical of classroom interaction, which Mehan (1979) called Initiation–Reply–Evaluation. What is relevant for our discussion is that when the instructor acknowledges the child's achievement by uttering *lelei*, the child does not reciprocate and acknowledge the instructor's accomplishments in the social event at hand. The child does not say, for example, *Lelei fo'i* or *Lelei fo'i 'oe* 'You did well too.' In contrast to *Maaloo*, *Lelei* closes an interactional sequence.

Simply in terms of their sequential organization, *maaloo* and *lelei* reflect differences in giving credit for task accomplishment. When a speaker uses *maaloo*, credit is typically reciprocally given (two-directional). When *lelei* is used, credit is unidirectional.

There are additional properties of *maaloo* that distinguish it from *lelei*. The *maaloo* exchange is not simply an exchange of compliments/praises. It expresses the idea that both parties to the *maaloo* exchange have contributed to the *same* task. As noted earlier, the initial expression of *maaloo* itself defines the speaker as a *taapua'i* 'supporter', and supporters should be given credit for accomplishing a task. Hence the speaker of *maaloo* 1 becomes the recipient of *maaloo* 2. The use of *lelei* apparently carries with it no such conditions. The instructor who uses *lelei* is not acknowledged by a child for his or her role in facilitating the achievement of literacy skills.

---

[4] Outside the classroom, *lelei* is used primarily to express agreement and conclude a topic, much like the English 'okay', 'sure', 'fine'. In these contexts, *lelei* is typically preceded by the particle *ia'*, a boundary marker of discourse units, roughly corresponding to the English 'well', 'so', 'then'. *Lelei* in the classroom also operates as a boundary marker, but performs a different speech act (praise rather than agreement). In addition, there are prosodic differences between the utterances in which *lelei* is used as a praise and those in which it is used as an agreement.

Outside this setting, the same child told *maaloo* does *maaloo* back, acknowledging the contribution of others in achieving a goal.

Young Samoan children experience a type of secondary socialization in the course of becoming literate. They learn sociolinguistic norms that differ from those operating in family interactions in the village. In their primary socialization, they learn not to expect praises and compliments for carrying out directed tasks. Children are expected to carry out these tasks for their elders and family. In their secondary socialization, they learn to expect recognition and positive assessments, given successful accomplishment of a task. In their primary socialization, Samoan children learn to consider tasks as cooperatively accomplished, as social products. In their secondary socialization, they learn to consider tasks as an individual's work and accomplishment.

This particular difference is not experienced by most Western middle-class children entering school. These children are accustomed to praise (LeVine 1980). Further, from infancy onward, these children are socialized through language to see tasks as interactions in which jointly accomplished tasks of adult and child are evaluated by the adult as an accomplishment of the child (Ochs & Schieffelin 1984). Adults provide the means for a child to accomplish a task, but then treat that task as the child's own achievement. Western middle-class caregivers repeat this pattern over and over in playing games, drawing, constructing (Bruner 1975), putting away toys, telling a story jointly with their children. The behavior of teachers in contemporary Western classrooms is continuous in this sense with that of caregivers. In both cases, the adult does not take (or get) credit for her or his part in accomplishing a task; instead, the child is given full credit through unidirectional praising.

We can see from this description that the secondary socialization of Samoan children may extend beyond norms of classroom interaction. Samoan children may be acquiring certain attitudes that characterize Western middle-class society. These attitudes dominate a wide range of social relationships, including, most important, economic relationships.

Rural Samoans acquire literacy skills primarily to be competent in reading the Bible and to be employable. The ability to read and write fluently is a requirement of most salaried jobs in the capital. But to participate successfully in the urban cash economy, a Samoan needs more than literacy skills in the strict sense of reading and writing. The urban economy is heavily influenced by Western values. In particular, the urban economic system relies on the notion of individual accomplishment. This is what a *salary* represents. The salary symbolizes recognition and approval of an individual's achievements, recognizes that an individual has done what was expected (or more than expected) of him. The Western-style pedagogic procedures used in transmitting literary skills prepare young children for the Western-style economy in which many will eventually participate. With a school certificate in hand, they have acquired (in some measure) both the social and linguistic competence demanded in these economic contexts. However, secondary socialization may be superseded by primary socialization as long as the traditional social context stays unchanged. When the emigrant Samoan comes back to his village for a visit, he is expected to share his earnings with his family, friends, and *taapua'i*. The fruits of his labor are redistributed among those who helped him at some earlier time in his life or were thinking of him while he was away.

V. CONCLUSIONS

In a recent collection on literacy and historical change, Graff (1981:258) wrote, 'Literacy's importance can not be understood in isolation, or in terms of self-advancement or skills; rather, its significance lies in its relation to the transmission of morals, discipline and social values.' Graff and other social scientists (e.g. Galtung 1981; Gintis 1971) have argued that in teaching literacy, educators have been simultaneously engaged in 'the reshaping of character, behavior, morality and culture' (Graff 1981:257). Industrialists apparently recognized this activity long before social scientists and in the nineteenth century encouraged schools to promote values that are harmonious with economic productivity, e.g. self-motivation, punctuality, regularity.

These observations are compatible with those of Scribner & Cole (1981). While the historians may ascribe more importance to social than to cognitive transformations (if such a distinction can be made), both perspectives indicate the importance of the *uses* of literacy. The consequences of literacy are related to the activities in which it is used in and outside the classroom. Children acquiring literacy are acquiring competence in these activities.

Through the examination described in this chapter, we come closer to understanding the effects of literacy and schooling on children. Children are socialized through participating in verbal interactions into certain perspectives and values. The extent to which the children of Western Samoa are affected depends on the extent of their education and the extent to which they continue to participate in village social life. Those who go on to secondary schools and those who leave the village to work or study elsewhere are obviously affected more than others. For the majority of rural Samoans, the Western view of adult–child relationships and task accomplishment is restricted to particular settings, namely school and work in the capital. This view coexists with more traditional views. Members of a Samoan village can shift their conduct and interpretive frame regarding children and tasks just as they can shift in and out of the literate register.

11. Language as symbol and tool

I. INTRODUCTION

The chapters in this book have detailed ways in which language expresses and generates meaning in the course of children's development. The book has not focused exclusively on one area of meaning, but rather has considered a range of concepts – from basic logical notions such as agent, causality, and patient to sociocultural notions of childhood, social control, knowledge, affect, task accomplishment, social activities, and social status. Fundamental to linguistic and sociocultural competence is the ability to relate linguistic structures to such a range of notions. Samoan children, as noted in Chapters 5 and 6, must come to understand how word order and case marking encode the transitive notions of agent and patient. But, as these chapters point out, they must also come to understand how word order and case marking encode socio-cultural information concerning social identity of speaker, formality of the situation, and keying of affective intensity (emphasis).

The bulk of this book has been devoted to the suggestion that as children become linguistically competent, they are becoming competent as members of a social group. Chapters 7 through 10 in particular articulate the process of *language socialization*, ways in which children are socialized through language and socialized to use language (Schieffelin & Ochs 1986a). When social scientists have looked to the relation between language and society, the preference has been to see language as expressive of local ideologies and social orders. That is, language is viewed as a repository of local meanings. A basic underlying tenet of language socialization is that language must be studied not only as a symbolic system that encodes local social and cultural structures, but also as a tool for establishing (i.e. maintaining, creating) social and psychological realities. Both the symbolic and the tool-like properties of language are exploited in the process of language socialization. Language socializes and in this sense it is a social tool. However, to a large extent, this socializing function relies upon the symbolic aspect of language. That is, among the many means through which language socialization is accomplished, symbolic function of language serves the social tool-like function of language.

In addition, language socialization relies on the manner in which utterances are delivered. By manner, I refer to a range of verbal phenomena such as grammatical forms; voice quality; codes; written, spoken, or signed modes; and the like. Such phenomena regulate the breadth and range of situational or social meanings a construction may convey, in much the same way as tones or chords function to circumscribe the key of a composition. For example, as noted in Chapter 9, in Samoan the imperative 'Give it to me' using the neutral first person pronoun form *a'u* 'me' (*Mai ia te a'u*) sets the meaning of the construction as a demand. If the speaker uses the sympathy-marked pronoun (*Mai taita*), a different meaning for the construction is established. Specifically, the sympathy-marked pronoun indexes that the speaker is begging. An important goal of this book has been to outline ways in which, among other routes, children and other novices gain sociocultural knowledge as they gain knowledge of such social indexes (Silverstein 1976a).

II. THE MICRO AND MACRO OF LANGUAGE SOCIALIZATION

In the remainder of this chapter, I shall draw on both Samoan data and data from other research studies to illustrate how the use of linguistic structures displays and creates sociocultural contexts for interlocutors. As such, these structures are powerful socializing tools. Analysis of language behavior at the microanalytical level leads both novice and researcher to more global understandings of sociocultural dispositions.

A. The linguistic index

Ultimately, as one delves into the process of language socialization, one is faced with specifying more precisely the relation of language to sociocultural context. Initially, one is faced with explicating more precisely how language form and content signal sociocultural dimensions of specific communicative events (e.g. social identities of participants, speech acts, etc.). But the task of relating language to socio-cultural context is not complete at this point. We have as well to account for how the sociolinguistic organization of these specific communicative events in turn interfaces with more general systems of social order and cultural knowledge. We know that particular communicative events relate to each other in systematic and complex ways within a defined speech community.

Although, as noted by Geertz (1973), cultures are not perfectly tidy systems, there are nonetheless dispositions, preferences, and dispreferences that cut across numerous communicative events and organize those events.

For example, as noted in Chapter 10, in traditional Samoan communities members view activities and tasks as social and not individual accomplishments. This perspective underlies several verbal activities, including verbal acknowledgments of physical labor, verbal response to oratory in chiefly councils, and judicial responses to acts of wrongdoing in court proceedings. In all these speech activities, one individual alone is neither praised nor blamed for his or her actions. It is not the individual but the social group who is responsible for accomplishments and transgressions.

Of particular importance to research on language socialization are (1) to specify what such overarching sociocultural dispositions are for particular social groups, (2) to account for how these sociocultural dispositions organize communicative practices, and (3) to account for how communicative practices generate sociocultural knowledge among novices in the course of their becoming members of a social group.

Intellectual headway on these issues is possible only as a multidisciplinary effort. Psychological models of mental representation and information processing, linguistic models of meaning and use, and sociological and anthropological models of social practices, social order, and cultural knowledge are all needed to understand the interface of language and sociocultural knowledge. The necessity and the immensity of this undertaking have been noted by several scholars. For example, Lyons's introduction to the field semantics states:

If linguistic semantics is taken to be that branch of semiotics which deals with the way in which meaning (of all kinds) is conveyed by language, it must be accepted that a comprehensive theory of linguistic semantics will need to be based upon, or include, a theory of contextual appropriateness. It is arguable, however, that, at the present time at least, the construction of such a comprehensive theory of contextual appropriateness is too ambitious a task. (1977:590)

B.   Properties of the index

A step beyond shaking in our boots or throwing up our hands at the complexity of sociocultural knowledge and its impact on language practice and interpretation is to begin considering how language signals or *indexes* sociocultural information at the level of particular communicative events. Children and other novices, after all, build up tacit knowledge of language use and other sociocultural phenomena through their participation in particular but recurrent communicative events. To go back to our earlier example, Samoan children may be socialized into an ideology of collective task accomplishment through receiving, producing, and overhearing verbal acknowledgments of completed actions. These acknowledgments index through linguistic form and message content sociocultural dispositions concerning responsibility for actions taken.

To this end, we have several theories of indexicality available, including those of Jacobson (1960), Lyons (1977), Morris (1946), Peirce (1931–58), and Silverstein (1976a). All of these approaches provide global frameworks for relating linguistic signs to some dimension of temporally and spatially located events. Lyons's definition of indexicality as 'some known or assumed connexion between a sign A and its significance C such that the occurrence of A can be held to imply [and indicate] the presence or existence of C' (1977:106) is clear and useful as a starting point for unraveling sociocultural deixis. Silverstein (1976a, 1985) has expanded this notion of index to include not only referential indexicals but nonreferential indexicals as well. Whereas a referential index contributes to the denotational or strict referential meaning of a sentence uttered in a context, a nonreferential index does not. The pronouns 'I' and 'you' are referential indexicals. They both index the communicative context (i.e. presence of speaker and addressee) and contribute to the referential meaning of propositions in which they appear. Choices of one dialect or one language rather than another, on the other hand, can be nonreferential indexes in that code choices may index the communicative context, e.g. the social status of the speaker, social relationship between speaker and addressee, etc., but do not contribute to the referential or literal meaning of propositions.

The pragmatic and sociolinguistic literature has provided us with a specification of *kinds of sociocultural information* that may be so indexed through linguistic signs – social status, roles, relationships, settings, actions, activities, genres, topics, affective and epistemological stances of participants, among others.

This literature as well has provided us with a wide range of *grammatical and discourse structures* that index sociocultural information in different speech communities. We know, for example, that phonological and morphological structures are widely used to key speakers' social status, role, and affect and epistemological perspective. Text structures such as repetition, reformulation, code switching, and various sequential units are also linguistic resources for indexing such local contextual dimensions.

Unfortunately, to get a grip on the process of language socialization, it is not enough to specify lists of contextual dimensions and lists of linguistic structures that index those dimensions. Indexical relations are more complex than one-to-one mappings between linguistic forms and contextual features. There are (1) mappings between a particular contextual dimension and sets of linguistic forms and (2) mappings between a particular linguistic form and several contextual dimensions; (3) further, an index or set of indexicals may recontextualize the past and precontextualize the future as well as contextualize the communicative context of the moment. Each of these indexical properties must be specified if we are to advance a model of language socialization. Let me consider each of these complexities in turn.

1.   Indexing through single features and through collocation of features

If we look through the pragmatic and sociolinguistic literature, two means of indexing sociocultural context stand out: (1) a single linguistic form may index some contextual dimension or (2) a set of linguistic forms may index some contextual dimension. Honorific morphology provides good examples of how single linguistic forms can index sociocultural context, in this case affective and social relationships between speaker and addressee or speaker and referent. Personal pronouns that index sex of speaker or hearer in many languages also illustrate how single linguistic items signal sociocultural context of the utterance.

While contextual information may be indexed by a single linguistic structure as just illustrated, in other cases contextual information is indexed not through one but a set of co-occurring structures. Let us call this process collocational indexing. The work of Andersen (1977), Biber (1986), Biber & Finegan (in press), Ferguson (1977), and others on registers, communicative styles, and text types illustrates this process. Here social identity of speaker or addressee, genre, communicative activity taking place, and the like are indexed through a set of linguistic features that systematically co-occur rather than through a single feature alone.

The important point here is that isolated linguistic features often have broad indexical scope. For example, in American standard-English-speaking communities, deletion of the copula (as in 'That bad') indexes a wide range of possible social contexts. It may index the social status of one's addressee as child, foreigner, patient, or elderly person, for example (Ferguson 1977). To narrow the scope of possible contexts to one of these social statuses, speaker–hearers must consider other linguistic forms that co-occur in the text. High pitch along with deletion of the copula, for example, might index that the addressee is a child, whereas loudness might index foreigner status of the addressee. It is the combination of indexes that narrows the indexical scope.

Another example of indexical narrowing through collocation concerns the domain of affect. Most linguistic constructions that index affect across the world's languages indicate a broad domain of speakers' or others' affective dispositions (Ochs & Schieffelin in press). For example, in many languages, particular features index only positive affect or negative affect. As noted in Chapter 9, the particle *e* in Samoan indicates a wide range of negative affects, including worry, sadness, and anger. Further specification of affective dispositions of participants lies in the relation of that feature to others expressed in the text (as well as to nonverbal features of the situation). Morpho-syntactic indexes of affect, for example, must be related to phonological and lexical indexes.

That context is indexed through collocation of indexes as well as through single indexes is a sociolinguistic generalization that must be incorporated into a developmental model of how sociocultural knowledge and linguistic knowledge interface in the course of language socialization. We must represent the fact that children come to understand constraints on co-occurrence and ordering of indexes and further come to understand how indexes interact to signal contextual information.

2.   Direct and indirect indexical relations

In addition, our model of language socialization needs to attend to another form of indexical complexity. In many examples of indexicality cited in the literature, there appears to be a direct, that is, unmediated, relation between one or more linguistic forms and some contextual dimension. A particular particle in one language may be described as a direct index of the speaker's feelings, for example, or a set of linguistic forms may be described as collectively directly indexing the activity of gossiping or lecturing or oratory.

In looking over numerous examples of indexical relations, I, together with a group of graduate students, have begun to discern a second, more complex type of indexical relation. In this second type, indexicality is achieved indirectly. A feature of the communicative event is evoked indirectly through the indexing of some other feature of the communicative event. In these cases, the feature of the communicative event directly indexed is conventionally linked to and helps to constitute some second feature of the communicative context, such that the indexing of one evokes or indexes the other.

Good examples of indirect indexes come from the work of Clancy (1986a), Cook (1987), Seki (1987), Uyeno (1971), and others on Japanese sentence-final particles. Certain particles, such as *ze* and *wa*, index both an affective disposition and gender. By gender I do not refer to biological distinctions between men and women but rather cultural constructs of men and women (Ortner & Whitehead 1981), i.e. local assumptions about being male and being female. With respect to the particles *ze* and *wa*, when speakers use these particles they index their gender identity along with their affective disposition. Using Bakhtin's framework, we can say that through these particles Japanese speakers index male or female 'voice', along with affect (Bakhtin 1981). *Ze*, for example, indexes both a disposition of affective intensity and male voice of speaker. *Wa* indexes almost the reverse: a more hesitant disposition in that it softens the force of an assertion and female voice of speaker.

Within the proposed framework, effect and gender stand in different indexical relations to the particles *zo*, *ze*, and *wa*. Specifically, the particles directly index affective dispositions and indirectly index gender of speaker. Speakers' gender is indirectly indexed through the indexing of speakers' affect in the sense that gender identity in Japanese society is partly defined in terms of these affective dispositions. Softness and hesitancy are expected constituents of female comportment, and forcefulness is part of local conceptions of being male. Because of the strong conventional and constitutive relations between affect and gender, the direct indexing of affect evokes gender identities or gender voices of participants as well. The relationship between the indexing of affect and gender identity is represented in Figure 11.1.

Another example of indirect indexing is the use of evidential particles in Samoan. Evidential particles directly index some property of the speaker's knowledge toward the proposition expressed. For example, in Samoan evidential particles directly index how certain the speaker's belief/knowledge is and the source of the speaker's knowledge (e.g. direct perception, reported speech, etc.). In addition, these particles may indirectly index types of speech acts performed. For examples, particles that directly index uncertainty of speaker's belief/knowledge may indirectly index that the speaker is speculating or guessing rather than declaring or claiming.

Particle	Direct meaning	Indirect meaning
Ze	Affective intensity	Male 'voice'
Wa	Affect of softness	Female 'voice'

Figure 11.1.   *Indexical meanings of* ze *and* wa.

In the perspective suggested here, features of a communicative event may be related to one another in *constitutive* ways, such that certain features help to define or constitute others. Participants' affect, for example, helps to constitute participants' gender identity, participants' uncertainty helps to constitute speech acts, speech acts help to constitute speech activities, and so on. The indexical potential of linguistic forms can thus extend to the contexts so constituted.

I want to suggest here that sociocultural dimensions of communicative events do not display themselves randomly with respect to being in a direct or indirect indexical relation to linguistic forms. Major sociocultural dimensions include social identities of participants, social relationships among participants, affective dispositions of participants, beliefs and knowledge (epistemological dispositions) of participants, social (including speech) acts, social (including speech) activities, and genre. Within this set, two contextual dimensions are recurrently used to constitute other contextual dimensions, namely *affective* and *epistemological* dispositions. Affective dispositions include feelings, moods, and attitudes of participants toward some proposition. Epistemological dispositions refer to some property of participants' beliefs or knowledge vis-à-vis some proposition, for example, the source of their knowledge or the degree of certainty of their knowledge. These two dispositions are directly indexed in all languages, are central dimensions of all communicative events, and are central constituents of other dimensions of communicative events. Furthermore, recent linguistic literature on affect and epistemological dispositions suggests that these two are probably the most highly grammaticized of the features that define sociocultural context (Besnier in press a, b; Biber & Finegan in press; Haviland in press; Labov 1984; Ochs & Schieffelin in press).

While other features can help define more complex contextual features, I propose that affect and epistemology are the most widely employed to this end. Participants' affect and participants' beliefs and knowledge help to establish their social identity, the social relationship obtaining between them, and the speech act or speech activity they are endeavoring to perform. In this sense, an understanding of indexes of affect and epistemological stance is basic to interpreting the sociocultural organization of a communicative event. And, following this line of thought, such indexes are building blocks of children's linguistic and sociocultural competence. The constitutive role of affect on the one hand and beliefs and knowledge on the other in defining sociocultural context is schematized in Figure 11.2.

$$
\begin{array}{ll}
\text{Affect} & ------\rangle \\
\text{Beliefs/knowledge} & ------\rangle
\end{array}
\left\{
\begin{array}{l}
\text{Social identity} \\
\text{Social relationship} \\
\text{Speech act} \\
\text{Speech activities} \\
\text{Genre}
\end{array}
\right\}
$$

Figure 11.2. *Constituting sociocultural context.*
  Key: $---\rangle$ = *constitutive relation*

To provide an exhaustive account of the ways in which affective and epistemological stances enter into the constitution of other contexts is beyond the scope of this final chapter. I briefly note, however, that affect is a strong component not only of gender identity but of social identity more generally. Many of the linguistic features previously analyzed solely as indexes of social status and role – for example, honorific marking and respect-vocabulary systems – can be reanalyzed as direct indexes of affective dispositions of speaker (e.g. humility, admiration, love), which in turn help to constitute or establish the social positions of participants in a communicative situation. As noted in Chapter 9, indexes of affect also help to define numerous speech acts such as praises, protests, begging, disagreement, teasing, accusations, compliments, and assessments.

Epistemological dispositions play an equally important role in constituting context. Indexes of source and certainty of speakers' beliefs and knowledge, for example, help to constitute communicative activities such as telling stories, gossiping, prophesying, confessing, interrogating, delivering messages, and writing academic papers. Similarly, as noted earlier, the indexing of beliefs and knowledge is fundamental to defining speech acts such as speculating, asking questions, accusing, and asserting. Epistemological dispositions also help to constitute social identities and social relationships. In many societies, for example, lower-status persons talking to higher-status persons are expected to evidence confused speech or to otherwise index that they do not know as much as their addressees (see Albert 1972).

Children come to an understanding of speech acts and speech activities taking place, genres in use, social identities and social relationships in play to a great extent through an understanding of linguistic forms that index affects and beliefs and knowledge. In becoming linguistically and socioculturally competent, children and other novices must learn the social work that these indexes perform, particularly their potential for establishing social personae and social goals.

3.   Vectors of indexicality

A third powerful socializing property of linguistic indexes is their capacity to index not only the ongoing or current context but past and future contexts as well. Thus far we have been considering cases in which one or more linguistic forms index some immediate contextual feature, such as the Japanese particles indexing affective stances and gender identities or the Samoan particles indexing epistemological stances and speech acts. And I have emphasized how children's understanding of the meanings of such indexes interfaces with their understanding of social order and cultural orientations. The power of indexicality, however, extends beyond the immediate situational context. Indexes also have the potential to redefine prior contexts, i.e. to *recontextualize*, and to anticipate future contexts, i.e. to *precontextualize*. And these additional vectors of indexicality augment the world-creating potential of language in the process of communication and socialization.

A good example of retrospective indexing comes from the use of linguistic forms that directly index epistemological stance, such as evidential markers in many languages. I mentioned that in Samoan, linguistic forms that directly index speakers' lack of certainty may indirectly index the speech act of speculation. So far, we are speaking only of indexing the immediate or current context. But speculation in Samoan, in turn, involves other contexts, particularly past events, and in so doing speculation functions to recontextualize those past events in a different light.

In Chapter 7, I concentrated on one of the many interesting aspects of recontextualization through speculation. I considered the type of object that is subjected to speculation across different societies. What does or does not become a topic of verbal speculation? What are the conditions under which verbal speculation is appropriate? In pursuing this concern, I have been considering perhaps the most basic recontextualizing function of speculation, namely the function of recontextualizing some object as an object of speculation. Comparative studies suggest that societies constrain what can or cannot be subject to speculation. In this sense, certain evidentials across languages and communities indirectly index for children and other novices the *limits of speculation* for the social group they are entering.

One of the most striking results of cross-cultural research is the finding that societies differ in their willingness to speculate verbally about what is in the mind of another person (see Ochs & Schieffelin 1984; Schieffelin and Ochs 1986a). As noted in Chapter 7, members of Western European societies generally show no dispreference with respect to explicitly guessing at what another person might be thinking or feeling. Indeed, members of these societies devote considerable attention to speculating about what is or was in someone's mind. Our legal system, for example, assesses the gravity of an action in terms of mental states and allows speculation concerning the premeditation of actions and the mental fitness of the actor at the time of the action. Further, a major pedagogical procedure in these societies is to get novices to explicitly guess what the instructor is thinking about. This procedure is codified in the test question, where the questioner knows the information and is eliciting from others the information the questioner already has in mind. The interest in this sort of mind probing is evident as well in riddles and in a series of games such as Twenty Questions and I Spy, which require others to hypothesize verbally about what is on the speaker's mind. As Chapter 9 points out, that the unclear mental state is an acceptable object of verbal speculation is made linguistically evident to children in the early period of their lives. Dozens of times a day caregivers in middle-class mainstream communities explicitly guess at unclearly formulated thoughts of young children. The caregivers make wild or educated guesses at what these children may have in mind and ask children to confirm or disconfirm their hypotheses. Through speech acts of this sort, caregivers contextualize some mental state of the child as an object of verbal speculation and in so doing specialize children through language into a component of the local epistemology.

Other societies, including Samoan, Kaluli of Papua New Guinea (Schieffelin in press), and Athapaskan (S. Scollon 1982) communities, strongly disprefer verbal speculation about what someone else might be thinking or feeling. In traditional Samoan households, interlocutors do not typically pose test questions, nor do they engage in mind-reading games or riddles. Legal assessments of wrongdoing do not rely on properties of mental states, and verbal conjectures on this topic are not part of legal proceedings. When Samoan caregivers hear an unclearly expressed thought of a young child, they do not engage the child in hypothesis testing vis-à-vis that thought. Rather, as in other societies, Samoan caregivers prefer to elicit a more intelligible reformation of the thought – asking for example, 'What did you say?' – or to terminate the topic.

Through speech-act responses of this sort, Samoan caregivers index mental states as uncertain objects, but they do not index mental states as objects of explicit speculation. In this way, Samoan caregivers, like mainstream middle-class caregivers and caregivers the world over, socialize young children into their particular epistemological perspective.

Evidential particles marking uncertainty in Samoan are not dedicated to speculating about mental states of others; they are, rather, dedicated to speculating about reported events, actions, and conditions. Speculation in these cases addresses the accuracy of the report and poses possible alternative accounts. The use of these particles by caregivers and others, then, indexes for Samoan children (1) a disposition of uncertainty (direct indexing of current context), (2) the speech act of speculation (indirect indexing of current context), and (3) the set of objects which speculation addresses (indirect indexing and recontextualization). Each of these contextual components is related to another in the sense that the indexing of uncertainty evokes the speech act of speculation, and the speech act of speculation evokes an object subjected to speculation.

Following the logic through, we can get a clearer picture of the impact of secondary socializing institutions such as formal schooling. Chapter 10 discussed contrastive patterns of adult–child verbal interaction in school and home settings. Among the many differences in conversational practice is the use of unidirectional praising in school but not in household interactions. Teachers, trained in Western pedagogy, praise young Samoan children if they answer correctly, regardless of whether the children received assistance from peers or instructor. In so praising, the instructor recontextualizes the activity as something accomplished by the child alone. Such recontextualization contrasts with the verbal acknowledgment of labor in other village settings. As noted in Chapter 10, task accomplishments outside the classroom are acknowledged through a verbal exchange known as the *maaloo* exchange. *Maaloo* 'well done' is exchanged by different parties involved in a task (those carrying out a particular action and supporters). Whereas praising recontextualizes the activity as an individual accomplishment, *maaloo* recontextualizes the activity as a joint or collective accomplishment. As Samoan children come to gain competence in the discourse of acknowledgment across settings, they are coming to an understanding of local conceptions of activities and accomplishment. Outside the classroom, *maaloo* exchanges retrospectively index for children the contribution of 'supporters'; inside the classroom, unidirectional praising by teachers retrospectively indexes for children the notion that individuals accomplish tasks.

C. Indexicality, discourse, and sociocultural knowledge

The examples of verbal speculation and praising/acknowledging just discussed display the relation among indexicality, discourse, and sociocultural knowledge advocated in this chapter. As children in different communities gain competence in the discourse of speculation and praising/acknowledging, they gain social–cultural knowledge as well. In each society, the norms, preferences, and expectations surrounding the activities of speculation and praising/acknowledging are tied to local theories of knowledge and task accomplishment, and children gaining competence in the discourse of these verbal activities are at the same time acquiring these folk epistemologies and dispositions. Through participating in the activity of speculation, for example, children in different communities are coming to understand what constitutes knowledge, what a person can know and what a person cannot know, what are the legitimate linguistic paths to knowledge, who can travel these paths and who cannot.

These examples are two of dozens that have been investigated in research into language socialization. We could see the same relation among indexicality, discourse, and socialization if we turned to the discourse of evidentials in Japanese (Clancy 1986a, Cook 1987, Seki 1987), Kaluli (Schieffelin 1986a, in press), Athapaskan (S. Scollon 1982), or Samoan (Ochs 1986b, in press); or to the discourse of Kaluli turned-over talk (Feld & Schieffelin 1982); or deictic verbs in Samoan (Platt 1980, 1982, 1986); or narratives among white working-class Americans (Heath 1982, 1983); or problem-solving talk among the Kwara'ae (Watson-Gegeo & Gegeo 1986). All of these examples illustrate the point that language and culture interface in the domain of discourse, particularly in the area of indexicality, and that as such linguistic and sociocultural knowledge organize each other.

III.   MEMBER AND NOVICE: ACTIVE, INTERACTIVE, AND VULNERABLE

A.   The Sapir–Whorf hypothesis

As noted in Chapter 1 and throughout this book, the view of language socialization advocated here resonates with several other perspectives. Most immediately it orients to Sapir's best-known statement, at the heart of the Sapir–Whorf hypothesis, that 'we see and hear and otherwise experience very largely as we do because the language habits of our community predispose certain choices of interpretation' (Mandelbaum 1949:162). The Sapir–Whorf hypothesis has had rather a bad beating in the annals of social science. One of the problems has been a deterministic reading of this hypothesis, a reading grounded in other remarks by Sapir that language does not just predispose but 'predetermines for us certain modes of obser-vation and interpretation' (Mandelbaum 1949:74). A second weak point has been the focus on grammar as the locus and source of culture.

I believe that the Sapir–Whorf hypothesis can be taken in other direc-tions, in particular to a focus on discourse and culture rather than on grammar and culture. Recall that in Chapter 1, discourse is defined not as a kind of structure but rather as a set of norms, preferences, and expectations relating language to context, which speaker–hearers draw on and modify in producing and making sense out of language in context. Knowledge of discourse is a part of our linguistic competence, but at the same time such knowledge is part of our sociocultural competence. This means that chil-dren developing discourse knowledge are developing a knowledge of both language and culture.

The deterministic reading of the Sapir–Whorf hypothesis has been roundly criticized by a two-decade-long list of psycholinguistic studies suggesting that indeed at least some features of world view cut across languages and cultures and are the outcome of psychological and biological processes common to our species. In the perspective on language socializa-tion taken throughout this book, linguistic determinism is to be discarded, but for reasons other than the arguments just mentioned. As noted in Chapter 7, such a strong interpretation of Sapir's statement gives the novice – here the child – very little control in the creation of linguistic and cultural understandings. The child is locked into a grammatical system and a cultural system that that grammar encodes. In this perspective, as well, members are little changed by their communication with children. It is the child and not the member who is psychologically altered by their social and linguistic experience with one another.

B.   The 'acquisition' problem

This diminishing of novices' impact on members is not unique to the so-called strong version of the Sapir–Whorf hypothesis. Indeed, many current theories of development, including theories of language development, consider the child as an individual; or, if environment is considered, its relation to children is viewed either as input or as a constraint on development. Figure 11.3 illustrates this perspective. In this perspective, the focus tends to be on how someone or something external to the child may affect the child, rather than the converse. In most current views, the child is highly active, busily constructing systems of knowledge (Piaget 1926, 1952). The child, however, is not viewed as actively modifying the system of competent speaker/members.

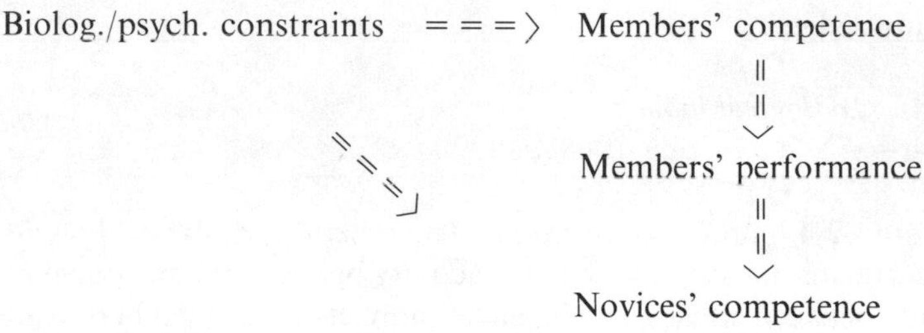

Biolog./psych. constraints $= = = \rangle$ Members' competence

$$\parallel$$
$$\parallel$$
$$\vee$$

Members' performance

$$\parallel$$
$$\parallel$$
$$\vee$$

Novices' competence

Figure 11.3.   *Unidirectional models.*
  Key: $= = = \rangle = direction\ of\ impact.$

The use of the term 'acquisition', as in 'language acquisition', codifies this perspective. I have used the term 'acquisition' many times throughout this book. In many cases, the term does not capture the process I am representing and I am in search of a more appropriate term. The terms 'acquirer' and 'acquisition' imply that little or no bidirectional transformation of knowledge and meaning takes place between members and novices. The notion of acquirer implies that there is a cognitive system out there (or perhaps I should say 'up there') and the role and goal of the child/novice is to reach a level of competence in this system. The course of development is seen as a movement toward the adult model. The adult model is not seen as moved through interactions with the child, as part of the process of negotiating reality. It must be that for certain areas of language and culture the term 'acquisition' is entirely appropriate. There are linguistic and sociocultural structures that are nonnegotiable and must be acquired. The term does not seem appropriate to all areas of knowledge, however, particularly not to all areas of discourse and sociocultural knowledge. Although I am in no position to say which areas of knowledge are relevant to this claim, I nonetheless wish to advocate a position that views both novices and more competent speaker/members as vulnerable to transforming their structures of knowledge and understanding vis-à-vis discourse and culture. As discussed in Chapter 1, such a position is dialogical and allows for bidirectional change, as represented in Figure 11.4.

Members' knowledge

Joint activity

Novices' knowledge

Figure 11.4. *Dialogical models.*
  Key: ⟨= = =⟩ = *direction of impact.*

Like Figure 1.2, Figure 11.4 indicates that members' and novices' knowledge impacts the nature of joint or social activity but at the same time that joint activity between novice and member impacts both members' and novices' tacit knowledge. For example, in many cases, members' understandings of family roles are modified through joint activities with infants and children. Despite the asymmetry of their relationship and their competence, children and caregivers may jointly construct these domains of knowledge with each other. In this sense, caregivers may be socialized by the children they are socializing. Teachers as well may be socialized by the students they are inducting into some area of expertise. Their understanding of the subject matter may be transformed by the responses and questions of students. Similarly, novices and members may impact each other's discourse knowledge. For example, in certain cases, children and caregivers may impact how they are to speak to one another in the course of their communications with each other. And teachers and students may in certain cases impact each other's knowledge of classroom communication. Language socialization has the potential, then, to be bidirectional, even though asymmetry exists between novice and member.

One of the charges into research into language socialization is to assess (1) the areas of members' language and culture more and less resistant to change from 'below' (from novices' influence) and (2) the communicative procedures that either discourage or stimulate such bidirectional socialization. A socialization procedure that allows question asking by novices may change members' behavior and world views more than a socialization procedure that relies on members modeling and novices repeating some form of knowledge or behavior. Do we find that certain societies more than others rely on particular forms of communication between member and novice? Do we find that certain forms of member–novice communication are linked to certain domains of knowledge within and across societies?

An integrated theory of language socialization, represented in Figure 11.5, excludes neither unidirectional, i.e. acquisition, nor bidirectional, i.e. dialogic, processes. This integrated perspective recognizes the social and psychological dominance of the member vis-à-vis the novice and the immense impact of this fact on novices' understanding of the world. This perspective also recognizes psychological and biological constraints on thought and behavior. At the same time, our model allows for members' knowledge to be impacted by novices through the medium of social activity and for social activity to alter biological and psychological parameters over evolutionary time. In this model, both members and novices are active, interactive, and vulnerable.

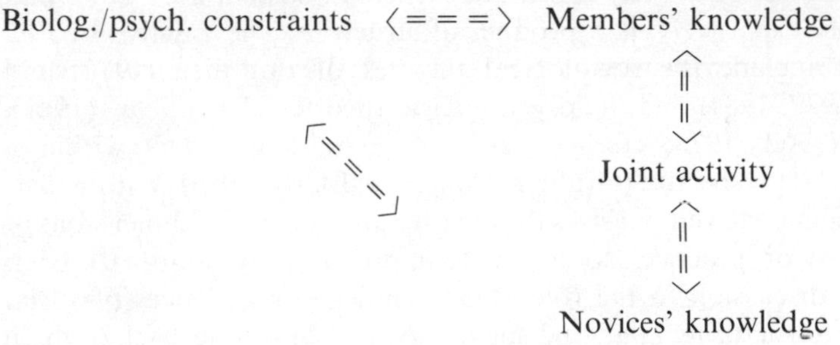

Biolog./psych. constraints $\langle = = = \rangle$ Members' knowledge

$$\wedge$$
$$\|$$
$$\|$$
$$\vee$$

$\lceil = = =$ Joint activity
$= = \rfloor$

$$\wedge$$
$$\|$$
$$\|$$
$$\vee$$

Novices' knowledge

Figure 11.5. *Integrated socialization model.*
  Key: $\langle = = = \rangle$ = *direction of impact.*

C.   Chaos theory

This view of language socialization is compatible with current scientific theories that envision systems as open-ended, active, and probabilistic. Chaos theory, proposed by the physicists Prigogine and Stengers (1984), is one such theory. They suggest first that matter is active and inherently unstable. This idea parallels our idea that both novice and knowing member are agents of change – no participant to a socializing interaction is passive. Prigogine further states that the active nature of matter may lead to irregular behavior, that is, to disorder. Whereas previous scientific paradigms looked at such disorder as detrimental, codified in the term 'entropy', Prigogine suggests that such disorder may lead to new dynamic states. A normal pattern is for matter to assume a new order and stability following the state of instability or chaos. While I am not suggesting that social relationships are inherently chaotic, I do advocate the idea that the structures of knowledge of both member and novice are vulnerable and that communication between them may lead to what Prigogine and others call 'far from equilibrium' conditions for both, which in turn lead to new organizations of knowledge for both. Questions by novices to members may reorder the thinking of both, despite their difference in knowledge and power. In other words, the relation between novice and member is not static and direction of change is not always unilateral.

D.   Language socialization and activity-centered social science

I noted in Chapter 1 that the view of language development and language socialization advocated in this book is compatible with a set of theories that are performance- or activity-based and critical of structuralist views that treat activity exclusively as a product of structure. These activity-based approaches include the sociological theories of Bourdieu (1977) and Giddens (1979, 1984) and the psychological theories of Leontyev (1981), Vygotsky (1962, 1978; cf. Wertsch 1985a, b), and others within a sociohistorical perspective (Griffin & Cole 1984; LCHC 1983). Within their own paradigms, each emphasizes the creative and generative dimensions of social activity or 'practice' (to use the term preferred by Bourdieu). Each gives some discussion to the role of unintended consequences of social activity in restructuring mind and society. At the same time, each of these approaches recognizes that psychological and social structures organize social activity. Structures are thus the source and the outcome of social behavior. These ideas parallel the notions in language socialization that both linguistic knowledge and sociocultural knowledge organize social activity and that at the same time such knowledge is the outcome of social activity. In this approach, linguistic and sociocultural knowledge of both novice and member is vulnerable and can be transformed through social activity.

IV.   CONCLUDING REMARKS

To know a language entails knowing how linguistic structures relate to meanings. Such knowledge includes not only knowledge of how language represents meanings but how language is a tool for generating meanings as well. As children come to understand sound–meaning correspondences, they come to understand what Gillian Sankoff calls the 'social life of language' (1980), that is, the web of social meanings, goals, actions, and conditions language helps to spin. Speakers of languages display to infants and young children linguistic strategies for expressing meanings. But speakers of languages are at the same time members of social groups and as such display to infants and young children local cultural strategies for representing, transforming, and otherwise engaging with the world. Particularly important to this process are linguistic structures that vary across socially constituted contexts and hence index these contexts. These indexes, either alone or in sets, either directly or indirectly, and either retrospectively, prospectively, or currently, establish contexts and as such are powerful socializing structures.

Appendix I.
Transcription conventions

ORTHOGRAPHY

In transcribing the Samoan tapes, I have used traditional Samoan orthography except for vowel length, which has been transcribed phonemically, that is, with a double (identical) vowel, rather than with a macron on a single vowel. The letter 'g' represents a velar nasal and the apostrophe represents a glottal stop.

The reader will notice that very often the standard spelling of a word is not found in the Samoan transcripts. Although the tapes were not transcribed phonetically, the transcribers tried to represent roughly how utterances were pronounced. As noted in Chapter 3, there is considerable variation in the expression of Samoan across settings and to some extent across groups of speakers. One hears in casual speech glottal stops dropped or added or vowel sounds shortened or lengthened where in careful speech they would be otherwise. Similarly, portions of words are often deleted and/ or elided. In casual speech, for example, one hears *laku* rather than *alu aku* 'go + deictic' and *faku* rather than *fai aku* 'say + deictic'. As noted in Chapter 3, grammatical markers are often deleted in casual speech. Thus, in our transcripts one will find case markers, tense/aspect markers, subject– verb agreement, and relative pronouns sometimes present and sometimes not. In the case of small children, very often their utterances were unrecognizable variants of adult speech. Where possible, I have reglossed the unintelligible forms of the children. The gloss is marked with an asterisk.

The reader should also note that most of the speech recorded and transcribed is in the phonological register that Samoans refer to as *tautala leaga* 'bad speech' (see Chapter 3). This register is not the register of written Samoan, and those who are familiar with Samoan may find it strange to read Samoan written in this form. The reader will find Samoan words written in *tautala lelei* 'good speech' primarily in general discussions about Samoan words and expressions. At times I present to the reader the Samoan form under discussion in both phonological registers.

TRANSLATION CONVENTIONS

Word-for-word glosses of Samoan utterances are placed immediately beneath the Samoan. Free glosses are written beneath the word-for-word gloss or immediately beneath the Samoan. Free glosses are marked by quotation marks.

LINGUISTIC CONVENTIONS

The following abbreviations are used throughout the text to specify grammatical information about Samoan utterances:

PRES   present tense
PST   past
PERF   perfect tense
INCPTPERF   inceptive perfect tense
IMPERF   imperfect
PRES PROG   present progressive tense
FUT   future

TRANS   transitive

NEG   negative

ERG   ergative marker
POSS   possessive marker
GEN   genitive marker
ALIEN   alienable
INALIEN   inalienable
DIR   directional marker
CAUS   causality marker
INSTR   instrument marker
TEMP   temporal marker
LOC   locative marker
OBJ   object marker
COMP   comparison marker
PREP   preposition
DEICT   deictic
EXCL   exclusive
INCL   inclusive

ART   article
SPEC   specific
NONSPEC   nonspecific

TOP   topic
PRT   particle
EMPH   emphasis
COMPL   complementizer
CONJ   conjunction

PERS   person
PL   plural

PRO   pronoun
CLIT   clitic
NP   noun phrase

OTHER TRANSCRIPTION CONVENTIONS

For the most part, the transcripts follow the conventions for representing conversational turns outlined in conversation analysis research (see for example Schenkein 1978). Overlap in adult–adult conversation is marked by square brackets ([ ]); overlap in household conversations with children is usually indicated by double slash marks (//). The double slash marks were appropriate, given the way in which children's turns are placed on the page (see below and Ochs 1979). Pause length is marked in parentheses, in tenths of seconds: '(1.8)'. Equal signs (=) indicate run-on utterances or a turn that continues over the turn of another. The dash indicates a cut-off word, but sometimes is used to indicate the process of separating words into syllables for teaching purposes in the speech of classroom instructors. Loudness is indicated by capitalization, emphatic stress by underlining. Information concerning tone of voice or other nonlinguistic information is indicated in double parentheses: (( )).

PAGE FORMAT

In our transcription notebooks written in the field, all contextual information and speech of the child we were primarily studying were transcribed on a left-hand notebook page and the speech of all others participating in household interactions was transcribed on the right-hand page. Although this format is difficult to reproduce in type, it is preserved in the chapters of this volume as follows:

Page format

| *Context* | *Speech of child* | *Speech of others* |

Utterances that overlap are placed on the same line, and the point of overlap is indicated with double slash marks.

Appendix II. Canonical transitive verb types in children's speech

MATU'U

Session I
'ai 'eat'
tai'i 'throw away'
ta'e 'break'
'aumai 'give'
fa'auma 'finish'
si'i 'carry'
'ave 'take'
fai 'do, make'
tu'u 'leave'
nana 'hide'

Session III
'aumai 'bring'
fasi 'hit'
fai 'do, make'
togi 'throw'
tu'u 'leave'
ta'u 'report, tell (on)'
'ai 'eat'

Session V
pu'e 'catch'
tu'u 'leave'
'ai 'eat'
ta'e 'break'
'ave 'take'
'avatu 'take away'
faga 'shoot'
fulu 'wash'
fai 'do, make'

Session VII
'ave 'take'
'ai 'eat'

> *pu'e* 'catch'
> *si'i* 'carry'
> *fai* 'do, make'
> *lulu* 'shake'
> *'aumai* 'bring'

IAKOPO

Session I   *togi* 'throw'

Session III   *poo* 'smack'
               pu'e 'catch'
               ta'e 'break'
               pa'a 'explode, burst'
               fai 'do, make'
               'ave 'take'
               tu'u 'leave'
               kaa/taa 'hit'

Session V   *fasi* 'hit'
               'u'u 'hold'
               poo 'smack'
               kogi 'throw'
               faia 'do, make (trans. suffix)'
               fai 'do, make'
               'ave 'take'
               fana 'shoot'
               sasa 'hit'
               a'a 'kick'

Session VIII   *susa* 'hit'
               inu 'drink'
               a'a 'kick'
               fai 'do, make'
               'ai 'eat'
               ta'e 'break'
               'u'u 'hold'
               selu 'comb'
               tia'i 'throw away'
               poo 'smack'
               'ave 'take'
               fasi 'hit'

fusi 'bind, lash'
kogi 'throw'
fa'akau 'buy'
'ai 'eat'
ka'u 'report, tell on'
tu'u 'leave'
fa'a'aka 'make laugh'
pu'e 'catch'
kaa 'hit'

PESIO

Session I   *pu'e* 'catch'
                    'u'u 'hold'
                    fai 'do, make'

Session III   *poo* 'smack'
                    'ave 'take'
                    kogi 'throw'
                    sasa 'hit'
                    fa'akau 'buy'
                    selu 'comb'
                    si'i 'carry'
                    fasi 'hit'
                    'u'u 'hold'

Session V   *igu* 'drink'
                    poo 'smack'
                    usu 'sing'
                    tusi 'write'
                    'ai 'eat'
                    'ave 'take'
                    faga 'shoot'
                    fai 'do, make'
                    pu'e 'catch'
                    gagaa 'hide'

Session VII   *nanaa* 'hide'
                    'ave 'take'
                    fa'akau 'buy'
                    fai 'do, make'

        fofoo 'rub'
        kia'i 'throw away'
        keu 'decorate'
        loke 'fidget with'
        ku'u 'leave'
        su'e 'search for'
        mai 'bring'
        fufulu 'clean'
        pese 'sing'
        vaelua 'divide'
        kusi 'write'

NAOMI

Session I   *taa* 'hit, strike'
                tape 'kill (an animal)'
                togi 'throw'
                poo 'smack'
                'ai 'eat'
                si'i 'carry'
                ufiufi 'cover'
                'ave 'take'
                tae 'pick up'
                sasa 'hit'
                inu 'drink'

Session III   *tu'u* 'leave'
                fasi 'hit'
                poo 'smack'
                sasa 'hit'
                'ai 'eat ERG'
                'ave 'take'
                koli 'twist off and fetch down'

Session V   *kiki* 'kick'
                kusi 'write'
                'ai 'eat'
                kui 'stab'
                fai 'do, make'
                fa'amoe 'make sleep'
                faga 'shoot'
                poo 'smack'

                  togi 'throw'
                  maua 'keep'

Session VII   *ku'u* 'leave'
                  'ai 'eat'
                  togi 'throw'
                  kipi 'cut'
                  fai 'do, make'
                  kaa 'hit'
                  poo 'smack'

NIULALA

Session I   *fasi* 'hit'
                  vaku 'take away'
                  kuli 'chase'
                  'ai 'eat'
                  kia'i 'throw away'
                  ofu 'wear'
                  tatala 'open'
                  'ave. 'take'
                  mai 'bring'
                  kogi 'throw'
                  fai 'do, make'
                  fau 'build'

Session III   *fa'amoe* 'make sleep'
                  kape 'kill (an animal)'
                  'ave 'take'
                  sui 'change'
                  kia'i 'throw away'
                  fao 'grab'
                  kaga 'hit (trans. suffix)'
                  po 'smack'
                  gagaa 'hide'
                  ku'u 'leave'
                  sulu 'put on (cloth)'
                  maua 'keep'
                  uku 'fill'

Session V *faga* 'shoot'
 'ave 'take'
 sua 'butt, crush ERG'
 ku'u 'leave'
 fai 'do, make'
 kogi 'throw'
 kaa 'hit'
 uu 'sting, bite'
 'ai 'eat'
 fa'akua 'buy'
 pu'e 'catch'
 koso 'pull'
 vaelua 'divide'
 fasioki 'kill (person)'
 kia'i 'throw away'
 'u'u 'hold'
 tuli 'chase'
 si'i 'carry'
 se'e 'put on, wear (shoes)'

Session VII *maua* 'keep'
 iloa 'know'
 misi 'know'
 'ave 'take'
 togi 'throw'
 fa'akau 'buy'
 kuli 'chase'
 faga 'shoot'
 gau 'break'
 fasi 'hit'
 'ai 'eat'
 tia'i 'throw away'

References

Albert, E. 1972. Cultural patterning of speech behavior in Burundi. In J. Gumperz and D. Hymes, eds., *Directions in sociolinguistics: the ethnography of communication*. New York: Holt, Rinehart & Winston, pp. 72–105.

Andersen, E. 1977. Learning how to speak with style. Unpublished Ph.D dissertation, Stanford University.

Anderson, S. R., and Chung, S. 1977. On grammatical relations and structure in verb-initial languages. In P. Cole and J. Sadock, eds., *Grammatical relations* (Syntax and semantics 8) 27. New York: Academic Press, pp. 1–27.

Antinucci, F., Duranti, A., and Gebert, L. 1979. Relative clause structure, relative clause perception, and the change from sov to svo. *Cognition* 7:145–76.

Austin, J. L. 1962. *How to do things with words*. Oxford: Oxford University Press.

Bakhtin, M. 1981. *The dialogic imagination*, ed. M. Holquist. Austin: University of Texas Press.

Barry, H., III, and Paxton, L. M. 1971. Infancy and early childhood: cross-cultural codes 2. *Ethnology* 15:409–30.

Bates, E., Camaioni, L., and Volterra, V. 1979. The acquisition of performatives prior to speech. In E. Ochs and B. Schieffelin, eds., *Developmental pragmatics*. New York: Academic Press, pp. 111–31.

Bateson, G. 1972. *Steps to an ecology of mind*. New York: Ballantine Books.
 1979. *Mind and nature*. New York: Bantam Press.

Bauman, R. 1977. *Verbal art as performance*. Rowley, Mass.: Newbury.

Besnier, N. In press a. Reported speech and affect on Nukulaelae. In J. H. Hill and J. Irvine, eds., *Responsibility and evidence in oral discourse*. Cambridge: Cambridge University Press.
 In press b. Conflict management, gossip and affective meaning on Nukulaelae. In K. Watson-Gegeo and G. White, eds., *Disentangling: the discourse of conflict and therapy in Pacific cultures*. New Brunswick, N.J.: Rutgers University Press.

Bever, T. 1970. The cognitive basis for linguistic structures. In J. R. Hayes, ed., *Cognition and the development of language*. New York: Wiley, pp. 279–352.

Biber, D. 1986, Spoken and written textual dimensions in English. *Language* 62(2):384–414.

Biber, D., and Finegan, E. In press. Adverbials as markers of stance: a multivariate approach *Discourse Processes*.

Bleicher, J. 1980. *Contemporary hermeneutics*. London: Routledge & Kegan Paul.
 1982. *The hermeneutic imagination: outline of a positive critique of scientism and sociology*. London: Routledge & Kegan Paul.

Blom, J.-P., and Gumperz, J. J. 1972. Social meaning in linguistic structures: code-switching in Norway. In J. Gumperz and D. Hymes, eds., *Directions in sociolinguistics: the ethnography of communication.* New York: Holt, Rinehart & Winston, pp. 407–34.

Bloom, L. 1973. *One word at a time: the use of single-word utterances before syntax.* The Hague: Mouton.

1970. *Language development: form and function in emerging grammars.* Cambridge, Mass.: MIT Press.

Boggs, S. 1985. *Speaking, relating and learning: a study of Hawaiian children at home and at school.* Norwood, N.J.: Ablex.

Bourdieu, P. 1977. *Outline of a theory of practice.* Cambridge: Cambridge University Press.

Bowerman, M. 1973. *Early syntactic development: a cross-linguistic study with special reference to Finnish.* Cambridge: Cambridge University Press.

Bowlby, J. 1969. *Attachment and loss,* vol. 1: *Attachment.* New York: Basic Books.

Brenneis, D. 1978. The matter of talk: political performances in Bhatgaon. *Language in Society* 7:159–70.

Bretherton, I., and Beeghly, M. 1982. Talking about internal states: the acquisition of an explicit theory of mind. *Development Psychology* 18:906–21.

Bretherton, I., McNew, S., and Beeghly-Smith, M. 1981. Early person knowledge as expressed in gestural and verbal communication: when do infants acquire a "theory of mind?" In M. E. Lamb and L. R. Sherwood, eds., *Infant social cognition.* Hillsdale, N.J.: Erlbaum.

Briggs, C. 1984. Learning how to ask: native metacommunicative competence and the incompetence of fieldworkers. *Language in Society* 13(1):1–28.

1986. *Learning how to ask.* Cambridge: Cambridge University Press.

Brown, P. 1979. Language, interaction, and sex roles in a Mayan community: a study of politeness and the position of women. Unpublished Ph.D. dissertation, University of California at Berkeley.

Brown, P., and Levinson, S. 1978. Universals in language usage: politeness phenomena. In E. Goody, ed., *Questions and politeness.* Cambridge: Cambridge University Press, pp. 56–289.

Brown, R. 1973. *A first language: the early stages.* Cambridge, Mass.: Harvard University Press.

1977. Introduction. In C. Snow and C. Ferguson, eds., *Talking to children.* Cambridge: Cambridge University Press, pp. 1–31.

Brown, R., and Bellugi, U. 1964. Three processes in the child's acquisition of syntax. *Harvard Educational Review* 34:133–51.

Brunner, J. S. 1972. Nature and uses of immaturity. In J. S. Bruner, A. Jolly, and K. Sylva, eds., *Play.* Harmondsworth: Penguin Books, pp. 28–64.

1975. The ontogenesis of speech acts. *Journal of Child Language* 2:1–21.

Burke, K. 1962. *A grammar of motives/a rhetoric of motives.* Cleveland, Ohio: Meridian Books.

Cazden, C. 1965. Environmental assistance to the child's acquisition of grammar. Unpublished Ph.D. dissertation, Harvard University.

1979. Language in education: variation in the teacher-talk register. In J. E. Alatis and R. Tucker, eds., *Language in public life.* Georgetown University Round Table on Languages and Linguistics. Washington, D.C.: Georgetown University Press.

Chafe, W. 1976. Givenness, contrastiveness, definiteness, subjects, topics and point of view. In C. Li, ed., *Subject and topic.* New York: Academic Press, pp. 25–56.

Chapin, P. 1970. Samoan pronominalization. *Language* 46(2):366–78.

Childs, C., and Greenfield, P. 1980. Informal modes of learning and teaching: the case of Zinacanteco weaving. In N. Warren, ed., *Studies in cross-cultural psychology* 2. London: Academic Press.

Chomsky, N. 1965. *Aspects of the theory of syntax*. Cambridge, Mass.: MIT Press.

1971. Deep structure, surface structure and semantic interpretation. In D. Steinberg and L. Jakobovits, eds., *Semantics*. Cambridge: Cambridge University Press, pp. 183–216.

1975. *Reflections of language*. New York: Pantheon Books.

1986. *Knowledge of language: its nature, origin, and use*. New York: Praeger Scientific.

Chung, S. 1973. The syntax of nominalizations in Polynesian. *Oceanic Linguistics* 12:641–86.

1978. *Case marking and grammatical relations in Polynesian*. Austin: University of Texas Press.

Churchward, S. 1951. *A new Samoan grammar*, 2nd ed. Melbourne: Spectator Press.

Cicourel, A. 1973. *Cognitive sociology*. Harmondsworth: Penguin Books.

Clancy, P. 1980. Referential choice in English and Japanese narrative discourse. In W. Chafe, ed., *The pear stories: cognitive, cultural and linguistic aspects of narrative production*. New York: Academic Press, pp. 127–202.

1986a. The acquisition of Japanese. In D. Slobin, ed., *The crosslinguistic study of language acquisition*. Hillsdale, N.J.: Erlbaum.

1986b. The acquisition of communicative style in Japanese. In B. B. Schieffelin and E. Ochs, eds. *Language socialization across cultures*. Cambridge: Cambridge University Press, pp. 213–49.

Clark, E. 1974. Some aspects of the conceptual basis for first language acquisition. In R. Schiefelbusch and L. Lloyd, eds., *Language perspective – acquisition, retardation and intervention*. Baltimore: University Park Press, pp. 105–28.

1978. From gesture to word: on the natural history of deixis in language acquisition. In J. Bruner and A. Garton, eds., *Human growth and development: Wolfson College Lectures 1976*. Oxford: Oxford University Press, pp. 85–120.

Clark, H., and Haviland, S. 1977. Comprehension and the given-new contract. In R. Freedle, ed. *Discourse production and comprehension*. Norwood, N.J.: Ablex, pp. 1–40.

Clark, H., and Lucy, P. 1975. Understanding what is meant from what is said: a study in conversationally conveyed requests. *Journal of Verbal Learning and Verbal Behavior* 14:56–72.

Cole, M. 1985. The zone of proximal development: where culture and cognition create each other. In J. Wertsch, ed., *Culture, communication and cognition: Vygotskian perspectives*. Cambridge: Cambridge University Press, pp. 146–61.

Cole, M., and Cole, S. In press. *Child development*. New York: Scientific American Books.

Comrie, B. 1978. Ergativity. In W. Lehmann, ed., *Syntactic typology: studies in the phenomenology of language*. Austin: University of Texas Press, pp. 329–94.

1979. Degrees of ergativity: some Chukchee evidence. In F. Plank, ed., *Ergativity*. London: Academic Press, pp. 219–40.

Conklin, I. 1962. Lexicographical treatment of folk taxonomics. In F. Householder and S. Saporta, eds., *Problems of lexicography*. Publication 21. Bloomington: Indiana University Research Center in Anthropology, Folklore and Linguistics.

Cook, H. 1987. Social voice and individual voice in Japanese: the particle NO and bare verbs. Manuscript. University of Southern California.

Cook, K. 1978. The mysterious Samoan transitive suffix. In J. Jaeger, A. Woodbury et al., eds., *Proceedings of the Fourth Annual Meeting of the Berkeley Linguistic Society*. Berkeley, Calif.: Berkeley Linguistic Society, pp. 53–66.

Cook-Gumperz, J. and Gumperz, J. 1981. From oral to written culture: the transition to literacy. In M. Whiteman, ed., *Writing: the nature, development and teaching of written communication*. Hillsdale, N.J.: Erlbaum, pp. 89–109.

Corsaro, W. 1977. The clarification request as a feature of adult interactive styles with young children. *Language in Society* 6:183–207.

1979. Sociolinguistic patterns in adult–child interaction. In E. Ochs and B. B. Schieffelin, eds., *Developmental pragmatics*. New York: Academic Press, pp. 373–89.

Coulthard, M. 1977. *An introduction to discourse analysis*. Harlow: Longman.

Cross, T. 1975. Some relationships between motherese and linguistic level in accelerated children. In *Papers and reports on child language development*, no. 10. Palo Alto, Calif.: Stanford University.

1977. Mothers' speech adjustments: the contribution of selected child listener variables. In C. Snow and C. Ferguson, eds., *Talking to children*. Cambridge: Cambridge University Press, pp. 151–88.

1978. Mothers' speech and its association with rate of linguistic acquisition in young children. In N. Waterson and C. Snow, eds., *The development of communication*. New York: Wiley, pp. 199–216.

1981. The linguistic experience of slow language learners. In Nesdale et al., eds., *Advances in child development*. Perth: University of Western Australia.

Cruttendon, A. 1982. How long does intonation acquisition take? Paper delivered at the Stanford University Child Language Forum, Palo Alto, Calif.

Demuth, C. 1986. Prompting routines in the language socialization of Basotho children. In B. B. Schieffelin and E. Ochs, eds., *Language socialization across cultures*. Cambridge: Cambridge University Press, pp. 51–78.

Derrida, J. 1977. Signature, event, context. *Glyph* 1:172–97.

Dixon, R. M. W. 1972. *The Dyirbal language of North Queensland*. Cambridge: Cambridge University Press.

1979. Ergativity. *Language* 55:59–138.

DuBois, J. 1981. Ergativity and preferred argument structure. Unpublished manuscript. Dept. of Linguistics, University of California, Los Angeles.

1984. Competing motivations. In J. Haiman, ed., *Iconicity in syntax: typological studies in language* 6. Amsterdam: John Benjamins.

Dunn, J., and Kendrick, C. 1982. The speech of two and three year olds to infant siblings. *Journal of Child Language* 9:579–95.

Duranti, A., 1981a. *The Samoan fono: a sociolinguistic study*. Pacific Linguistics, ser. B, vol. 80. Canberra: Department of Linguistics, Research School of Pacific Studies, Australian National University.

1981b. Speechmaking and the organization of discourse in a Samoan *fono*. *Journal of the Polynesian Society* 90:357–400.

1983. Samoan speechmaking across social events: one genre in and out of a *fono*. *Language in Society* 12:1–22.

1984a. Sociocultural dimensions of discourse. In T. A. Van Dijk, ed., *Handbook of discourse analysis*. London: Academic Press, pp. 193–230.

1984b. *Intentions, self, and local theories of meaning: words and social action in a Samoan context*. Center for Human Information Processing Technical Report 122. La Jolla: University of California, San Diego.

1984c. *Lauga* and *talanoaga*: structure and variation in the language of a Samoan speech event. In D. Brenneis and F. Meyers, eds., *Dangerous words: language*

and politics in the Pacific. New York: New York University Press, pp. 217–37.
In press. Ethnography of speaking: toward a linguistics of the praxis. In F.
Newmeyer, ed., *The Cambridge survey*, vol. 3: *Language: the socio-cultural
context*. Cambridge: Cambridge University Press.

Duranti, A., and Brenneis, D., eds. 1986. *The audience as co-author. Text* 6(3)
(special issue).

Duranti, A., and Ochs, E. 1979. Left-dislocation in Italian conversation. in T.
Givón, ed., *Syntax and semantics*, vol. 12: *Discourse and syntax*. New York:
Academic Press, pp. 377–416.
1983. Word order in Samoan discourse: a conspiracy toward a two-constituent
pattern. Lecture presented in Discourse Seminar at the Summer Institute of
Linguistics, University of California, Los Angeles.

Eibl-Eiblesfeldt, I. 1970. *Ethnology: the biology of behavior*. New York: Holt,
Rinehart & Winston.

Eisenberg, A. 1982. Language acquisition in cultural perspective: talk in three
Mexicano homes. Unpublished Ph.D. dissertation, University of California,
Berkeley.
1986. Teasing: verbal play in two Mexican homes. In B. B. Schieffelin and E.
Ochs, eds., *Language socialization across cultures*. Cambridge: Cambridge
University Press, pp. 182–98.

Ellis, J., and Ure, J. 1969. Language variety: register. In A. Meetham, ed., *Encyclo-
pedia of linguistics information and control*. London: Pergamon Press, pp. 251–
9.

Ervin-Tripp, S. 1972. On sociolinguistic rules: alteration and co-occurrence. In J.
Gumperz and D. Hymes, eds., *Directions in sociolinguistics: the ethnography of
communication*. New York: Holt, Rinehart & Winston, pp. 213–50.
1979. Children's verbal turn-taking. In E. Ochs and B. B. Schieffelin, eds.,
Developmental pragmatics. New York: Academic Press, pp. 391–415.

Feld, S., and Schieffelin, B.B. 1982. Hard words: a functional basis for Kaluli
discourse. In D. Tannen, ed., *Analyzing discourse: text and talk*. Georgetown
University Round Table on Languages and Linguistics 1981. Washington,
D.C.: Georgetown University Press, pp. 350–70.

Ferguson, C. 1977. Baby talk as a simplified register. In C. Snow and C. Ferguson,
eds., *Talking to children*. Cambridge: Cambridge University Press, pp. 219–37.

Fillmore, C. 1968. The case for case. In E. Bach and R. Harms, eds., *Universals in
linguistic theory*. New York: Holt, Rinehart & Winston, pp. 1–88.

Frake, C. 1964. A structural description of Subanun 'religious behavior'. In W.
Goodenough, ed., *Explorations in cultural anthropology*. New York: McGraw-
Hill, pp. 111–29.

Freeman, D. 1983. *Margaret Mead and the making of Samoa*. Cambridge, Mass.:
Harvard University Press.

Gadamer, H.-G. 1976. *Philosophical hermeneutics*, trans. and ed. D. Linge. Berkeley
and Los Angeles: University of California Press.

Gallagher, T. 1981. Contingent query sequences within adult–child discourse.
Journal of Child Language 8:51–62.

Gallimore, R., Boggs, J., and Jordan, C. 1974. *Culture, behavior and education: a
study of Hawaiian-Americans*. Beverly Hills, Calif.: Sage Publications.

Galtung, J. 1981. Literacy, education and schooling – for what? In H. Graff, ed.,
Literacy and social development in the West. Cambridge: Cambridge University
Press, pp. 271–85.

Garfinkel, H. 1967. *Studies in ethnomethodology*. New York: Prentice-Hall.

Garnica, O. 1977. Some prosodic and paralinguistic features of speech to young
children. In C. Snow and C. Ferguson, eds., *Talking to children*. Cambridge:
Cambridge University Press, pp. 63–89.

Garvey, C. 1977. The contingent query: a dependent act in conversation. In M. Lewis and L. Rosenblum, eds., *Interaction, conversation, and the development of language* 5. New York: Wiley, pp. 63–94.

1979. Contingent queries and their relations in discourse. In E. Ochs and B. B. Schieffelin, eds., *Developmental pragmatics*. New York: Academic Press, pp. 363–72.

Geertz, C. 1973. *The interpretation of cultures*. New York: Basic Books.

Gerber, E. 1975. The cultural patterning of emotions in Samoa. Unpublished Ph.D. dissertation, University of California, San Diego.

Giddens, A. 1979. *Central problems in social theory: action, structure and contradiction in social analysis*. Berkeley and Los Angeles: University of California Press.

1984. *The constitution of society*. Berkeley and Los Angeles: University of California Press.

Gintis, H. 1971. Education, technology and the characteristics of worker productivity. *American Economic Review* 61:266–79.

Givón, T. 1979. *On understanding grammar*. New York: Academic Press.

Gleason, J., and Greif, E. 1983. Men's speech to young children. In B. Thorne, C. Kramerae, and N. Henley, eds., *Language, gender, and society*. Rowley, Mass.: Newbury.

Gleason, J., and Weintraub, S. 1976. The acquisition of routines in child language. *Language in Society* 5:129–36.

Goffman, E. 1959. *The presentation of self in everyday life*. Garden City, N.Y.: Doubleday (Anchor Books).

1963. *Behavior in public places*. New York: Free Press.

1967. *Interaction ritual: essays on face-to-face behavior*. Garden City, N.Y.: Doubleday (Anchor Books).

1974. *Frame analysis*. New York: Harper & Row.

1981. *Forms of talk*. Philadelphia: University of Pennsylvania Press.

Goldin-Meadow, S. 1975. *The representation of semantic relations in a manual language created by deaf children of hearing parents: a language you can't dismiss out of hand*. Technical Report XXVI. Philadelphia: University of Pennsylvania. (Dissertation.)

Golinkoff, R. 1983. The pre-verbal negotiation of failed messages: insights into the transition period. In R. Golinkoff, ed., *The transition from prelinguistic to linguistic communication*. Hillsdale, N.J.: Erlbaum, pp. 57–78.

Goodenough, W. 1957. Cultural anthropology and linguistics. In P. Garvin, ed., *Report of the Seventh Annual Round Table on Linguistics and Language Study*. Washington, D.C.: Georgetown University Monograph Serial Language and Linguistics 9.

Goodwin, C. 1981. *Conversational organization: interaction between speakers and hearers*. New York; Academic Press.

1986. Audience diversity, participation and interpretation. In A. Duranti and D. Brenneis, eds., *The audience as co-author. Text* 6(3) (special issue).

Goody, E. 1978. Towards a theory of questions. In E. Goody, ed., *Questions and politeness*. Cambridge: Cambridge University Press, pp. 17–43.

Goody, J. 1977. *Domestication of the savage mind*. Cambridge: Cambridge University Press.

Graff, H. J. 1981. Literacy, jobs, and industrialization: the nineteenth century. In H. J. Graff, ed. *Literacy and social development in the West*. Cambridge: Cambridge University Press, pp. 231–60.

Greenberg, J. H. 1966. *Universals of language*, 2nd ed. Cambridge, Mass.: MIT Press.

Greenfield, P. 1972. Oral and written language: the consequences for cognitive development in Africa, the United States, and England. *Language and Speech* 15:169–78.

Greenfield, P., and Bruner, J. 1966. Culture and cognitive growth. *International Journal of Psychology* 1(2):89–107.

Greenfield, P., and Smith, J. 1976. *The structure of communication in early language development*. New York: Academic Press.

Greif, E., and Gleason, J. 1980. Hi, thanks, and goodbye: more routine information. *Language in Society* 9(2):159–66.

Grice, H. P. 1968. Utterer's meaning, sentence-meaning, and word-meaning. *Foundations of Language* 4:1–18.

1975. Logic and conversation. In P. Cole and J. Morgan, eds., *Syntax and semantics*, vol. 3: *Speech acts*. New York: Academic Press.

Griffin, P., and Cole, M. 1984. Current activity for the future: the zo-ped. In B. Rogoff and J. Wertsch, eds., *New directions for child development*. Children's Learning in the 'Zone of Proximal Development' 23. San Francisco: Jossey-Bass.

Gumperz, J. 1972. Introduction. In J. Gumperz and D. Hymes, eds., *Directions in sociolinguistics*. New York: Holt, Rinehart & Winston, pp. 26–33.

1977. Sociocultural knowledge in conversational inference. In M. Saville-Troike, ed., *Linguistics and anthropology*. Georgetown University 28th Round Table on Languages and Linguistics. Washington D.C.: Georgetown University Press, pp. 191–211.

1982. *Discourse strategies*. Cambridge: Cambridge University Press.

Gumperz, J., and Cook-Gumperz, J. 1982. Introduction: language and the communication of social identity. In J. Gumperz, ed., *Language and social identity*. Cambridge: Cambridge University Press, pp. 1–21.

Gumperz, J., and Wilson, R. 1971. Convergence and creolization: a case from the Indo-Aryan/Dravidian border. In D. Hymes, ed., *Pidginization and creolization of languages*. Cambridge: Cambridge University Press, pp. 151–67.

Halliday, M. 1967. Notes on transitivity and theme in English II. *Journal of Linguistics* 3:199–244.

1973. *Exploration in the functions of language*. London: Arnold.

Haviland, J. In press. 'Sure, sure': evidence and affect. *Text*.

Hawkins, J. In press. Competence and performance in the explanation of language universals. In M. Atkinson and J. Durand, eds., *Commemorative volume for David Kilby* (working title).

Heath, S. 1982. What no bedtime story means: narrative skills at home and school. *Language in Society* 11:49–77.

1983. *Ways with words: language, life and work in communities and classrooms*. Cambridge: Cambridge University Press.

Heidegger, M. 1962. *Being and time*. New York: Harper & Row.

Hickman, M. 1985. The implication of J. Wertsch, ed., *Culture, communication and cognition: Vygotskian perspectives*. Cambridge: Cambridge University Press, pp.236–57.

Hoffman, M. 1981. Perspectives on the difference between understanding people and understanding things: the role of affect. In J. Flavell and L. Ross, eds., *Social cognitive development: frontiers and possible futures*. Cambridge: Cambridge University Press, pp. 67–81.

Holquist, M. 1983. The politics of representation. *Laboratory of Comparative Human Cognition Newsletter* 5(1):2–9.

Hopper, P. 1979. Acpect and foregrounding in discourse. In T. Givón, ed., *Syntax and semantics*, vol. 12: *Discourse and syntax*. New York: Academic Press, pp. 213–41.

Hopper, P., and Thompson, S. A. 1980. Transitivity in grammar and discourse. *Language* 56:251–300.

Husserl, E. 1970. *Logical investigations*. 2 vols. London: Routledge & Kegan Paul.

Hymes, D. 1962. The ethnography of speaking. In T. Gladwin and W. Sturtevant, eds., *Anthropology and human behavior*. Washington, D.C.: Anthropological Society of Washington, pp. 15–53.

   1972. On communicative competence. In J. Pride and J. Holmes, eds., *Sociolinguistics*. Harmondsworth: Penguin Books, pp. 269–85.

   1974. *Foundations in sociolinguistics: an ethnographic approach*. Philadelphia: University of Pennsylvania Press.

Irvine, J. 1979. Formality and informality in communicative events. *American Anthropologist* 81:773–90.

   1982. Language and affect: some cross-cultural issues. In H. Burns, ed., *Contemporary perceptions of language: interdisciplinary dimensions*. Georgetown Round Table on Languages and Linguistics. Washington, D.C.: Georgetown University Press.

Jakobson, R. 1960. Concluding statement: linguistics and poetics. In T. Sebeok, ed. *Style in language*. Cambridge, Mass.: MIT Press, pp. 350–73.

Jefferson, G. 1974. Error-correction as an interactional resource. *Language in Society* 3(2):181–200.

Karmiloff-Smith, A. 1979. Micro- and macrodevelopmental changes in language acquisition and other representational systems. *Cognitive Science* 3:91–118.

Keenan, E., Ochs, E., and Schieffelin, B.B. 1976. Topic as a discourse notion: a study of topic in the conversations of children and adults. In C. Li, ed., *Subject and topic*. New York: Academic Press, pp. 335–85.

Keesing, F. 1934. *Modern Samoa*. London: Allen & Unwin.

Keesing, F., and Keesing, M. 1956. *Elite communication in Samoa*. Palo Alto, Calif.: Stanford University Press.

Keesing, R. 1974. Theories of culture. In B. Siegel, ed., *Annual review of anthropology*, vol. 3. Palo Alto, Calif.: Annual Reviews, pp. 73–97.

Kernan, K. 1969. The acquisition of language by Samoan children. Unpublished Ph.D. dissertation, University of California, Berkeley.

   1974. The acquisition of formal and colloquial styles of speech by Samoan children. *Anthropological Linguistics* 16:107–19.

Klinnert, M., Campos, J., Sorce, J., Emde, R., and Svejda, M. 1983. Emotions as behavior regulators: social referencing in infancy. In R. Plutchnik and H. Kellerman, eds., *Emotions: theory, research and experience*, vol. 2: *The emotions*. New York: Academic Press, pp. 57–86.

Kochman, T. 1981. *Black and white styles in conflict*. Chicago: University of Chicago Press.

   1983. The boundary between play and nonplay in black verbal dueling. *Language in Society* 12(3):329–38.

Krämer, A. 1902/3. *Die Samoa-Inseln*. 2 vols. Stuttgart: Schwertzerbartsche Verlag.

Kuno, S. 1972. Functional sentence perspective: a case study from Japanese and English. *Linguistic Inquiry* 3:161–95.

Labov, W. 1963. The social motivation of a sound change. *Word* 19:273–309.

   1966. *The social stratification of English in New York City*. Washington, D.C.: Center for Applied Linguistics.

1972. *Sociolinguistic patterns*. Philadelphia: University of Pennsylvania Press.

1984. Intensity. In D. Schiffrin, ed., *Meaning, form and use in context: linguistic applications*. Georgetown University Round Table on Languages and Linguistics. Washington, D.C.: Georgetown University Press, pp. 43–70.

Lakoff, G. 1972. Hedges: a study in meaning criteria and the logic of fuzzy concepts. In *Papers from the Eighth Regional Meeting of the Chicago Linguistics Society*. Chicago: University of Chicago Press, pp. 183–228.

Lakoff, G., and Johnson, M. 1980. *Metaphors we live by*. Chicago: University of Chicago Press.

Lakoff, R. 1973. The logic of politeness: or minding your p's and q's. *Proceedings of the Ninth Regional Meeting of the Chicago Linguistics Society*, pp. 292–305.

Lambrecht, K. 1985. On the status of svo sentences in French discourse. In R. Tomlin, ed., *Coherence and grounding in discourse*. Proceedings of the Symposium on Discourse Relations and Cognitive Units, University of Oregon, Eugene. Amsterdam: John Benjamins.

Langness, L., and Frank, G. 1981. *Lives: an anthropological approach to biography*. Novato, Calif.: Chandler & Sharp.

Lavandera, B. 1978. Where does the sociolinguistic variable stop? *Language in Society* 7:171–82.

Lave, J. 1977. Tailor-made experiments and evaluating the intellectual consequences of apprenticeship training. *Quarterly Newsletter of the Institute for Comparative Human Development* 1:1–3.

LCHC (Laboratory of Comparative Human Cognition). 1983. Culture and cognitive development. In W. Kessen, ed., *Mussen's handbook of child psychology*, 4th ed., vol. 1. New York: Wiley.

Leach, E. 1982. *Social anthropology*. Oxford University Press.

Lee, B. 1985. The intellectual origins of Vygotsky's semiotic analysis. In J. Wertsch, ed., *Culture, communication and cognition: Vygotskian perspectives*. Cambridge: Cambridge University Press, pp. 66–93.

Lehmann, W. P. 1973. A structural principle of language and its implications. *Language* 49:47–66.

Leontyev, A. N. 1981. *Problems of the development of the mind*. Moscow: Progress Publishers.

LeVine, R. 1980. Anthropology and child development. In *Anthropological perspectives on child development. New Directions for Child Development* 8:71–86 (special issue).

Levinson, S. 1979. Activity types and language. *Linguistics* 17:365–99.

Lévi-Strauss, C. 1968. *Structural anthropology*, vol. 1. Harmondsworth: Penguin Books.

Levy, R. 1973. *Tahitians: mind and experience in the Society Islands*. Chicago: University of Chicago Press.

1984. Emotion, knowing, and culture. In R. Shweder and R. LeVine, eds., *Culture theory: Essays on mind, self, and emotion*. Cambridge: Cambridge University Press, pp. 214–37.

Lock, A. 1981. *The guided reinvention of language*. London: Academic Press.

Luria, R. 1976. *Cognitive development: its cultural and social foundations*. Cambridge, Mass.: Harvard University Press.

1981. *Language and cognition*, ed. J. V. Wertsch. New York: Wiley Intersciences.

Lutz, C. 1982. The domain of emotion words on Ifluk. *American Ethnologist* 9(1):113–28.

Lyons, J. 1977. *Semantics*, vols. 1–2. Cambridge: Cambridge University Press.

McNeill, D. 1970. *The acquisition of language: the study of developmental psycholinguistics*. New York: Harper & Row.

MacWhinney, B. 1977. Starting points. *Language* 53:152–78.

1984. Grammatical devices for sharing points. In R. Schiefelbusch and J. Picka, eds., *The acquisition of communicative competence*. Baltimore: University Park Press, pp. 323–74.

Malinowski, B. 1978. *Coral gardens and their magic*, vol. 11: *The language of magic and gardening*. New York: Dover.

Mandelbaum, D., ed. 1949. *Selected writings of Edward Sapir*. Berkeley and Los Angeles: University of California Press.

Mandler, G. 1975. *Mind and emotion*. New York: Wiley.

Marsack, C. 1962. *Samoan*. London: Hodder & Stoughton.

Marx, K. 1959. *Marx and Engels: basic writings on politics and philosophy*, ed. L. S. Feurer. Garden City, N.Y.: Doubleday.

Mead, M. 1928. *Coming of age in Samoa*. New York: Morrow.

1930. *Social organization of Manu'a*. Bulletin 76. Honolulu: B. P. Bishop Museum.

1937. The Samoans. In M. Mead, ed., *Cooperation and competition among primitive people*. Boston: Beacon Press, pp. 282–312.

1963. Socialization and enculturation. *Current Anthropology* 4(2):184–8.

Mehan, H. 1979. *Learning lessons*. Cambridge, Mass.: Harvard University Press.

Miller, P. 1982. *Amy, Wendy and Beth: learning language in South Baltimore*. Austin: University of Texas Press.

1986. Teasing as language socialization and verbal play in a white working-class community. In B. B. Schieffelin and E. Ochs, eds., *Language socialization across cultures*. Cambridge: Cambridge University Press, pp. 199–211.

Milner, G. B. 1961. The Samoan vocabulary of respect. *Journal of the Royal Anthropological Institute* 91:296–317.

1962. Active, passive, or perfective in Samoan: a fresh appraisal of the problem. *Journal of Polynesian Society* 71:151–61.

1966. *Samoan dictionary*. London: Oxford University Press.

1973. It is aspect (not voice) which is marked in Samoan. *Oceanic Linguistics* 12(1–2):621–39.

Mitchell-Kernan, C., and Kernan, K. 1975. Children's insults: American and Samoan. In M. Sanches and B. Blount, eds., *Sociocultural dimensions of language use*. New York: Academic Press, pp. 307–15.

Morris, C.W. 1946. *Signification and significance*. Cambridge, Mass.: MIT Press.

Much, N., & Shweder, R. 1978. Speaking of rules: the analysis of culture in breach. In W. Damon, ed., *Moral development*. San Francisco: Jossey-Bass.

Neffgen, H. 1918. *Grammar and vocabulary of the Samoan language*. London: Kegan Paul, Trench, Tubner.

Nelson, K. 1981. Social cognition in a script framework. In J. Flavell and L. Ross, eds., *Social cognitive development*. Cambridge: Cambridge University Press.

Newport, E. 1976. Motherese: the speech of mothers to young children. In N. Castellan, D. Pisoni, and G. Potts, eds., *Cognitive theory*, vol. 2. Hillsdale, N.J.: Erlbaum.

Norman, D. 1979. *Twelve issues for cognitive science*. Center for Human Information Processing Report 87. University of California, San Diego.

Ochs, E. 1979. Transcription as theory. In E. Ochs and B. B. Schieffelin, eds., *Developmental pragmatics*. New York: Academic Press, pp. 43–72.

1982a. Talking to children in Western Samoa. *Language in Society* 11:77–104.

1982b. Ergativity and word order in Samoan child language: a sociolinguistic study. *Language* 58:646–71.

1986a. Variation and error: a sociolinguistic study of language acquisition in Samoa. In D. Slobin, ed., *The crosslinguistic study of language acquisition*. Hillsdale, N.J.: Erlbaum, pp. 783–838.

1986b. From feelings to grammar: a Samoan case study. In B. B. Schieffelin and E. Ochs, eds., *Language socialization across cultures*. Cambridge: Cambridge University Press, pp. 251–72.

Ochs, E., and Schieffelin, B. B. 1984. Language acquisition and socialization: three developmental stories and their implications. In R. Shweder and R. LeVine, eds., *Culture theory: essays on mind, self, and emotion*. Cambridge: Cambridge University Press, pp. 276–320.

In press. Language has a heart. *Text*.

Ochs, E., Schieffelin, B. B., and Platt, M. 1979. Propositions across utterances and speakers. In E. Ochs and B. B. Schieffelin, eds., *Developmental pragmatics*. New York: Academic Press, pp. 251–68.

Olson, D. R. Some social aspects of meaning in oral and written language. In D. R. Olson, ed., *The social foundations of language and thought*. New York: Norton.

Ortner, S., and Whitehead, H. 1981. *Sexual meanings: the cultural construction of gender and sexuality*. Cambridge: Cambridge University Press.

Pawley, A. 1966. Polynesian languages: a sub-grouping based on shared innovations in morphology. *Journal of Polynesian Society* 75:39–64.

1967. The relationships of Polynesian outlier languages. *Journal of Polynesian Society* 76:259–96.

Peirce, C. S. 1931–58. *Collected papers*, vols. 1–8, ed. C. Hartshorne and P. Weiss. Cambridge, Mass.: Harvard University Press.

Peters, A. 1977. Language learning strategies. *Language* 53:560–73.

1983. *The results of language acquisition*. Cambridge: Cambridge University Press.

Peters, A., and Boggs, S. 1986. Interactional routines as cultural influences upon language acquisition. In. B. B. Schieffelin and E. Ochs, eds., *Language socialization across cultures*. Cambridge: Cambridge University Press, pp. 80–96.

Petersen, C., Danner, F., and Flavell, J. 1972. Developmental changes in children's responses to three indications of communicator failure. *Child Development* 43:1463–81.

Philips, S. 1970. Acquisition of rules for appropriate speech usage. In G. Alatis, ed., *Bilingualism and language contact: anthropological, linguistic and sociological aspects*. Monograph Series No. 23, Languages and Linguistics. Washington, D.C.: Georgetown University Press.

1983. *The invisible culture: communication in classroom and community on the Warm Springs Indian reservation*. New York: Longman.

Piaget, J. 1926. *The language and thought of the child*. London: Routledge & Kegan Paul.

1929. *The child's conception of the world*. London: Routledge and Kegan Paul.

1951. *Play, dreams, and imitation in childhood*. New York: Norton.

1952. *The origins of intelligence in children*. New York: Norton.

Piatelli-Palmarini, M., ed. 1980. *Language and learning: the debate between Jean Piaget and Noam Chomsky*. Cambridge, Mass.: Harvard University Press.

Piers, G., and Singer, M. 1971. *Shame and guilt*. New York: Norton.

Plank, F., ed. 1979. *Ergativity*. London: Academic Press.

Platt, M. 1980. The acquisition of 'come', 'give', and 'bring' by Samoan children. In

Papers and reports on child language development, no. 19. Palo Alto, Calif.: Stanford University Dept. of Linguistics.

1982. Social and semantic dimensions of deictic verbs and particles in Samoan child language. Unpublished Ph.D. dissertation, University of Southern California.

1986. Social norms and lexical acquisition: a study of deictic verbs in Samoan child language. In B. B. Schieffelin and E. Ochs, eds., *Language socialization across cultures*. Cambridge: Cambridge University Press, pp. 127–51.

Pratt, G. 1911. *Grammar and dictionary of the Samoan language*, 4th ed., rev. and enlarged by the Rev. J. E. Newell. Apia: Malua, Samoa.

Prigogine, I., and Stengers, I. 1984. *Order out of chaos*. New York: Bantam.

Pye, C. 1979. The acquisition of grammatical morphemes in Quiché Mayan. Unpublished Ph.D. dissertation, University of Pittsburgh.

1980. The acquisition of person markers in Quiché Mayan. In *Papers and reports on child language development*, no. 19. Palo Alto, Calif.: Stanford University Dept. of Linguistics, pp. 53–9.

Radulovic, L. 1975. Acquisition of language: studies of Dubrovnik children. Unpublished Ph.D. dissertation, University of California, Berkeley.

Ricoeur, P. 1981. *Hermeneutics and the human sciences*, ed. and trans. John B. Thompson. Cambridge: Cambridge University Press.

Rogoff, B. 1984. Introduction: thinking and learning in social context. In B. Rogoff and J. Lave, eds., *Everyday cognition*. Cambridge, Mass.: Harvard University Press, pp. 1–8.

Romaine, S., ed. 1982. *Sociolinguistic variation in speech communities*. London: Arnold.

Rosaldo, M. 1982. The things we do with words: Ilongot speech acts and speech act theory in philosophy. *Language in Society* 11:203–37.

Ryle, G. 1949. *The concept of mind*. London: Hutchinson.

1953. Ordinary language. *Philosophical Review 62*.

Sachs, J. 1977. The adaptive significance of linguistic input to prelinguistic infants. In C. Snow and C. Ferguson, eds., *Talking to children*. Cambridge: Cambridge University Press, pp. 51–63.

Sachs, J., and Devin, J. 1976. Young children's use of age-appropriate speech styles in social interaction and role-playing. *Journal of Child Language* 3:81–98.

Sacks, H., and Schegloff, E. 1979. Two preferences in the organization of reference to persons in conversation and their interaction. In G. Psathas, ed., *Everyday language: studies in ethnomethodology*. New York: Irvington, pp. 15–21.

Sacks, H., Schegloff, E., and Jefferson, G. 1974. A simplest systematics for the organization of turn-taking in conversation. *Language* 50(4):696–735.

Sahlins, M. 1958. *Social stratification in Polynesia*. Seattle: University of Washington Press.

Sankoff, G. 1980. *The social life of language*. Philadelphia: University of Pennsylvania Press.

Sapir, E. 1921. *Language*. New York: Harcourt Brace.

1924. Culture, genuine and spurious. *American Journal of Sociology* 29:401–92.

1927. The unconscious patterning of behavior in society. In E. S. Dummer, ed., *The unconscious*. New York: Knopf, pp. 114–42.

Schank, R., and Abelson, R. 1977. *Scripts, plans, goals and understanding*. Hillsdale, N.J.: Erlbaum.

Scheff, T. 1977. The distancing of emotion in ritual. *Current Anthropology* 18(3):483–505.

Schegloff, E. 1984. On some questions' ambiguities in conversation. In J. Atkinson and J. Heritage, eds., *Structures of social action*. Cambridge: Cambridge University Press, pp. 28–52.

Schegloff, E., Jefferson, G., and Sacks, H. 1977. The preference for self-correction in the organization of repair in conversation. *Language* 53:361–82.

Schenkein, J. 1978. *Studies in the organization of conversational interaction*. New York: Academic Press.

Schieffelin, B. B. 1979. How Kaluli children learn what to say, what to do, and how to feel: an ethnographic study of the development of communicative competence. Unpublished Ph.D. dissertation, Columbia University.

    1986a. The acquisition of Kaluli. In D. Slobin, ed., *The crosslinguistic study of language acquisition*. Hillsdale, N.J.: Erlbaum, pp. 525–95.

    1986b. Teasing and shaming in Kaluli children's interactions. In B. B. Schieffelin and E. Ochs, eds., *Language socialization across cultures*. Cambridge: Cambridge University Press, pp. 165–81.

    In press. *How Kaluli children learn what to say, what to do, and how to feel*. Cambridge: Cambridge University Press.

Schieffelin, B. B., and Cochran-Smith, M. 1984. Learning to read culturally: literacy before schooling. In H. Goelman, A. Oberg, and F. Smith, eds., *Awakening to literacy*. London: Heinemann Educational, pp. 3–23.

Schieffelin, B. B., and Gilmore, P. 1986. *The acquisition of literacy: ethnographic perspectives*. Advances in Discourse Processes, vol. 21. Norwood, N.J.: Ablex.

Schieffelin, B. B., and Ochs, E. 1983. Cultural perspective on the transition from pre-linguistic to linguistic communication. In R. Golinkoff, ed., *The transition from pre-linguistic to linguistic communication*. Hillsdale, N.J.: Erlbaum.

    1986a. Language socialization. In B. Siegel, ed., *Annual review of anthropology*. Palo Alto, Calif.: Annual Reviews, pp. 163–91.

Schieffelin, B. B., and Ochs, E., eds, 1986b. *Language socialization across cultures*. Cambridge: Cambridge University Press.

Schneider, D. 1968. *American kinship: a cultural account*. Englewood Cliffs, N.J.: Prentice-Hall.

Schutz, A. 1967. *The phenomenology of the social world*. Evanston, Ill.: Northwestern University Press.

Scollon, R. 1976. *Conversations with a one year old*. Honolulu: University of Hawaii Press.

Scollon, R., and Scollon, S. 1981. The literate two-year-old: the fictionalization of self. In R. Scollon and S. Scollon, eds., *Narrative, literacy and face in interethnic communication*. Norwood, N.J.: Ablex, pp. 57–98.

Scollon, S. 1982. Reality set, socialization and linguistic convergence. Unpublished Ph.D. dissertation, University of Hawaii, Honolulu.

Scribner, S., and Cole, M. 1973. Cognitive consequences of formal and informal education. *Science* 182:553–9.

    1981. *The psychology of language*. Cambridge, Mass.: Harvard University Press.

Searle, J. 1969. *Speech acts*. Cambridge: Cambridge University Press.

    1979. *Expression and meaning*. Cambridge: Cambridge University Press.

    1983. *Intentionality: an essay in the philosophy of mind*. Cambridge: Cambridge University Press.

Seiter, W. 1980. *Studies in Niuean syntax*. New York: Garland.

Seki, M. 1987. Final particles in the speech of 2-year-old Japanese children and their mothers. Manuscript. University of Southern California.

Shatz, M., and Gelman, R. 1973. *The development of communication skills: modifica-*

tions in the speech of young children as a function of the listener. SRCD Monographs 5, 38.

Shore, B. 1977. A Samoan theory of action: social control and social order in a Polynesian paradox. Unpublished Ph.D. dissertation, University of Chicago.

1982. *Sala'ilua: a Samoan mystery.* New York: Columbia University Press.

Shotter, J. 1974. The development of personal powers. In M. Richards, ed., *The integration of the child into a social world.* Cambridge: Cambridge University Press, pp. 83–98.

1978. The cultural context of communication studies: theoretical and methodological issues. In A. Lock, ed., *Action, gesture and symbol: the emergence of language.* London: Academic Press, 43–79.

Shweder, R. 1984. Anthropology's romantic rebellion against the enlightenment; or there's more to thinking than reason and evidence. In R. Shweder and R. LeVine, eds., *Culture theory: essays on mind, self, and emotion.* Cambridge: Cambridge University Press, pp. 27–66.

Silverstein, M. 1976a. Shifters, linguistic categories, and cultural description. In K. Basso and H. Selby, eds., *Meaning and anthropology.* Albuquerque: University of New Mexico Press, pp. 11–55.

1976b. Hierarchy of features and ergativity. In R. Dixon, ed., *Grammatical categories in Australian languages.* Canberra: Australian Institute of Aboriginal Studies, pp. 112–71.

1981a. *The limits of awareness.* Sociolinguistic Working Paper 84. Austin, Texas: Southwest Educational Development Laboratory.

1981b. Metaforces of power in traditional oratory. Manuscript. Dept. of Anthropology, University of Chicago.

1985. The functional stratification of language and ontogenesis. In J. Wertsch, ed., *Culture, communication and cognition: Vygotskian perspectives.* Cambridge: Cambridge University Press, pp. 205–35.

Skinner, B. 1957. *Verbal behavior.* New York: Appleton–Century–Crofts.

Slobin, D., 1973. Cognitive prerequisites for the acquisition of grammar. In C. A. Ferguson and D. I. Slobin, eds., *Studies of child language development.* New York: Holt, Rinehart & Winston, pp. 175–208.

1975. The more it changes . . . on understanding language by watching it more through time. In *Papers and reports on child language development,* no. 10. Palo Alto, Calif.: Stanford University Dept. of Linguistics, pp. 1–30.

1982. Universal and particular in the acquisition of language. In L. Gleitman, ed., *Language acquisition: state of the art.* Cambridge: Cambridge University Press, pp. 128–70.

1986. Crosslinguistic evidence for the language-making. In D. I. Slobin, ed. *The crosslinguistic study of language acquisition.* Hillsdale, N.J.: Erlbaum.

Slobin, D., and Bever, T. 1982. Children use canonical sentence schemas: a crosslinguistic study of word order and inflections. *Cognition* 12:229–65.

Smith, C. 1983. A theory of aspectual choice. *Language* 59(3):479–501.

Snow, C. 1972. Mothers' speech to children learning language. *Child Development* 43:549–65.

Snow, C., and Ferguson, C., eds. 1977. *Talking to children.* Cambridge: Cambridge University Press.

Stern, D. 1977. *The first relationship: infant and mother.* London: Fontana/Open Books 33.

Tindall, B. 1976. Theory in the study of cultural transmission. In B. Siegel, ed., *Annual review of anthropology,* vol. 5. Palo Alto, Calif.: Annual Reviews, pp. 195–208.

Trevarthen, C. 1979. Communication and co-operation in early infancy: a description of primary intersubjectivity. In M. Bullowa, ed., *Before speech*. Cambridge: Cambridge University Press, pp. 321–49.

Trudgill, P. 1974. *Sociolinguistics: an introduction*. Harmondsworth: Penguin Books.

Tuitele, M. T., and Kneubuhl, J. 1978. *'Upu Saamoa/Samoan words*. Pago-Pago: Bilingual/Bicultural Education Project of American Samoa, Department of Education, Government of American Samoa.

Tuitele, M. T., Sapolu, M. and Kneubuhl, J. 1978. *La taatou gagana: tusi muamua* [Our language: first volume]. Pago-Pago: Bilingual/Bicultural Education Project of American Samoa, Department of Education, Government of American Samoa.

Turner, G. 1884. *Samoa: a hundred years ago and long before*. London: Macmillan.

Tyler, S. 1969. Introduction. In S. Tyler, ed., *Cognitive anthropology*. New York: Holt, Rinehart & Winston, pp. 1–23.

Uyeno, T. 1971. A study of Japanese modality: a performative analysis of sentence particles. Unpublished Ph.D. dissertation, University of Michigan.

Violette, le R. 1879. *Dictionnaire Samoa–français–anglais*. Paris.

Voloshinov, V. N. 1973. *Marxism and the philosophy of language*, trans. L. Matejka and I. R. Titunik, New York: Seminar Press. (Original publication in Russian, 1929.)

Vygotsky, L. S. 1962. *Thought and language*. Cambridge, Mass.: MIT Press.

1978. *Mind in society: the development of higher psychological processes*, ed. M. Cole, V. John-Steiner, S. Scribner, and E. Souberman. Cambridge, Mass.: Harvard University Press.

Wallace, A. 1970. *Culture and personality*, 2nd ed. New York: Random House.

Watson-Gegeo, K., and Boggs, S. 1977. From verbal play to talk story: the role of routines in speech events among Hawaiian children. In S. Ervin-Tripp and C. Mitchell-Kernan, eds., *Child discourse*. New York: Academic Press, pp. 67–90.

Watson-Gegeo, K., and Gegeo, D. 1986. Calling-out and repeating routines in Kwara'ae children's language socialization. In B. B. Schieffelin and E. Ochs, eds., *Language socialization across cultures*, pp. 17–50.

Weisner, T., and Gallimore, R. 1977. My brother's keeper: child and sibling caretaking. *Current Anthropology* 18(2):169–90.

Wentworth, W. M. 1980. *Context and understanding*. New York: Elsevier.

Wertsch, J. 1980. The significance of dialogue in Vygotsky's account of social, egocentric, and inner speech. *Contemporary Educational Psychology* 5:150–62.

1985a. *Vygotsky and the social formation of mind*. Cambridge, Mass.: Harvard University Press.

Wertsch, J., ed. 1985b. *Culture, communication and cognition: Vygotskian perspectives*. Cambridge: Cambridge University Press.

Whorf, B. 1941. The relations of habitual thought and behavior to language. In L. Spier, A. Hallowell, and S. Newman, eds. *Language, culture and personality: essays in memory of Edward Sapir*. Menasha, Wis.: Banta.

Wittgenstein, L. 1958. *Philosophical investigations*. Oxford: Blackwell.

Zahn-Waxler, C., Radke-Yarrow, M., and King, R. 1979. Child-rearing and children's pro-social initiations toward victims of distress. *Child Development* 50:319–30.

Zajonc, R. B. 1980. Feeling and thinking: preferences need no inference. *American Psychologist* 35:151–75.

Index

acquisition, vii–ix, 4–5, 8, 14, 102–3, 105,
  127
  affect, 3, 33, 38, 145, 168, 183–8
  ergative case marking, 3, 31, 86–7, 96,
    100-1, 122, 127
  knowledge, 17–18, 20, 26, 29, 38, 144, 205
  language, 17, 22–4, 29, 32, 34, 38, 49,
    51–2, 60, 86–8, 105, 121, 132, 223–4
  linguistic structures, 29–30, 100, 133
  literacy, xii, 48, 189, 192–4, 200–1, 208
  meaning, 12, 18
  order of, 31–2
  word order, 117, 127
activity, 14–18, 21–2, 27, 129, 198, 224–5
adult speech study, 49–51, 53, 86, 90–1, 95,
  104, 106–8, 113, 116, 118–22, 125–6,
  187, 228
affect, ix, x, 4, 8–9, 13, 30–3, 38, 63, 76,
  106, 145–6, 150, 154–5, 166–88, 210,
  214, 216–18
  in adult communication, 170
  -marked pronoun, 178–81, 183, 185–7
  Samoan concepts of, 146–7
  working definition, 145–6
American, 13; see also social class
Athapaskan, 220–1
audience, vii, 92, 142, 175, 178
  primary, 165
  secondary, 165–7

behaviorism, 18–19

caregiving, 22–4, 30–1, 47, 72, 198, 204–5
  control strategies of, 38, 72, 145, 147–57
  of younger siblings, xi, 21, 25, 72, 76,
    79–85, 128, 133, 136, 138, 140, 147,
    156–8, 162–5
  register, x, 1–2, 22–3, 89, 103–4, 131–5,
    204
  Samoan, 24, 32, 143–4, 156–68, 220
  social organization of, 78–85, 103–4,
    144, 148, 155–8

chaos theory, 225–6
childhood
  concept of, x, 51, 159
  Samoan, 33, 49, 71, 145, 156–67
  social identity of the child, ix, 157, 190
clarification, 28–9, 38, 128–40, 143–4,
  203–5, 219–20
classroom study, 48
competence, 11, 24, 29, 33–7, 38, 49, 50–1,
  57, 70–1, 105, 153, 199, 208–10, 222–3
concept of person, 38, 54, 129, 140, 170
contextualization, x, 3, 8–9, 11, 21–2, 31,
  35–6, 54–7, 65, 69–70, 85–6, 90–3,
  103–4, 107–10, 114, 126, 133, 135,
  141–2, 161, 166–7, 171, 191, 208–9,
  211–14, 218–22
conversation
  analysis, 20, 26–7, 50, 132, 142
  structures, 55, 129–30
culture, 5–7, 15, 23, 130–1, 141, 146,
  211–12, 222

deconstructionist theory, 19, 142
discourse, 20–1, 29–30
  structures, 3, 8, 110–11, 129, 213, 224
  theory, 17

egocentrism, 5, 24–5, 185–6
enculturation, 5
epistemology, 22, 26–8, 47, 76, 131, 140,
  144, 217–19, 221
ergativity, 31–3, 36, 38, 55, 58–60, 69,
  86–93, 95–107, 113–15, 121–2, 125–6,
  146, 229

first words, 159, 169, 184
frames, 3, 5, 9–11, 21, 130, 169, 200, 204,
  209

gender, 43–5, 71, 76–7, 79, 108, 168,
  177–83, 197, 215–16, 218
grammar, x, 8, 29, 33, 53, 69, 93

grammar (*cont.*)
  case marking, 86, 89–90, 92, 228
  deictic verbs, 30–1, 64, 66, 85, 170,
    228–9
  genitive, 60, 63, 101, 111, 121, 126, 178,
    229
  linguistic structures, x, 3–4, 11–13, 17,
    35, 38, 51, 86, 105, 169, 183, 213, 224
  major constituents, 67–9, 99–100, 105,
    107–10, 112–22, 125–7
  subject–verb agreement, 66–9, 228
  tense–aspect, 36–7, 64–6, 68, 70, 170,
    228
  two-constituent preference, 105–6, 110,
    113, 117
  verb complex, 64
  verbal suffix, 67, 69
  word order, 3, 30, 36, 38, 55, 62–3, 67–9,
    86, 92, 100, 105–8, 113–17, 119–25,
    127, 170

hermeneutic philosophy, 20, 28, 142

indexicality, 3–4, 8–9, 13, 21–2, 58, 211–16,
  218–22
innatism, vii–viii, 19
intentionality, 29, 140–4

Japanese, 215–16, 221

Kaluli, x, 10, 12–13, 23, 25, 32, 88, 100–3,
  162, 220–1
keys, 153, 167–8, 171; *see also* frames
knowledge, 12–18, 131, 140, 210–11, 218
  linguistic, vii, 2, 4–5, 8, 35–6, 128
  sociocultural, 4–6, 33, 128, 168, 221, 224
  theory of, 26, 144
Kwara'ae, 10, 12–13, 221

language socialization, ix–xi, 14, 42, 128,
  130, 168–9, 189–90, 210–13, 218–19,
  221, 224
literacy, ix, 55, 57, 59, 78, 196, 209
  activities, 129, 190
  instruction, xii, 39, 48, 49, 189, 191,
    194–5, 200–3, 205
  register, 195
longitudinal study, 42–6, 49, 50, 96, 119,
  122

Mead–Freeman debate, 145, 147–8
meaning, x, 4–5, 7, 13–14, 18–22, 27, 31,
  38, 132, 136, 139–44, 159, 168, 188,
  210–11, 218
metacommunication, 8–10
methodology, ix–x, 1–2, 40–51, 57–8
multiparty interaction, x, 21, 72, 76, 165

particles, 36, 59–62, 65, 89–90, 102, 107,
  115, 126, 149, 151, 154–5, 167, 170,
  172, 174–5, 177–8, 187, 215–16, 218,
  230
  evidential, 140, 216, 220–1
perceptual saliency, 100, 102
performance, 22, 29–30, 32, 145, 161,
  165–7, 194, 200
perspective taking, 24, 137–8, 162; *see also*
  sociocentric
phonology, 11, 53–7, 62, 69, 170, 185
play, 9–10, 22
practice theory, 16–17, 128
preference relations, 13–14, 28, 43, 106–7,
  112, 115–16, 120, 123–4, 135–6

registers, xii, 8, 11, 23–4, 31–3, 37, 53,
  55–8, 65, 70, 88–9, 109, 121, 171–2,
  176, 183, 195–6, 228
  'bad speech', vii, 1, 36, 51, 54–8, 61,
    66–7, 196, 228
  'good speech', vii, 1, 36, 51, 54–8, 61, 66,
    196, 228
  literate, 209; *see also* literacy
  teacher talk, 204
respect vocabulary, 30, 58, 69, 72, 85, 138,
  161–5, 174–5, 199, 218

Sapir–Whorf hypothesis, 14, 22, 29, 130–1,
  222–3
schools, ix, 36–7, 48–9, 55, 57, 78–80,
  129, 143, 189, 196, 201, 203–4, 209,
  220
shaming, 134, 153–5
simplification, 22–3, 25, 170, 204–5
social
  distance, 13, 59–60, 65, 67, 69, 88, 92–3,
    103–4, 109
  organization, 2, 14, 30, 37–8, 40, 51,
    71–5, 129, 211
  rank, 28–30, 40–1, 43, 47, 49–50, 58,
    71–8, 81–2, 85, 92, 102, 130, 136–9,
    142–4, 161–2, 168, 171, 177–83,
    197–9, 217–18
  referencing, x, xii, 169
  stratification, xi, 9, 50, 57, 80–1, 197–8
social class
  black/white-working, 10, 12, 141–2, 221
  white-middle, 10–12, 23–6, 28–9, 38, 54,
    131, 135, 137, 140–3, 190, 198, 204–5,
    208, 219–20
socialization, 5, 134
  of children, vii, x, 5–7, 38–9, 47, 71–2,
    76, 78, 129, 137–8, 144, 158, 161, 164,
    198–9
  secondary, 208–9
sociocentric, 24, 28, 85, 137, 170

sociocultural, viii, 21–2, 30
  context, 34, 38–9, 129
  framework, x, 3, 14, 128, 217
sociohistorical approaches to development,
  12, 15–16, 19–21, 129–30, 142, 189
speech-act, 11, 13, 18, 21, 27, 32, 85, 154,
  177, 185, 217
speech activity, 7–9, 12–13, 50, 108, 217;
  see also activity
structuration theory, 16
syntagmatic relations, 11–12

task accomplishment, 49, 78, 190–1, 194,
  197–200, 205, 208–10, 221
teasing, 10, 57, 134, 153–5, 218
transcription procedures, 46–8, 50–1, 194,
  228–31

variation, vii, 10, 33, 53–4, 59, 91–3, 105,
  121, 127, 129, 189, 196

Western-based institutions, ix, 55, 78–9,
  194–6, 204, 209